North Carolina EOG Grade 6 Math for Beginners

The Ultimate Step by Step Guide to Preparing for the North Carolina EOG Math Test

By

Reza Nazari

Copyright © 2023
Effortless Math Education Inc.

All rights reserved. No part of this publication may be reproduced, stored in a retrieval system, or transmitted in any form or by any means, electronic, mechanical, photocopying, recording, scanning, or otherwise, except as permitted under Section 107 or 108 of the 1976 United States Copyright Ac, without permission of the author.

Effortless Math provides unofficial test prep products for a variety of tests and exams. It is not affiliated with or endorsed by any official organizations.

All inquiries should be addressed to:
info@effortlessMath.com
www.EffortlessMath.com

ISBN: 978-1-63719-314-3

Published by: Effortless Math Education Inc.

For Online Math Practice Visit www.EffortlessMath.com

Welcome to
North Carolina EOG Grade 6 Math Prep 2023

Thank you for choosing Effortless Math for your North Carolina EOG Grade 6 Math test preparation and congratulations on making the decision to prepare for the North Carolina EOG Grade 6 test!

It's a remarkable move you are taking, one that shouldn't be diminished in any capacity. That's why you need to use every tool possible to ensure you succeed on the test with the highest possible score, and this extensive study guide is one such tool.

This study guide will help you prepare for (and even ACE) the North Carolina EOG Grade 6 test's math section. As test day draws nearer, effective preparation becomes increasingly more important. Thankfully, you have this comprehensive study guide to help you get ready for the test. With this guide, you can feel confident that you will be more than ready for the North Carolina EOG Grade 6 Math test when the time comes.

First and foremost, it is important to note that this book is a study guide and not a textbook. It is best read from cover to cover. Every lesson of this "self-guided math book" was carefully developed to ensure that you are making the most effective use of your time while preparing for the test. This up-to-date guide reflects the 2023 test guidelines and will put you on the right track to hone your math skills, overcome exam anxiety, and boost your confidence, so that you can have your best to succeed on the North Carolina EOG Grade 6 Math test.

This study guide will:

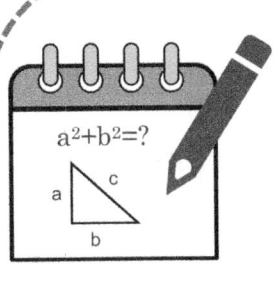

- ☑ Explain the format of the North Carolina EOG Grade 6 Math test.
- ☑ Describe specific test-taking strategies that you can use on the test.
- ☑ Provide North Carolina EOG Grade 6 Math test-taking tips.
- ☑ Review all North Carolina EOG Grade 6 Math concepts and topics you will be tested on.
- ☑ Help you identify the areas in which you need to concentrate your study time.
- ☑ Offer exercises that help you develop the basic math skills you will learn in each section.
- ☑ Give **2 realistic and full-length practice tests** (featuring new question types) with detailed answers to help you measure your exam readiness and build confidence.

This resource contains everything you will ever need to succeed on the North Carolina EOG Grade 6 Math test. You'll get in-depth instructions on every math topic as well as tips and techniques on how to answer each question type. You'll also get plenty of practice questions to boost your test-taking confidence.

In addition, in the following pages you'll find:

➢ **How to Use This Book Effectively** – This section provides you with step-by-step instructions on how to get the most out of this comprehensive study guide.

➢ **How to study for the North Carolina EOG Grade 6 Math Test** – A six-step study program has been developed to help you make the best use of this book and prepare for your North Carolina EOG Grade 6 Math test. Here you'll find tips and strategies to guide your study program and help you understand North Carolina EOG Grade 6 Math and how to ace the test.

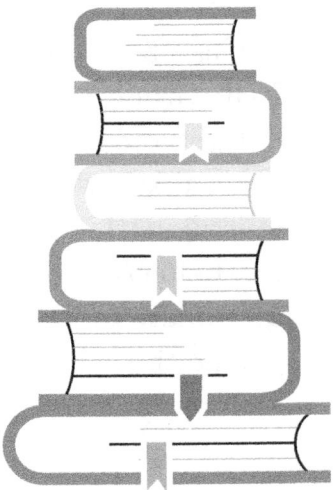

- ➤ **North Carolina EOG Grade 6 Math Review** – Learn everything you need to know about the North Carolina EOG Grade 6 Math test.

- ➤ **North Carolina EOG Grade 6 Math Test-Taking Strategies** – Learn how to effectively put these recommended test-taking techniques into use for improving your North Carolina EOG Grade 6 Math score.

- ➤ **Test Day Tips** – Review these tips to make sure you will do your best when the big day comes.

Effortless Math's North Carolina EOG Grade 6 Online Center

Effortless Math Online North Carolina EOG Grade 6 Center offers a complete study program, including the following:

- ✓ Step-by-step instructions on how to prepare for the North Carolina EOG Grade 6 Math test
- ✓ Numerous North Carolina EOG Grade 6 Math worksheets to help you measure your math skills
- ✓ Complete list of North Carolina EOG Grade 6 Math formulas
- ✓ Video lessons for all North Carolina EOG Grade 6 Math topics
- ✓ Full-length North Carolina EOG Grade 6 Math practice tests
- ✓ And much more...

No Registration Required.

Visit effortlessmath.com/NorthCarolinaEOG6 to find your online North Carolina EOG Grade 6 Math resources.

How to Use This Book Effectively

Look no further when you need a study guide to improve your math skills to succeed on the math portion of the North Carolina EOG Grade 6 test. Each chapter of this comprehensive guide to the North Carolina EOG Grade 6 Math will provide you with the knowledge, tools, and understanding needed for every topic covered on the test.

It's imperative that you understand each topic before moving onto another one, as that's the way to guarantee your success. Each topic provides you with examples and a step-by-step guide of every concept to better understand the content that will be on the test. To get the best possible results from this book:

- ➢ **Begin studying long before your test date.** This provides you ample time to learn the different math concepts. The earlier you begin studying for the test, the sharper your skills will be. Do not procrastinate! Provide yourself with plenty of time to learn the concepts and feel comfortable that you understand them when your test date arrives.
- ➢ **Practice consistently.** Study North Carolina EOG Grade 6 Math concepts at least 20 to 30 minutes a day. Remember, slow and steady wins the race, which can be applied to preparing for the North Carolina EOG Grade 6 Math test. Instead of cramming to tackle everything at once, be patient and learn the math topics in short bursts.
- ➢ Whenever you get a math problem wrong, **mark it off, and review it later** to make sure you understand the concept.
- ➢ Start each session by **looking over the previous material.**
- ➢ Once you've reviewed the book's lessons, **take the practice test at the back of the book** to gauge your level of readiness. Then, review your results. Read detailed answers and solutions for each question you missed.
- ➢ **Take another practice test** to get an idea of how ready you are to take the actual exam. Taking the practice tests will give you the confidence you need on test day. Simulate the North Carolina EOG Grade 6 testing environment by sitting in a quiet room free from distraction. Make sure to clock yourself with a timer.

How to Study for the North Carolina EOG Grade 6 Math Test

Studying for the North Carolina EOG Grade 6 Math test can be a really daunting and boring task. What's the best way to go about it? Is there a certain study method that works better than others? Well, studying for the North Carolina EOG Grade 6 Math can be done effectively. The following six-step program has been designed to make preparing for the North Carolina EOG Grade 6 Math test more efficient and less overwhelming.

Step 1 - Create a study plan.
Step 2 - Choose your study resources.
Step 3 - Review, Learn, Practice
Step 4 - Learn and practice test-taking strategies.
Step 5 - Learn the North Carolina EOG Grade 6 Test format and take practice tests.
Step 6 - Analyze your performance.

STEP 1: Create a Study Plan

It's always easier to get things done when you have a plan. Creating a study plan for the North Carolina EOG Grade 6 Math test can help you to stay on track with your studies. It's important to sit down and prepare a study plan with what works with your life, school, and any other obligations you may have. Devote enough time 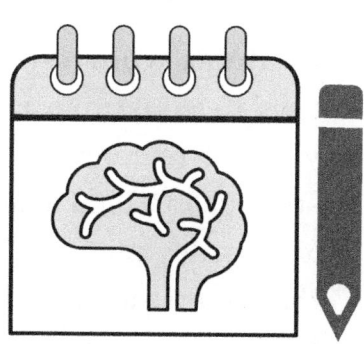 each day to studying. It's also a great idea to break down each section of the exam into blocks and study one concept at a time.

It's important to understand that there is no "right" way to create a study plan. Your study plan will be personalized based on your specific needs and learning style.

Follow these guidelines to create an effective study plan for your North Carolina EOG Grade 6 Math test:

- ★ **Analyze your learning style and study habits** – Everyone has a different learning style. It is essential to embrace your individuality and the unique way you learn. Think about what works and what doesn't work for you. Do you prefer North Carolina EOG Grade 6 Math prep books or a combination of textbooks and video lessons? Does it work better for you if you study every night for thirty minutes or is it more effective to study in the morning before going to school?

- ★ **Evaluate your schedule** – Review your current schedule and find out how much time you can consistently devote to North Carolina EOG Grade 6 Math study.

- ★ **Develop a schedule** – Now it's time to add your study schedule to your calendar like any other obligation. Schedule time for study, practice, and review. Plan out which topic you will study on which day to ensure that you're devoting enough time to each concept. Develop a study plan that is mindful, realistic, and flexible.

- ★ **Stick to your schedule** – A study plan is only effective when it is followed consistently. You should try to develop a study plan that you can follow for the length of your study program.

- ★ **Evaluate your study plan and adjust as needed** – Sometimes you need to adjust your plan when you have new commitments. Check in with yourself regularly to make sure that you're not falling behind in your study plan. Remember, the most important thing is sticking to your plan. Your study plan is all about helping you be more productive. If you find that your study plan is not as effective as you want, don't get discouraged. It's okay to make changes as you figure out what works best for you.

STEP 2: Choose Your Study Resources

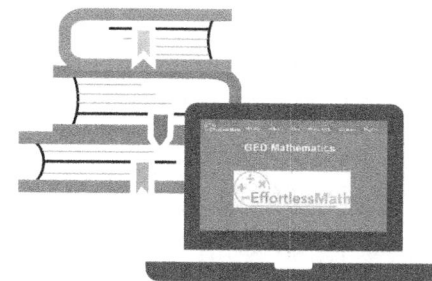

There are numerous textbooks and online resources available for the North Carolina EOG Grade 6 Math test, and it may not be clear where to begin. Don't worry! This study guide provides everything you need to fully prepare for your North Carolina EOG Grade 6 Math test. In addition to the book content, you can also use Effortless Math's online resources. (Video lessons, worksheets, formulas, etc.)

You can also visit EffortlessMath.com/NorthCarolinaEOG6 to find your online North Carolina EOG Grade 6 Math resources.

STEP 3: Review, Learn, Practice

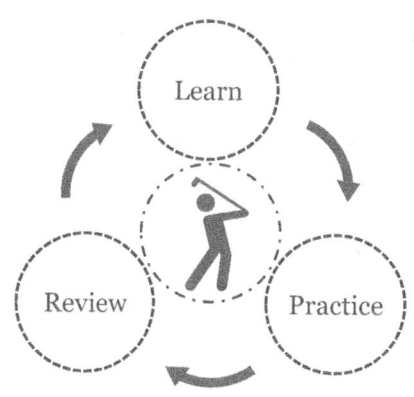

This North Carolina EOG Grade 6 Math study guide breaks down each subject into specific skills or content areas. For instance, the percent concept is separated into different topics–percent calculation, percent increase and decrease, percent problems, etc. Use this study guide and Effortless Math online North Carolina EOG Grade 6 center to help you go over all key math concepts and topics on the North Carolina EOG Grade 6 Math test.

As you read each topic, take notes or highlight the concepts you would like to go over again in the future. If you're unfamiliar with a topic or something is difficult for you, visit Effortless Math North Carolina EOG center to learn more about that topic. For each math topic, plenty of instructions, step-by-step guides, and examples are provided to ensure you get a good grasp of the material.

Quickly review the topics you do understand to get a brush-up of the material. Be sure to do the practice questions provided at the end of every chapter to measure your understanding of the concepts.

STEP 4: Learn and Practice Test-taking Strategies

In the following sections, you will find important test-taking strategies and tips that can help you earn extra points. You'll learn how to think strategically and when to guess if you don't know the answer to a question. Using North Carolina EOG Grade 6 Math test-taking strategies and tips can help you raise your score and do well on the test. Apply test taking strategies on the practice tests to help you boost your confidence.

STEP 5: Learn the North Carolina EOG Grade 6 Test Format and Take Practice Tests

The North Carolina EOG *Test Review* section provides information about the structure of the North Carolina EOG test. Read this section to learn more about the North Carolina EOG test structure. When you have a prior understanding of the test format and different types of North Carolina EOG Grade 6 Math questions, you'll feel more confident when you take the actual exam.

Once you have read through the instructions and lessons and feel like you are ready to go – take advantage of both of the full-length North Carolina EOG Grade 6 Math practice tests available in this study guide. Use the practice tests to sharpen your skills and build confidence.

The North Carolina EOG Grade 6 Math practice tests offered at the end of the book are formatted similarly to the actual North Carolina EOG Grade 6 Math test. When you take each practice test, try to simulate actual testing conditions. To take the practice tests, sit in a quiet space, time yourself, and work through as many of the questions as time allows. The practice tests are followed by detailed answer explanations to help you find your weak areas, learn from your mistakes, and raise your North Carolina EOG Grade 6 Math score.

STEP 6: Analyze Your Performance

After taking the practice tests, look over the answer keys and explanations to learn which questions you answered correctly and which you did not. Never be discouraged if you make a few mistakes. See them as a learning opportunity. This will highlight your strengths and weaknesses.

You can use the results to determine if you need additional practice or if you are ready to take the actual North Carolina EOG Grade 6 Math test.

Looking for more?

Visit effortlessMath.com/NorthCarolinaEOG6 to find hundreds of North Carolina EOG Grade 6 Math worksheets, video tutorials, practice tests, North Carolina EOG Grade 6 Math formulas, and much more.

No Registration Required.

North Carolina EOG Test Review

The North Carolina End-of-Grade Tests (EOG) is a standardized assessment program administered to public school students in grades 3-8 in the state of North Carolina. The EOG test is designed to measure student achievement in core academic subjects, including reading, math, and science.

The EOG tests are developed by the North Carolina Department of Public Instruction and are aligned with the North Carolina Standard Course of Study, which outlines the academic content and skills that students are expected to learn in each grade level. The purpose of the EOG test is to provide a measure of student achievement and to help educators identify areas where students may need additional support.

The EOG tests are administered in two parts. The first part is a multiple-choice section, which is designed to assess students' knowledge and understanding of the academic content in each subject area. The second part is a performance task section, which requires students to demonstrate their ability to apply what they have learned in a real-world context.

The EOG tests are typically administered in the spring of each school year, and results are used to evaluate the effectiveness of individual schools and school districts in achieving academic goals. In addition, EOG results are used to inform decisions about instructional strategies and to identify areas where students may need additional support.

Overall, the North Carolina End-of-Grade Tests (EOG) is an important component of the state's assessment program, providing valuable information about student achievement and helping educators identify ways to improve academic outcomes for all students.

Section: Ratios and Proportional Relationships	
Understand ratio concepts and use ratio reasoning to solve problems.	
Standard Code	Standard
6. RP. A. 1	Understand the concept of a ratio and use ratio language to describe a ratio relationship between two quantities.
6. RP. A. 2	Understand the concept of a unit rate a/b associated with a ratio $a:b$ with b is not equal to 0 and use rate language in the context of a ratio relationship.
6. RP. A. 3	Use ratio and rate reasoning to solve real-world and mathematical problems, e.g., by reasoning about tables of equivalent ratios, tape diagrams, double number line diagrams, or equations.

Section: The Number System	
Apply and extend previous understandings of multiplication and division to divide fractions by fractions.	
Standard Code	Standard
6. NS. A. 1	Interpret and compute quotients of fractions and solve word problems involving division of fractions by fractions, e.g., by using visual fraction models and equations to represent the problem.
Compute fluently with multi-digit numbers and find common factors and multiples.	
Standard Code	Standard
6. NS. B. 2	Fluently divide multi-digit numbers using the standard algorithm.
6. NS. B. 3	Fluently add, subtract, multiply, and divide multi-digit decimals using the standard algorithm for each operation.
6. NS. B. 4	Find the greatest common factor of two whole numbers less than or equal to 100 and the least common multiple of two whole numbers less than or equal to 12. Use the distributive property to express a sum of two whole numbers 1–100 with a common factor as a multiple of a sum of two whole numbers with no common factor.
Apply and extend previous understandings of numbers to the system of rational numbers.	
Standard Code	Standard
6. NS. C. 5	Understand that positive and negative numbers are used together to describe quantities having opposite directions or values (e.g., temperature above/below zero, elevation above/below sea level, credits/debits, positive/negative electric charge); use positive and negative numbers to represent quantities in real-world contexts, explaining the meaning of 0 in each situation.
6. NS. C. 6	Understand a rational number as a point on the number line. Extend number line diagrams and coordinate axes familiar from previous grades to represent points on the line and in the plane with negative number coordinates.

Standard Code	Standard
6.NS.C.7	Understand ordering and absolute value of rational numbers.
6.NS.C.8	Solve real-world and mathematical problems by graphing points in all four quadrants of the coordinate plane. Include use of coordinates and absolute value to find distances between points with the same first coordinate or the same second coordinate.

Section: Expressions and Equations

Apply and extend previous understandings of arithmetic to algebraic expressions.

Standard Code	Standard
6.EE.A.1	Write and evaluate numerical expressions involving whole-number exponents.
6.EE.A.2	Write, read, and evaluate expressions in which letters stand for numbers.
6.EE.A.3	Apply the properties of operations to generate equivalent expressions.
6.EE.A.4	Identify when two expressions are equivalent (i.e., when the two expressions name the same number regardless of which value is substituted into them).

Reason about and solve one-variable equations and inequalities.

Standard Code	Standard
6.EE.B.5	Understand solving an equation or inequality as a process of answering a question: which values from a specified set, if any, make the equation or inequality true? Use substitution to determine whether a given number in a specified set makes an equation or inequality true.
6.EE.B.6	Use variables to represent numbers and write expressions when solving a real-world or mathematical problem; understand that a variable can represent an unknown number, or depending on the purpose at hand, any number in a specified set.
6.EE.B.7	Solve real-world and mathematical problems by writing and solving equations of the form $x + p = q$ and $px = q$ for cases in which p, q and x are all nonnegative rational numbers.
6.EE.B.8	Write an inequality of the form $x > c$ or $x < c$ to represent a constraint or condition in a real-world or mathematical problem. Recognize that inequalities of the form $x > c$ or $x < c$ have infinitely many solutions; represent solutions of such inequalities on number line diagrams.

Represent and analyze quantitative relationships between dependent and independent variables.

Standard Code	Standard
6.EE.C.9	Use variables to represent two quantities in a real-world problem that change in relationship to one another; write an equation to express one quantity, thought of as the dependent variable, in terms of the other quantity, thought of as the independent variable. Analyze the relationship between the dependent and independent variables using graphs and tables and relate these to the equation.

Section: Geometry	
Solve real-world and mathematical problems involving area, surface area, and volume.	
Standard Code	Standard
6. G. A. 1	Find the area of right triangles, other triangles, special quadrilaterals, and polygons by composing into rectangles or decomposing into triangles and other shapes; apply these techniques in the context of solving real-world and mathematical problems.
6. G. A. 2	Find the volume of a right rectangular prism with fractional edge lengths by packing it with unit cubes of the appropriate unit fraction edge lengths and show that the volume is the same as would be found by multiplying the edge lengths of the prism. Apply the formulas $V = l\,w\,h$ and $V = b\,h$ to find volumes of right rectangular prisms with fractional edge lengths in the context of solving real-world and mathematical problems.
6. G. A. 3	Draw polygons in the coordinate plane given coordinates for the vertices; use coordinates to find the length of a side joining points with the same first coordinate or the same second coordinate. Apply these techniques in the context of solving real-world and mathematical problems.
6. G. A. 4	Represent three-dimensional figures using nets made up of rectangles and triangles and use the nets to find the surface area of these figures. Apply these techniques in the context of solving real-world and mathematical problems.

Section: Statistics and Probability	
Develop understanding of statistical variability.	
Standard Code	Standard
6. SP. A. 1	Recognize a statistical question as one that anticipates variability in the data related to the question and accounts for it in the answers.
6. SP. A. 2	Understand that a set of data collected to answer a statistical question has a distribution which can be described by its center, spread, and overall shape.
6. SP. A. 3	Recognize that a measure of center for a numerical data set summarizes all of its values with a single number, while a measure of variation describes how its values vary with a single number.
Summarize and describe distributions.	
Standard Code	Standard
6. SP. B. 4	Display numerical data in plots on a number line, including dot plots, histograms, and box plots.
6. SP. B. 5	Summarize numerical data sets in relation to their context.

North Carolina EOG Grade 6 Math Test-Taking Strategies

Here are some test-taking strategies that you can use to maximize your performance and results on the North Carolina EOG Grade 6 Math test.

#1: Use This Approach To Answer Every North Carolina EOG Math Question

- Review the question to identify keywords and important information.
- Translate the keywords into math operations so you can solve the problem.
- Review the answer choices. What are the differences between answer choices?
- Draw or label a diagram if needed.
- Try to find patterns.
- Find the right method to answer the question. Use straightforward math, plug in numbers, or test the answer choices (backsolving).
- Double-check your work.

#2: Use Educated Guessing

This approach is applicable to the problems you understand to some degree but cannot solve using straightforward math. In such cases, try to filter out as many answer choices as possible before picking an answer. In cases where you don't have a clue about what a certain problem entails, don't waste any time trying to eliminate answer choices. Just choose one randomly before moving onto the next question.

As you can ascertain, direct solutions are the most optimal approach. Carefully read through the question, determine what the solution is using the math you have learned before, then coordinate the answer with one of the choices available to you. Are you stumped? Make your best guess, then move on.

Don't leave any fields empty! Even if you're unable to work out a problem, strive to answer it. Take a guess if you have to. You will not lose points by getting an answer wrong, though you may gain a point by getting it correct!

#3: BALLPARK

A ballpark answer is a rough approximation. When we become overwhelmed by calculations and figures, we end up making silly mistakes. A decimal that is moved by one unit can change an answer from right to wrong, regardless of the number of steps that you went through to get it. That's where ballparking can play a big part.

If you think you know what the correct answer may be (even if it's just a ballpark answer), you'll usually have the ability to eliminate a couple of choices. While answer choices are usually based on the average student error and/or values that are closely tied, you will still be able to weed out choices that are way far afield. Try to find answers that aren't in the proverbial ballpark when you're looking for a wrong answer on a multiple-choice question. This is an optimal approach to eliminating answers to a problem.

#4: BACKSOLVING

A majority of questions on the North Carolina EOG Grade 6 Math test will be in multiple-choice format. Many test-takers prefer multiple-choice questions, as at least the answer is right there. You'll typically have four answers to pick from. You simply need to figure out which one is correct. Usually, the best way to go about doing so is "backsolving."

As mentioned earlier, direct solutions are the most optimal approach to answering a question. Carefully read through a problem, calculate a solution, then correspond the answer with one of the choices displayed in front of you. If you can't calculate a solution, your next best approach involves "backsolving."

When backsolving a problem, contrast one of your answer options against the problem you are asked, then see which of them is most relevant. More often than not, answer choices are listed in ascending or descending order. In such cases, try out the choices B or C. If it's not correct, you can go either down or up from there.

#5: Plugging In Numbers

"Plugging in numbers" is a strategy that can be applied to a wide range of different math problems on the North Carolina EOG Grade 6 Math test. This approach is typically used to simplify a challenging question so that it is more understandable. By using the strategy carefully, you can find the answer without too much trouble.

The concept is fairly straightforward–replace unknown variables in a problem with certain values. When selecting a number, consider the following:

- Choose a number that's basic (just not too basic). Generally, you should avoid choosing 1 (or even 0). A decent choice is 2.
- Try not to choose a number that is displayed in the problem.
- Make sure you keep your numbers different if you need to choose at least two of them.
- More often than not, choosing numbers merely lets you filter out some of your answer choices. As such, don't just go with the first choice that gives you the right answer.
- If several answers seem correct, then you'll need to choose another value and try again. This time, though, you'll just need to check choices that haven't been eliminated yet.
- If your question contains fractions, then a potential right answer may involve either an LCD (least common denominator) or an LCD multiple.
- 100 is the number you should choose when you are dealing with problems involving percentages.

North Carolina EOG Grade 6 Math – Test Day Tips

After practicing and reviewing all the math concepts you've been taught, and taking some North Carolina EOG Grade 6 mathematics practice tests, you'll be prepared for test day. Consider the following tips to be extra-ready come test time.

Before Your Test

What to do the night before:

- **Relax!** One day before your test, study lightly or skip studying altogether. You shouldn't attempt to learn something new, either. There are plenty of reasons why studying the evening before a big test can work against you. Put it this way–a marathoner wouldn't go out for a sprint before the day of a big race. Mental marathoners–such as yourself–should not study for any more than one hour 24 hours before a North Carolina EOG Grade 6 test. That's because your brain requires some rest to be at its best. The night before your exam, spend some time with family or friends, or read a book.

- **Avoid bright screens** - You'll have to get some good shuteye the night before your test. Bright screens (such as the ones coming from your laptop, TV, or mobile device) should be avoided altogether. Staring at such a screen will keep your brain up, making it hard to drift asleep at a reasonable hour.

- **Make sure your dinner is healthy** - The meal that you have for dinner should be nutritious. Be sure to drink plenty of water as well. Load up on your complex carbohydrates, much like a marathon runner would do. Pasta, rice, and potatoes are ideal options here, as are vegetables and protein sources.

- **Get your bag ready for test day** - The night prior to your test, pack your bag with any gear that you need. Keep the bag right by your front door.

The Day of the Test

- **Get up reasonably early, but not too early.**

- **Have breakfast** - Breakfast improves your concentration, memory, and mood. As such, make sure the breakfast that you eat in the morning is healthy. The last thing you want to be is distracted by a grumbling tummy. If it's not your own stomach making those noises, another test taker close to you might be instead. Prevent discomfort or embarrassment by consuming a healthy breakfast. Bring a snack with you if you think you'll need it.

- **Follow your daily routine** - Do you watch TV each morning while getting ready for the day? Don't break your usual habits on the day of the test. Likewise, if coffee isn't something you drink in the morning, then don't take up the habit hours before your test. Routine consistency lets you concentrate on the main objective—doing the best you can on your test.

- **Wear layers** - Dress yourself up in comfortable layers. You should be ready for any kind of internal temperature. If it gets too warm during the test, take a layer off.

- **Get there on time** - The last thing you want to do is get to the test site late. Rather, you should be there 45 minutes prior to the start of the test. Upon your arrival, try not to hang out with anybody who is nervous. Any anxious energy they exhibit shouldn't influence you.

- **Leave the books at home** - No books should be brought to the test site. If you start developing anxiety before the test, books could encourage you to do some last-minute studying, which will only hinder you. Keep the books far away—better yet, leave them at home.

- **Make your voice heard** - If something is off, speak to a proctor. If medical attention is needed or if you'll require anything, consult the proctor prior to the start of the test. Any doubts you have should be clarified. You should be entering the test site with a state of mind that is completely clear.

- **Have faith in yourself** - When you feel confident, you will be able to perform at your best. When you are waiting for the test to begin, envision yourself receiving an outstanding result. Try to see yourself as someone who knows all the answers, no matter what the questions are. A lot of athletes tend to use this technique–particularly before a big competition. Your expectations will be reflected by your performance.

During your test

- **Be calm and breathe deeply** - You need to relax before the test, and some deep breathing will go a long way to help you do that. Be confident and calm. You got this. Everybody feels a little stressed out just before an evaluation of any kind is set to begin. Learn some effective breathing exercises. Spend a minute meditating before the test starts. Filter out any negative thoughts you have. Exhibit confidence when having such thoughts.

- **Concentrate on the test** - Refrain from comparing yourself to anyone else. You shouldn't be distracted by the people near you or random noise. Concentrate exclusively on the test. If you find yourself irritated by surrounding noises, earplugs can be used to block sounds off close to you. Don't forget–the test is going to last several hours. Some of that time will be dedicated to brief sections. Concentrate on the specific question you are working on during a particular moment.

- **Skip challenging questions** - Optimize your time when taking the test. Lingering on a single question for too long will work against you. If you don't know what the answer is to a certain question, use your best guess, and mark the question so you can review it later on. There is no need to spend time attempting to solve something you aren't sure about. That time would be better served handling the questions you can actually answer well. You will not be penalized for getting the wrong answer on a test like this.

- **Try to answer each question individually** - Focus only on the question you are working on. Use one of the test-taking strategies to solve the problem. If you aren't able to come up with an answer, don't get frustrated. Simply skip that question, then move onto the next one.

- **Don't forget to breathe!** Whenever you notice your mind wandering, your stress levels boosting, or frustration brewing, take a thirty-second break. Shut your eyes, drop your pencil, breathe deeply, and let your shoulders relax. You will end up being more productive when you allow yourself to relax for a moment.

- **Review your answer.** If you still have time at the end of the test, don't waste it. Go back and check over your answers. It is worth going through the test from start to finish to ensure that you didn't make a sloppy mistake somewhere.

After your test

- **Take it easy** - You will need to set some time aside to relax and decompress once the test has concluded. There is no need to stress yourself out about what you could've said, or what you may have done wrong. At this point, there's nothing you can do about it. Your energy and time would be better spent on something that will bring you happiness for the remainder of your day.

Contents

Chapter 1: Expressions and Equations — 1

- Identifying Expressions and Equations 2
- Identify Equivalent Expressions 3
- Using Properties to Write Equivalent Expressions 4
- Using Strip Models to Identify Equivalent Expressions................ 5
- Using Algebra Tiles to Identify Equivalent Expressions............... 6
- Using Exponents to Write down Multiplication Expressions 7
- Using Exponents to Write Powers of Ten 8
- Prime Factorization with Exponents 9
- Identifying Errors Involving the Order of Operations 10
- Writing down Variable Expressions Involving Two Operations... 11
- Using Area Models to Factor Variable Expressions.................... 12
- Using Distributive Property to Factor Variable Expressions 13
- Using Distributive Property to Factor Numerical Expressions... 14
- Chapter 1: Practices 15
- Chapter 1: Answers... 22

Chapter 2: One-Step Operation — 25

- One–Step Adding and Subtracting of Decimals and Fractions ... 26
- One–Step Multiplying and Dividing of Decimals and Fractions.. 27
- Graphing One-Step Multiplication and Division Equations....... 28
- Graphing One-Step Inequalities with Rational Numbers 29
- One–Step Equations 30
- Matching Word Problems with the One-Step Equation............ 31
- Word Problems of the One-Step Equation................................ 32
- Chapter 2: Practices 33
- Chapter 2: Answers... 36

Chapter 3: Inequalities — 39

- Write Inequalities from Number Lines 40
- Graphing Single–Variable Inequalities....................................... 41
- One–Step Inequalities 42
- Word Problems Involving One-step Inequalities 43
- Chapter 3: Practices 44
- Chapter 3: Answers... 46

Chapter 4: Variables and Equations — 47

- Independent and Dependent Variables in Tables and Graphs... 48
- Independent and Dependent Variables in Word Problems....... 49
- Using Algebra Tiles to Model and Solve Equations 50
- Using Diagrams to Model and Solve Equations 51
- Evaluating One Variable 52
- Chapter 4: Practices 53
- Chapter 4: Answers... 57

Contents

Chapter 5: Two-Variable Equation — 59
- Using a Table to Write down a Two-Variable Equation 60
- Complete a Table and Graph a Two-Variable Equation 61
- Evaluating Two Variables 62
- Solving Word problems by Finding Two-Variable Equation...................... 63
- Chapter 5: Practices 64
- Chapter 5: Answers 66

Chapter 6: Geometry and Solid Figures — 67
- Triangles 68
- Triangle Inequality 69
- Relationships Between Sides and Angles in a Triangle............................ 70
- Definition of the Area of a Triangle 71
- Polygons 72
- Cubes 73
- Rectangular Prisms.. 74
- Definition of the Area of a Parallelogram 75
- Word Problems Involving Area of Quadrilaterals and Triangles 76
- Definition of the Area of a Trapezoid 77
- Finding Area of Compound Figures 78
- Finding Area Between Two Rectangles... 79
- Finding Area Between Two Triangles... 80
- Volume of Cubes and Rectangular Prisms: Word Problems 81
- Chapter 6: Practices... 82
- Chapter 6: Answers.. 92

Chapter 7: Ratios and Proportions — 93
- Write a Ratio.. 94
- Ratio Tables 95
- Using a Fraction to Write down a Ratio.. 96
- Matching a Model with a Ratio... 97
- Word Problems Involving Writing a Ratio 98
- Finding Equivalent Ratio 99
- Word Problems Involving Comparing Ratio... 100
- Word Problems Involving Equivalent Ratio... 101
- Similarity and Ratios.. 102
- Equivalent rates.. 103
- Word Problems Involving Comparing Rates 104
- Word Problems Involving Rates and Ratios.. 105
- Make a Graph of Ratios and Rates.. 106
- Chapter 7: Practices... 107
- Chapter 7: Answers.. 116

Contents

Chapter 8: Percentage — 119

- Representing Percentage 120
- Using Number Line to Graph Percentages 121
- Using Grid models to Represent Percent 122
- Using Strip Models to Explain Percent 123
- Using Grid Models to Solve Percentage Problems 124
- Using Strip Models to Solve Percentage Problems 125
- Word Problems of Determining Percentage of a Number 126
- Solving Percentage Word Problems 127
- Fractional and Decimal Percentages 128
- Using Grid Models to Convert Fractions to Percentages 129
- Word Problems: Comparing Percent and Fractions 130
- Word Problems: conversion of Percent, Fractions, and Decimals 131
- Percent Problems 132
- Chapter 8: Practices 133
- Chapter 8: Answers 140

Chapter 9: Measurement System — 144

- Mixed Customary Units Operations 145
- Mixed Numbers and Fractions Customary Unit Conversions 146
- Using Proportions to Convert Traditional and Metric Units 147
- Compare the Temperatures Above and Below Zero 148
- Chapter 9: Practices 149
- Chapter 9: Answers 151

Chapter 10: Statistics and Data Analysis — 152

- Pie Graph 153
- Graph The Line Plot 154
- Distributions in Line Plot 155
- Relative Frequency Tables 156
- Frequency Charts 157
- Mean, Median, Mode, and Range of the Given Data 158
- Interpreting Charts to find mean, median, mode, and range 159
- Finding an Outlier 160
- Finding Range, Quartiles, and Interquartile Range 161
- Interpreting Categorical Data 162
- Identifying Statistical Questions 163
- Completing a Table and Making a Graph: Word Problems 164
- Chapter 10: Practices 165
- Chapter 10: Answers 173

Chapter 11: Fundamentals of Computations — 177

- Additive and multiplicative relationships 178
- Properties of addition 179
- Using Area Models and the Distributive Property to Multiply 180
- Reciprocals 181
- Chapter 11: Practices 182

EffortlessMath.com

Contents

Chapter 12: Operations of Fraction, Decimal, and Mixed Numbers — 187

- Chapter 11: Answers 184
- Scaling whole numbers by fractions 188
- Using Models to Divide Whole Numbers by Unit Fractions 189
- Dividing fractions by whole numbers in recipes 190
- Using Models to Multiply Two Fractions 191
- Multiplying and Dividing Fractions 192
- Word Problem for Explaining Fractions as Division 193
- Word Problem of Dividing Fractions 194
- Multiplication and Division of Decimals by Powers of Ten 195
- Estimate Products of Mixed Numbers 196
- Scaling by Fractions and Mixed Numbers 197
- Multiplying Mixed Numbers 198
- Dividing Mixed Numbers 199
- Word Problem of Multiplying Mixed Numbers 200
- Multiplying and Dividing Decimals 201
- Multiplying Three Rational Numbers, and Whole Numbers 202
- Chapter 12: Practices 203
- Chapter 12: Answers 210

Chapter 13: Fraction, Decimals and Mixed Numbers — 213

- Using Number Lines to Represent Fractions 214
- Using Strip Diagrams to Represent Fractions 215
- Fractions Word Problems 216
- Word Problems Involving Fractions of a Group 217
- Simplifying Fractions 218
- Using Number Lines to Present Decimal 219
- Repeating Decimals 220
- Convert Between Fractions and Decimals 221
- Unit Prices with Decimals and Fractions 222
- Convert Between Decimals and Mixed Numbers 223
- Convert Between Improper Fractions and Mixed Numbers 224
- Order of Decimals, Mixed Numbers and Fractions 225
- Chapter 13: Practices 226
- Chapter 13: Answers 232

Chapter 14: Rational Numbers and Integers — 235

- Using a Diagram to Classify Rational Numbers 236
- Opposite integers 237
- Using Number Lines to Present Integers 238
- Integers and Vertical and Horizontal Number Lines 239
- Chapter 14: Practices 240
- Chapter 14: Answers 242

Contents

Chapter 15: **Coordinate Plane** — 245
- Objects on a Coordinate Plane 246
- Understanding Quadrants 247
- Coordinate Planes as Maps 248
- Chapter 15: Practices 249
- Chapter 15: Answers 251

Chapter 16: **Rational Numbers** — 253
- Using Number Lines to Represent Rational Numbers 254
- Using Number Lines to Order Rational Numbers 255
- Word Problems of Ordering Rational Numbers 256
- Convert Rational Numbers to a Fraction 257
- Chapter 16: Practices 258
- Chapter 16: Answers 260

Chapter 17: **Absolute Value** — 263
- Absolute Value Definition 264
- Integers and Absolute Value 265
- Using Number Lines to Present Absolute Value 266
- Integer Inequalities Involving Absolute Values 267
- Word Problems of Absolute Value and Integers 268
- Absolute Value of Rational Numbers 269
- Absolute Values and Opposites of Rational Numbers 270
- Chapter 17: Practices 271
- Chapter 17: Answers 274

Time to Test -- 276
North Carolina EOG Grade 6 Math Practice Test 1 -------------------------- 277
North Carolina EOG Grade 6 Math Practice Test 2 -------------------------- 293
North Carolina EOG Grade 6 Math Practice Tests Answer Keys ----------- 307
North Carolina EOG Grade 6 Math Practice Tests Answers and Explanations ------- 309

CHAPTER 1
Expressions and Equations

Math topics that you'll learn in this chapter:

- ☑ Identifying Expressions and Equations
- ☑ Identify Equivalent Expressions
- ☑ Using Properties to Write Equivalent Expressions
- ☑ Using Strip Models to Identify Equivalent Expressions
- ☑ Using Algebra Tiles to Identify Equivalent Expressions
- ☑ Using Exponents to Write down Multiplication Expressions
- ☑ Using Exponents to Write Powers of Ten
- ☑ Prime Factorization with Exponents
- ☑ Identifying Errors Involving the Order of Operations
- ☑ Writing down Variable Expressions Involving Two Operations
- ☑ Using Area Models to Factor Variable Expressions
- ☑ Using Distributive Property to Factor Variable Expressions
- ☑ Using Distributive Property to Factor Numerical Expressions

Identifying Expressions and Equations

- Expressions are mathematical phrases that have numbers, variables, or both.

- Expressions may additionally contain operations; however, they don't ever have an equal sign. Equations are mathematical sentences showing that 2 expressions are equal. Equations will always have an equal sign. Here, for instance, $3x + 13$ is the expression on the left-hand side, and it is equal to the expression 28 on the right-hand side.

$$3x + 13 = 28$$

Examples:

Example 1. Determine if this is an expression or an equation.

$$(x + 8) \div 3$$

Solution: This is an expression. Because it does not have an equal sign and just it has contained numbers and variable, actually contain the operations without the equal sign.

Example 2. Is this an expression or an equation?

$$w = 88 - 19$$

Solution: This is an equation. Because it has an equal sign.

Identify Equivalent Expressions

- Usually, if 2 things are equal, then it's called equivalent.

- In math, equivalent expressions are expressions that are the same, even if the expression doesn't look the same. However, if the values are placed into the expression, both expressions provide the same answer. For example, $3(x + 2)$ and $3x + 6$ are equivalent expressions since the value of both stays the same for any value of x.

Examples:

Example 1. Determine the equivalent expression below.

$$8r - 3r$$

Solution: Combine like terms to form the standard form:

$$8r - 3r = 5r$$

So, the expression $8r - 3r$ is equivalent to $5r$.

Example 2. Determine the equivalent expression below.

$$1u + ((u + 2u) \div 3u)$$

Solution: Combine like terms to form the standard form:

$$1u + ((u + 2u) \div 3u) = 1u + (3u \div 3u) = 1u + 1$$

So, the expression $1u + ((u + 2u) \div 3u)$ is equivalent to $1u + 1$.

Example 3. Determine the equivalent expression below.

$$4k + 2k$$

Solution: Combine like terms to form the standard form:

$$4k + 2k = 6k$$

So, the expression $4k + 2k$ is equivalent to $6k$.

Using Properties to Write Equivalent Expressions

- It's possible to write equivalent expressions via a combination of like terms. A like term is a term that has the same variables raised to the same powers.

- Properties are utilized to simplify algebraic expressions.

- You can use properties of operations to write equivalent expressions. Here are some common properties:

Commutative property of addition	$a + b = b + a$
Commutative property of multiplication	$a \times b = b \times a$
Associative property of addition	$(a + b) + c = a + (b + c)$
Associative property of multiplication	$(a \times b)c = a(b \times c)$
Distributive property	$a(b + c) = a \times b + a \times c$

Examples:

Example 1. Complete and solve the expressions.

$12 + 7d + 5 = 7d + \boxed{} + 5 = ?$

Solution: According to the two expressions, the commutative property of addition shows changing the order of addends does not change the sum. So, these expressions are equivalent if the missing number is 12. And add 12 to 5, to solve the expression. Therefore, it will be:

$$12 + 7d + 5 = 7d + 12 + 5 = 7d + 17$$

Example 2. Complete and solve the expressions.

$4x \times 8 = 8 \times \boxed{} = ?$

Solution: According to the two expressions, the commutative property of multiplication shows changing the order of factors does not change the product. So, these expressions are equivalent if the missing factor is $4x$. And multiply $4x$ by 8, to solve the expression. Therefore, it will be:

$$4x \times 8 = 8 \times 4x = 32x$$

Using Strip Models to Identify Equivalent Expressions

- Two expressions are equal if you can simplify them to the same third expression or if one of them is able to be written like the other one.

- One may additionally figure out if 2 expressions are equivalent whenever values are substituted in for the variable and both get you the same answer.

- This model signifies the expression:

| n | n | n | n | n | n | n | d | d | d |

$$n+n+n+n+n+n+n+d+d+d = 7n+3d$$

Examples:

Example 1. What expression does this model represent?

Solution: This model represents $1+1+1+1+1+d+d+d+d$. There are 5 times 1 and 4 times d in the model. Which can also write as 5 and $4d$.

| 1 | 1 | 1 | 1 | 1 | d | d | d | d |

So, the total length of the model is $5+4d$.

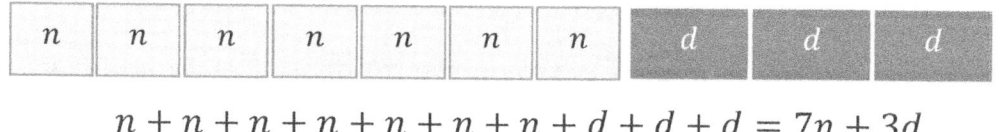

Example 2. What expression does this model represent?

| a | a | a | x | x | x | x | x | x | x |

Solution: This model represents $a+a+a+x+x+x+x+x+x+x$. There are 3 times a and 7 times x in the model. Which can also write as $3a$ and $7x$.

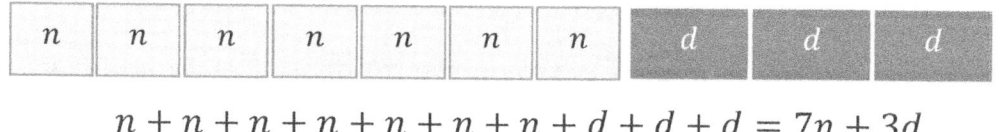

So, the total length of the model is $3a+7x$.

Using Algebra Tiles to Identify Equivalent Expressions

- An algebra tile is a square or rectangle-shaped tile or a tile that signifies numbers and variables.

- For instance, you may utilize square tiles to signify numbers. Each of the square tiles equals one. Thus, you can represent four using four tiles.

- If both of the expressions have the same amount of rectangular variable tiles along with the same amount of positive or negative tiles, then these expressions are equivalent.

- If there's any difference between the number of rectangular variable tiles or square plus or minus 1 tile, then these expressions aren't equivalent.

$3x + 12$

Examples:

Example 1. What expression do these tiles represent?

Solution: Count and write each set of tiles, $2x + 5 + 3x$. Combine like terms. There are 5 of (x) tiles and 5 of (1) tiles in all.

So, **$5x + 5$** is equivalent to algebra tiles.

Example 2. These tiles represent the expression $2x + 8 + 4x$. Write the equivalent expression.

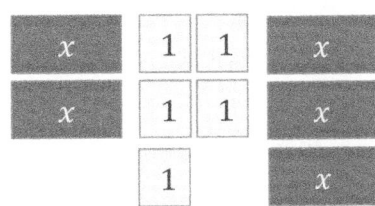

Solution: First, combine like terms. There are 6 of (x) tiles and 8 of (1) tiles in all.

So, **$6x + 8$** is equivalent to algebra tiles.

Using Exponents to Write down Multiplication Expressions

- Exponential expressions are merely a method of writing down powers in a short form.

- The base number shows which number gets multiplied. The exponent, a small number placed above and to the right-hand side of the base number, explains the number of times the base number gets multiplied.

- The exponent signifies the number of times the base is utilized as a factor. Thus, in the example of 64, it may be written as $4 \times 4 \times 4 = 4^3$, where 4 is the "base" and 3 is the "exponent". You will read this expression as "four to the third power".

Examples:

Example 1. Write the expression using an exponent.

$$5 \times 5 \times 5 \times 5 = ?$$

Solution: Since 5 is used 4 times, so the base is 5 and the exponent is repeat times, that is, 4.

$$5 \times 5 \times 5 \times 5 = 5^4$$

Example 2. Write the expression using an exponent.

$$6 \times 6 \times 6 = ?$$

Solution: Since 6 is used 3 times, so the base is 6 and the exponent is repeat times, that is, 3.

$$6 \times 6 \times 6 = 6^3$$

Using Exponents to Write Powers of Ten

- A power is a product of multiplying a number by itself. Generally, power is signified using a base number as well as an exponent.

- A base number shows the number getting multiplied. An exponent, a small number placed above and to the right-hand side of the base number, explains the number of times the base number gets multiplied.

- Whenever 10 gets raised to a whole number exponent, its value will have a leftmost digit of 1 and all of the other digits are 0. The exponent shows the number of 0s which come after the 1.

- To determine a missing exponent, you must look at the right-hand side of an equation and count how many zeros are after the 1. For example, $10^? = 1,000,000 \rightarrow$ There's six. Therefore, the missing exponent is 6.

$$10^6 = 1,000,000$$

Examples:

Example 1. Find the exponent.

$$10^? = 10,000,000$$

Solution: Since when 10 is raised to a whole number exponent, the value of the leftmost digit is 1 and all other digits are 0. The exponent tells you how many 0's come after the 1. So, count the number of 0s. There are 7 of them. Then, $10^7 = 10,000,000$.

Example 2. Write the number as an exponent based on 10.

$$100 = ?$$

Solution: Count the number of 0s. There are 2 of them. Then, $100 = 10^2$.

Prime Factorization with Exponents

- A prime factorization shows how to write a number as the product of prime factors.

- Prime factorization is when you break down a number into prime numbers which multiply by the original number.

- For instance, 40 is equal to $2 \times 2 \times 2 \times 5$. You were tasked with giving the answer in an exponent format. $2 \times 2 \times 2$ is equal to 2 cubed. The prime factorization of 40 in exponent format is 2 cubed multiplied by 5.

$$40 = 8 \times 5 \rightarrow 40 = 2 \times 2 \times 2 \times 5 \rightarrow 40 = 2^3 \times 5$$

Examples:

Example 1. Write the prime factorization of 25 with exponents.

5	25
5	5
	1

Solution: Divide by prime factors. And the final quotient must be 1.

$$25 \div 5 = 5$$

The prime factorization of 25 is 5×5. And write down the repeated factor (5) with exponent, 5^2.

Example 2. Write the prime factorization of 60 with exponents.

Solution: Divide by prime factors. And the final quotient must be 1.

$$60 = 5 \times 12 \rightarrow 60 = 5 \times 3 \times 4 \rightarrow 60 = 5 \times 3 \times 2 \times 2$$

5	60
3	12
2	4
2	2
	1

The prime factorization of 60 is $2 \times 2 \times 3 \times 5$. And write down the repeated factor (5) with exponent, $2^2 \times 3 \times 5$.

Identifying Errors Involving the Order of Operations

- To assess an expression having multiple operations, one may follow the order of operations:

  1. Do the operations inside the parentheses and the brackets. Begin with the operations inside the inner parentheses or brackets, calculating the expression from the inside out.

  2. Calculate the exponents.

  3. Multiply and divide from left to right.

  4. Add and subtract from left to right

Examples:

Example 1. How can you simplify $7 \times 2 + (20 - 2) \div 3^2 + 3$?

Solution: First, perform operations inside parentheses $(20 - 2) = 18$. Second, calculate exponents, $3^2 = 9$. Thus, you have $7 \times 2 + 18 \div 9 + 3$

Third, multiply and divide from left to right, $7 \times 2 = 14$ and $18 \div 9 = 2$. Thus, $14 + 2 + 3$. You finally add from left to right, $14 + 2 + 3 = 19$.

So, $7 \times 2 + (20 - 2) \div 3^2 + 3 = 19$

Example 2. Is it correct to use the order of operations in this expression?

$$5 \times 2^3 - 6 \div 2 + 4$$
$$= 10^3 - 6 \div 6$$
$$= 1000 - 1$$
$$= 999$$

Solution: For doing an operation on this expression, first, you have to calculate exponents such as $2^3 = 8$, and then multiply with 5. And other side, should divide 6 by 2, then add to 4 or subtract from the answer 5×2^3. So, the order of operations in this expression is not correct. Therefore, it must be:

$$5 \times 2^3 - 6 \div 2 + 4 = 5 \times 8 - 6 \div 2 + 4 = 40 - 3 + 4 = 41$$

Writing down Variable Expressions Involving Two Operations

- Variables are letters in which you don't know the value.

- For instance, x is the variable in the expression: $3x + 45$.

- The coefficient is a numerical value utilized along with a variable. For instance, 3 is the variable in the expression $3x + 45$.

- Whenever you write down a mathematical expression, find the keywords to assist you in identifying the operations.

- Utilize the keywords for converting the description into an expression, doing one operation at a time.

Examples:

Example 1. Write an expression for the sequence of operations described below.

Divide 6 by x, then add 5 to the result.

Solution: See the keywords. Keywords are 'divide' and 'add'. Then use keywords to write an expression. Convert the first keyword: divide 6 by x, $\frac{6}{x}$. Then convert the second keyword: then add 5 to the result, result + 5.

So, $\frac{6}{x} + 5$.

Example 2. Write an expression for the sequence of operations described below.

Multiply g by 7, then multiply u by the result.

Solution: See the keywords. Keywords are 'multiply'. Then use keywords to write an expression. Convert the first keyword: multiply g by 7, $g \times 7$. Then convert the second keyword: then multiply u by the result, $u \times$ (result).

So, $u \times (g \times 7)$.

Using Area Models to Factor Variable Expressions

- Factors are an expression where something is multiplied by something else.

- Factors may be numbers, variables, terms, or any additional longer expression. For instance, the factors for $2xy$ are 2, x, and y.

- The area model of solving multiplication and division problems is derived from the concept of finding the area of a rectangle.

Area of a rectangle $= Length \times Width$

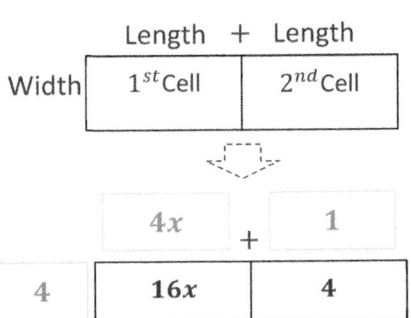

- First, find the terms of the missing factor: $16x + 4$
- Divide each term by the factor given to you in the model: $4(4x + 1)$

Examples:

Example 1. Use the area model for factoring $16d + 12n$.

Solution: First, find the greatest common factor (GCF) of $16d$ and $12n$. For finding GCF that appears in both lists, list the factors of both numbers:

Factor of 16: 1, 2, 4, 8, 16

Factor of 12: 1, 2, 3, 4, 6, 12

Divide each term by the factor, $16d \div 4 = 4d$, $12n \div 4 = 3n$. Now, you can write $16d + 12n$ in factored form. The area model shows it is equal to the product of 4 and $4d + 3n$.

Example 2. Use the area model for factoring $50 + 25x$.

Solution: First, divide each term by the factor given in the model, $50 \div 5 = 10$, $25 \div 5 = 5$.

Then complete the model. Now, you can write $50 + 25x$ in factored form. The area model shows it is equal to the product of 5 and $10 + 5x$.

Using Distributive Property to Factor Variable Expressions

- Use these four steps:

    • Distribute or multiply the outer term to the inner terms.

    • Combine the like terms.

    • Place terms so the constants and variables are on the opposite sides of the equal's sign.

    • Resolve the equation and simplify, if you need to.

Examples:

Example 1. Factor the expression, $3s + 6t$. Write a product with a whole number greater than 1.

Solution: First, find the greatest common factor (GCF) of $3s$ and $6t$. For finding GCF that appears in both lists, list the factors of both numbers:

Factor of 3: $1, 3$

Factor of 6: $1, 2, 3, 6$

Divide each number by 3. And now use the distributive property to write an equivalent expression, $3s + 6t = 3 \times s + 3 \times 2t = 3(s + 2t)$

Example 2. Factor the expression, $55x + 22x$. Write product with a whole number greater than 1.

Solution: First, find the greatest common factor (GCF) of $55x$ and $22x$. For finding GCF that appears in both lists, list the factors of both numbers:

Factor of $55x$: $1x, 5x, 11x, 55x$

Factor of $22x$: $1x, 2x, 11x, 22x$

Divide each number by $11x$. And now use the distributive property to write an equivalent expression, $55x + 22x = 11x \times 5 + 11x \times 2 = 11x(5 + 2)$

Using Distributive Property to Factor Numerical Expressions

- In order to factor a polynomial, firstly discover the greatest common factor of the monomial terms.

- Utilize the distributive property for rewriting the polynomial as the product of the *GCF* and the additional parts of the polynomial.

- To "distribute" requires dividing something or giving a share or a part of something. Based on the rules of the distributive property, multiplying the sum of two or more addends via a number is going to give the exact same answer as multiplying each of the addends individually by the number and afterward adding the products together.

$$a(b + c) = a \times b + a \times c$$

Examples:

Example 1. Using distributive property, factor the expression, $24 + 20$.

Solution: First, find the greatest common factor (*GCF*) of 24 and 20. For finding *GCF* that appears in both lists, list the factors of both numbers:

Factor of 24: 1, 2, 3, 4, 6, 8, 12, 24

Factor of 20: 1, 2, 4, 5, 10, 20

Divide each number by 4 and now use the distributive property to write an equivalent expression, $24 + 20 = 4 \times 6 + 4 \times 5 = 4(6 + 5)$

Example 2. Using distributive property, factor the expression, $42 + 36$.

Solution: First, find the greatest common factor (*GCF*) of 42 and 36. For finding *GCF* that appears in both lists, list the factors of both numbers:

Factor of 42: 1, 2, 3, 6, 7, 14, 21, 42

Factor of 36: 1, 2, 3, 4, 6, 9, 12, 18, 36

Divide each number by 6 and now use the distributive property to write an equivalent expression, $42 + 36 = 6 \times 7 + 6 \times 6 = 6(7 + 6)$

Chapter 1: Practices

✏️ **Determine if this is an expression or an equation.**

1) $(6-2) \div 5$

2) $\dfrac{2}{9-u}$

3) $4 \times (7-2) = 20$

4) $(c \times 10) - 12 = 8$

5) $\dfrac{4}{x} \times 77$

6) $60 + 9w$

7) $h = 8f$

8) $1 + u$

✏️ **Write the equivalent of the following expressions.**

9) $2p + p + 2$

10) $2(5x - 3)$

11) $7t - 2t + 8$

12) $-4(3k - 5)$

13) $21d - 12d + 6 - 7d$

14) $(6 \div (4x + 2x)) - 15$

15) $18 - 12y - 25 + 15y$

16) $-3(-4g - 2g) + 8g$

✏️ **Complete and solve the expressions.**

17) $3 + 15p + 8 = 15p + 8 + \boxed{} = \boxed{}$?

18) $5r + 3 + 8r = 5r + \boxed{} + 3 = ?$

19) $w(15 + 9) = 15 \times w + 9 \times \boxed{} = ?$

20) $3s + (5s + 9) = (3s + \boxed{}) + 9 = ?$

21) $f \times 88 = 88 \times \boxed{} = ?$

22) $4 \times (5 \times 12a) = (4 \times 5) \times \boxed{} = ?$

23) $9g \times 11 = \boxed{} \times 9g = ?$

24) $(5t + 2) \times 5 = \boxed{} \times 5 + 2 \times 5 = ?$

✏️ **Write an expression that represents the model.**

25) $7x + 7n$

26) $e + 3j$

27) $13y$

28) $\frac{5}{a} + 3b$

29) $4z + 2$

30) $5f + 22$

31) $\frac{4t}{a} + 9$

32) $2 + 6v$

Chapter 1: Expressions and Equations

✍ **Write the equivalent of the following expressions, using algebra tiles.**

33) $5 + x + 2$

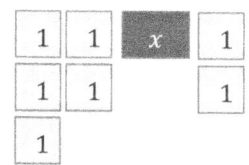

34) $4 + 3x + 8 + x$

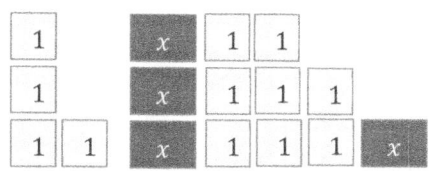

35) $4x + 12 + 6x$

36) $3 + 2x + 3 - x$

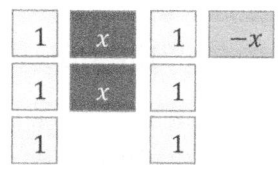

37) $2x + 10 + 6x$

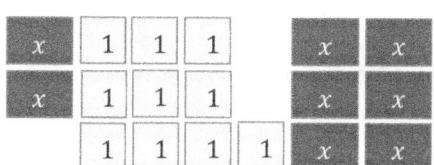

38) $3x + 2 + 5x$

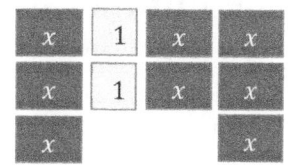

39) $-10 + 5x + 5$

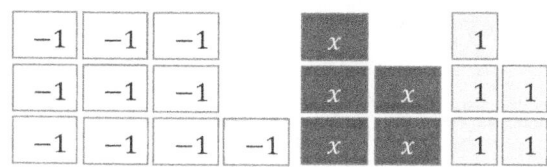

40) $2x + 2 + 2x - 2$

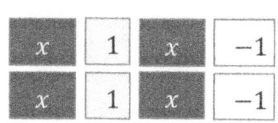

✎ **Write the expression using an exponent.**

41) $8 \times 8 =$ ___

42) $2 \times 2 \times 2 \times 2 =$ ___

43) $3 \times 3 \times 3 =$ ___

44) $4 \times 4 \times 4 \times 4 =$ ___

45) $10 \times 10 =$ ___

46) $7 \times 7 \times 7 \times 7 \times 7 =$ ___

47) $11 \times 11 \times 11 \times 11 =$ ___

48) $1 \times 1 \times 1 =$ ___

✎ **Find the exponent.**

49) $10^{} = 10{,}000{,}000{,}000$

50) $10^{} = 100{,}000$

51) $10^{} = 1{,}000{,}000{,}000$

52) $10^{} = 100{,}000{,}000$

✎ **Write the number as an exponent based on 10.**

53) $1{,}000 =$ ___

54) $10{,}000 =$ ___

55) $10 =$ ___

56) $1 =$ ___

✎ **Write the prime factorization with exponents.**

57) $75 =$ ___

58) $256 =$ ___

59) $45 =$ ___

60) $147 =$ ___

61) $405 =$ ___

62) $600 =$ ___

63) $80 =$ ___

64) $112 =$ ___

Chapter 1: Expressions and Equations

✎ **Tell which operation is to be done first. Then calculate.**

65) $12 \div 3 + 5$

66) $\frac{2+4}{3} \times 7$

67) $2^5 \div 4$

68) $20 \div \frac{4 \times 4}{2+6}$

✎ **Which operation is true?**

69) $36 \div 3^2 - 1 + 9 = 12^2 - 1 + 9 = 152$

70) $2 \times -2 + \frac{10}{2} = -4 + 5 = +1$

71) $(3.6 + 5.4) \times 4^2 \div 2 = 9 \times 16 \div 2 = 144 \div 2 = 72$

72) $3 \times \frac{4 \times 4}{2+6} - 15 + 3 = \frac{48}{8} - 15 + 3 = 6 - 15 + 3 = 6 - 18 = -12$

✎ **Write the expression for the sequence of operations described.**

73) Divide 7 by g, then subtract 15 from the result.

74) 4 multiplied by x.

75) Subtract 3 from g, then divide 2 by the result.

76) Multiply a by 8, then subtract 9 from the result.

77) Add 7 and a, then subtract 1 from the result.

78) Subtract 8 from y

79) Add 12 to a, then subtract b from the result.

80) Add 8 to g, then divide h by the result.

81) 6 divided by x.

82) Divide *g* by *h*, then multiply 6 by the result.

83) Add *y* to 9.

84) Multiply 11 by *a*, then add 4 to the result.

✎ **Use the area model for factoring variable expressions.**

85) $30s + 12t$

	?	+	?
6	30s		12t

86) $5a + 24a$

	?	+	?
a	5a		24a

87) $9d + 21d$

	?	+	?
3	9d		21d

88) $65 + 25d$

	?	+	?
5	65		25d

89) $77b + 35$

	?	+	?
?	77b		35

90) $49 + 21k$

	?	+	?
?	49		21k

91) $27j + 15$

	?	+	?
?	27j		15

92) $16z + 56z$

	?	+	?
?	16z		56z

✎ **Using distributive property, factor the expressions.**

93) $35 + 15p$

94) $144r + 24r$

95) $17a + 34b$

96) $105 + 21z$

97) $12s - 88$

98) $42d + 18d$

99) $85c + 65n$

100) $50 + 20n$

Using distributive property, factor the numerical expressions.

101) $45 + 75$

102) $33 + 24$

103) $12 + 28$

104) $15 + 99$

105) $9 - 99$

106) $48 + 18$

107) $14 + 42$

108) $125 + 15$

Chapter 1: Answers

1) This is an **expression**.
2) This is an **expression**.
3) This is an **equation**.
4) This is an **equation**.
5) This is an **expression**.
6) This is an **expression**.
7) This is an **equation**.
8) This is an **expression**.
9) $3P + 2$
10) $10x - 6$
11) $5t + 8$
12) $-12k + 20$
13) $2d + 6$
14) $\frac{1}{x} - 15$
15) $-7 + 3y$
16) $26g$
17) $15p + 8 + 3 = 15p + 11$
18) $5r + 8r + 3 = 13r + 3$
19) $15 \times w + 9 \times w = 24w$
20) $(3s + 5s) + 9 = 8s + 9$
21) $88 \times f = 88f$
22) $(4 \times 5) \times 12a = 240a$
23) $11 \times 9g = 99g$
24) $5t \times 5 + 2 \times 5 = 25t + 10$
25) $7x + 7n$
26) $e + 3j$
27) $13y$
28) $6\frac{1}{a} + 3b$
29) $4z + 2$
30) $5f + 24$
31) $4\frac{t}{a} + 9$
32) $2 + 6v$
33) $x + 7$
34) $4x + 12$
35) $10x + 12$
36) $x + 6$
37) $8x + 10$
38) $8x + 2$
39) $5x - 5$
40) $4x$
41) 8^2
42) 2^4
43) 3^3
44) 4^4
45) 10^2
46) 7^5
47) 11^4
48) 1^3
49) 10^{10}
50) 10^5
51) 10^9
52) 10^8
53) 10^3
54) 10^4
55) 10^1
56) 10^0
57) $5^2 \times 3$
58) 2^8
59) $3^2 \times 5$
60) $7^2 \times 3$
61) $3^4 \times 5$
62) $2^3 \times 5^2 \times 3$
63) $2^4 \times 5$
64) $2^4 \times 7$

Chapter 1: Expressions and Equations

65) $4 + 5 = 9$

66) $\frac{6}{3} \times 7 = 2 \times 7 = 14$

67) $32 \div 4 = 8$

68) $20 \div \frac{16}{8} = 10$

69) False

70) True

71) True

72) False

73) $\frac{7}{g} - 15$

74) $4x$

75) $\frac{2}{3-g}$ or $2 \div (3 - g)$

76) $(a \times 8) - 9$

77) $(7 + a) - 1$

78) $y - 8$

79) $(12 + a) - b$

80) $\frac{h}{8+g}$ or $h \div (8 - g)$

81) $\frac{6}{x}$

82) $\frac{g}{h} \times 6$

83) $y + 9$

84) $(11 \times a) + 4$

85) $6(5S + 2t)$

86) $a(5 + 24)$

87) $3(3d + 7d)$

88) $5(13 + 5d)$

89) $7(11b + 5)$

90) $7(7 + 3k)$

91) $3(9j + 5)$

92) $8z(2 + 7)$

93) $5(7 + 3p)$

94) $24r(6 + 1)$

95) $17(a + 2b)$

96) $21(5 + z)$

97) $4(3s - 22)$

98) $6d(7 + 3)$

99) $5(17c + 13n)$

100) $10(5 + 2n)$

101) $15(3 + 5)$

102) $3(11 + 8)$

103) $4(3 + 7)$

104) $3(5 + 33)$

105) $9(1 - 11)$

106) $6(8 + 3)$

107) $14(1 + 3)$

108) $5(25 + 3)$

CHAPTER 2
One-Step Operation

Math topics that you'll learn in this chapter:

- ☑ One–Step Adding and Subtracting of Decimals and Fractions
- ☑ One–Step Multiplying and Dividing of Decimals and Fractions
- ☑ Graphing One-Step Multiplication and Division Equations
- ☑ Graphing One-Step Inequalities with Rational Numbers
- ☑ One-Step Equations
- ☑ Matching Word Problems with the One-Step Equation
- ☑ Word Problems of the One-Step Equation

One-Step Adding and Subtracting of Decimals and Fractions

- The subtraction and addition properties of equality state one is able to subtract or add a value from both sides of an equation with no change in the meaning of an equation. The key is that you have to do the identical thing to both sides of an equation.

- In order to add 2 decimal numbers with opposite signs, discover their differences. The sign of the solution will be identical to the sign of the bigger number.

- Do not forget whenever adding decimals to line up the decimal points.

Examples:

Example 1. Solve the equation for y, $y - \frac{1}{5} = 5$. Write your answer as a fraction or as a whole or mixed number.

Solution: First add $\frac{1}{5}$ to both sides. Then write 5 as a fraction.

$$y - \frac{1}{5} = 5 \rightarrow y - \frac{1}{5} + \frac{1}{5} = 5 + \frac{1}{5} \rightarrow y = \frac{25}{5} + \frac{1}{5} \rightarrow y = \frac{26}{5}$$

Then convert the answer as a mixed number, $y = 5\frac{1}{5}$.

Example 2. Solve the equation for x, $x + 7.5 = 12$. Write your answer as a fraction or as a whole or mixed number.

Solution: First, use the inverse operation to undo the operations in the equation, to get the variable x alone on the side of the equation. Then subtract 7.5 from both sides.

$$x + 7.5 = 12 \rightarrow x + 7.5 - 7.5 = 12 - 7.5 \rightarrow x = 4.5$$

So, x is equal to 4.5.

One-Step Multiplying and Dividing of Decimals and Fractions

- One-step equations are equations requiring merely a single step to solve. Only one operation is needed to resolve or isolate the variable.

- To divide fractions:
  - Figure out the reciprocal (by reversing its numerator and denominator) of the 2nd fraction.
  - Multiply the 2 numerators.
  - Multiply the 2 denominators.
  - Simplify the fractions if you need to.

- You can convert a fraction to a decimal using division: Divide its numerator by its denominator.

Examples:

Example 1. Solve the equation for q, $q \div \frac{1}{3} = 8$. Write your answer as a fraction or as a whole or mixed number.

Solution: Use inverse the operation to get the variable q alone on the side of the equation. Therefore, multiply $\frac{1}{3}$ by both sides.

$$q \div \frac{1}{3} = 8 \to q \div \frac{1}{3} \times \frac{1}{3} = 8 \times \frac{1}{3} \to q = \frac{8}{1} \times \frac{1}{3} \to q = \frac{8}{3}$$

Then convert the answer as a mixed number, $q = 2\frac{2}{3}$.

Example 2. Solve the equation for e, $e \times 2.5 = 7$. Write your answer as a fraction or as a whole or mixed number.

Solution: Use inverse the operation to get the variable e alone on the side of the equation. Therefore, divide 2.5 by both sides.

$$e \times 2.5 = 7 \to e \times 2.5 \div 2.5 = 7 \div 2.5 \to e = 2.8$$

So, e is equal to 2.8.

Graphing One-Step Multiplication and Division Equations

- One-Step equations are equations that merely need one calculation to be solved.

- There are four methods of solving one-step equations:
  - If you add the same number to both sides of an equation, both sides stay equal.
  - If you subtract the same number from both sides of an equation, both sides stay equal.
  - If you divide both sides of an equation by the same number, both sides stay equal.
  - If you multiply both sides of an equation by the same number, both sides stay equal.

$$10m = 30 \rightarrow \frac{10m}{10} = \frac{30}{10} \rightarrow m = 3$$

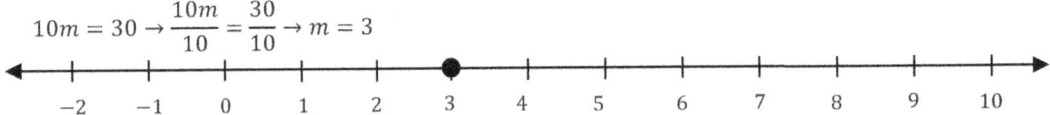

Examples:

Example 1. Solve the equation. And graph the solution, $12x = 36$.

Solution: First, solve the equation, using inverse operations for x. And since x is multiplied by 12 in this equation, then its inverse is divided by 12 on both sides, $\frac{12x}{12} = \frac{36}{12} \rightarrow x = 3$. Now, graph $x = 3$ on the number line.

Example 2. Solve the equation. And graph the solution, $\frac{x}{3} = 2$.

Solution: First, solve the equation, using inverse operations for x. And since x is divided by 3 in this equation, then its inverse is multiplied by 3 on both sides, $\frac{x}{3} \times 3 = 2 \times 3 \rightarrow x = 6$. Now graph $x = 6$ on the number line.

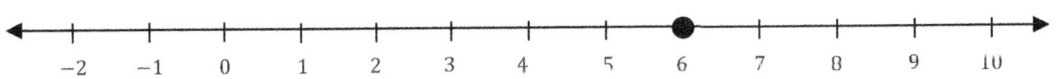

Graphing One-Step Inequalities with Rational Numbers

- Whenever you're graphing an inequality on a number line, you must pick between utilizing a filled-in or open circle.

- Utilize a filled-in circle whenever an inequality shows ≤ or ≥.

  $x \geq -1$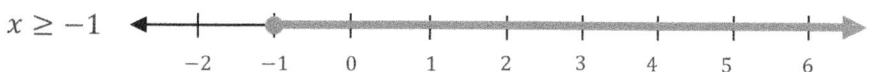

- Utilize an open circle whenever an inequality shows < or >.

  $x > -1$

- You must utilize inverse operations for solving these problems.

Examples:

Example 1. Solve the inequality. And graph the solution, $-13x < -26$.

Solution: First, solve the inequality, using inverse operations for x. And since x is multiplied by -13 in this inequality, then its inverse is divided by -13 on both sides, $\frac{-13x}{-13} = \frac{26}{-13} \rightarrow x > 2$. Remember to reverse the inequality symbol when you multiply both sides by a negative number.

Now graph $x > 2$ on the number line. The inequality $x > 2$ means that x can be any number greater than 2. So, draw an open circle on 2. Then, draw a line on the right of the open circle.

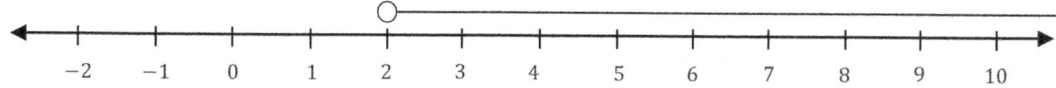

Example 2. Solve the inequality. And graph the solution, $\frac{y}{7} \geq -1$.

Solution: First, solve the inequality, using inverse operations for y. And since y is divided by 7 in this inequality, then its inverse is multiplied by 7 on both sides to find the solution, $\frac{y}{7} \times 7 \geq -1 \times 7 \rightarrow y \geq -7$.

Now graph $y \geq -7$ on the number line. The inequality $y \geq -7$ means that y can be any number greater than or equal to -7. So, draw a filled-in circle on -7. Then, draw a line on the right of the filled-in circle.

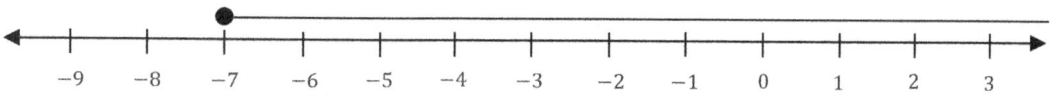

One−Step Equations

- The values of two expressions on both sides of an equation are equal. Example: $ax = b$. In this equation, ax is equal to b.
- Solving an equation means finding the value of the variable.
- You only need to perform one Math operation to solve the one-step equations.
- To solve a one-step equation, find the inverse (opposite) operation is being performed.
- The inverse operations are:
  - ❖ Addition and subtraction
  - ❖ Multiplication and division

Examples:

Example 1. Solve this equation for x. $4x = 16 \to x = ?$

Solution: Here, the operation is multiplication (variable x is multiplied by 4) and its inverse operation is division. To solve this equation, divide both sides of equation by 4: $4x = 16 \to \frac{4x}{4} = \frac{16}{4} \to x = 4$

Example 2. Solve this equation. $x + 8 = 0 \to x = ?$

Solution: In this equation, 8 is added to the variable x. The inverse operation of addition is subtraction. To solve this equation, subtract 8 from both sides of the equation: $x + 8 - 8 = 0 - 8$. Then: $x + 8 - 8 = 0 - 8 \to x = -8$

Example 3. Solve this equation for x. $x - 12 = 0$

Solution: Here, the operation is subtraction, and its inverse operation is addition. To solve this equation, add 12 to both sides of the equation: $x - 12 + 12 = 0 + 12 \to x = 12$

Matching Word Problems with the One-Step Equation

- One-step equations are algebraic equations that can be solved in just a single step.

- The equation has been resolved whenever you have the variable by itself, and there are not any numbers in front of it, on 1 side of the equal sign.

Examples:

Example 1. How many packages of popcorn can you buy for $18 if one package costs $2? Write the equation for it, then solve it.

Solution: First look for words and phrases in the sentences that tell you what equation will model it.

The total money is 18 dollars. The cost of each package is 2 dollars. How many packages can buy is x. And modeled by the multiply equation $2x = 18$.

Now solve it, $x = 9$. By 18 dollars can buy 9 packages of popcorn.

Example 2. A recipe for cookies calls for 7 cups of flour. Olivia has already put in 4 cups. How many more cups does she need to put in? Write the equation for it, then solve it.

Solution: First look for words and phrases in the sentences that tell you what equation will model it.

The total of flour is 7 cups. Already there are 4 cups. How many more cups need is x. And modeled by the add equation $x + 4 = 7$.

Now solve it, $x = 3$. She needs 3 cups more.

Word Problems of the One-Step Equation

- Equations are mathematical sentences showing that 2 expressions are identical.
- To obtain the solution for one-step equations, utilize inverse operations. It's vital not to forget that whatever is done to one side of this equation, is additionally done to the other one.

  • Addition ↔ Subtraction

  • Multiplication ↔ Division

Examples:

Example 1. Jessika gets to feed the dolphins! The dolphin trainer gives Jessika a bucket of fish to divide evenly among 7 dolphins. Each dolphin gets 4 fish. Which equation can you use to find the number of fish f in the bucket?

Solution: There are 7 dolphins, and there are 4 fish per dolphin. To find the total number of fish in the bucket you can display by an equation using division. Total number of fishes $\frac{f}{7} = 4$ Number of fishes per dolphin / Number of dolphins

And solve this equation: $\frac{f}{7} = 4 \rightarrow f = 4 \times 7 = 28$

Example 2. John and his friend rake his farm all day and fill a number of wheat bags. Then, when John isn't looking, his friend empty 8 of the bags to make a giant Wheat pile! John is frustrated that only 12 bags of wheat remain. Which equation can you use to find the total number of bags b?

Solution: After John and his friend fill b number bags with wheats, his friend empty 8 of them. Now only 12 bags remain. This can be represented by an equation using subtraction.

Total number of bags they fill $b - 8 = 12$ Number of bags that remain / Number of bags they empty

And solve this equation: $b - 8 = 12 \rightarrow b = 12 + 8 \rightarrow b = 20$

Chapter 2: Practices

✎ Solve.

1) $d + 9.8 = 7$

2) $t - 2.6 = 6.6$

3) $\frac{3}{8} - \frac{8}{5} = n$

4) $u + \frac{1}{3} = 6$

5) $8 + \frac{7}{6} = p$

6) $h - \frac{4}{5} = 1.6$

7) $r = 5 + 2.5$

8) $7 + x = \frac{2}{7}$

✎ Solve.

9) $d \times 4 = 6.5$

10) $4 \times 2.5 = z$

11) $t \div \frac{8}{5} = \frac{1}{10}$

12) $u \times \frac{2}{3} = \frac{4}{6}$

13) $7 \div \frac{7}{6} = p$

14) $h \div 1.5 = 3$

15) $m \times \frac{6}{9} = 2$

16) $r \div 5 = \frac{2}{7}$

✎ Solve the equation, then graph on the number line.

17) $6v = 24$

18) $\frac{n}{2} = 5$

19) $3p = 27$

20) $\frac{z}{4} = -2$

21) $\frac{u}{2} = 2$

22) $-\frac{f}{5} = 1$

23) $4w = 28$

24) $12d = -72$

✍ Solve the inequality, then graph on the number line.

25) $2w \geq 12$

26) $\frac{x}{3} > -3$

27) $-4y \leq 16$

28) $\frac{z}{4} > -2$

29) $8m < 32$

30) $-\frac{t}{8} \geq -1$

31) $-9k > 18$

32) $-\frac{s}{2} \leq -5$

✍ Solve each equation. (One–Step Equations)

33) $x + 6 = 3 \rightarrow x =$ ____

34) $5 = 11 - x \rightarrow x =$ ____

35) $-3 = 8 + x \rightarrow x =$ ____

36) $x - 2 = -7 \rightarrow x =$ ____

37) $-15 = x + 6 \rightarrow x =$ ____

38) $10 - x = -2 \rightarrow x =$ ____

39) $22 - x = -9 \rightarrow x =$ ____

40) $-4 + x = 28 \rightarrow x =$ ____

41) $11 - x = -7 \rightarrow x =$ ____

42) $35 - x = -7 \rightarrow x =$ ____

✍ Write the one-step equation for the word problem. Then solve.

43) A hotel has a parking lot with enough space for 65 cars. There are 27 cars in the parking lot right now. How many more cars can park in the lot?

44) Kate has $29. E-book downloads cost $2.5 each. How many E-books can she download and still have $1.5 left?

45) If the weight of five bags of grain is 75 pounds, find the weight of one bag of grain.

46) Sarah bought muffins in boxes of 16. The cost of a box is $20. What is the price of each muffin?

47) Liam has $42 to spend at the amusement park. The ticket to each game is $5 and the rides cost to the amusement park $12. How many tickets can he buy?

48) For a trip, Daniel gave her brother $12.30 to buy some groceries. This covered $\frac{3}{11}$ of the cost. How much did the trip cost?

49) In an examination, Mia ran 30 miles more than Emma. Mia ran 47 miles. How many miles did Emma run?

50) After using 3 cucumbers for a salad, Johnny has 8 cucumbers in the basket. How many cucumbers did he have before using the salad?

Write the equation and solve.

51) How many packs of chips (p) can you buy for $65 if one package costs $5?

52) At a cafe, frank and his four friends decided to divide the bill evenly. If each person paid $18 then what was the total bill (b)?

53) Maria is practicing baking skills and bakes cupcakes with sugar powder. After baking the cupcakes, 9 of them will burn. In total she baked 40 cupcakes. How many cupcakes (c) are completely baked?

54) If the weight of a package is multiplied by $\frac{5}{8}$ the result is 43.75 pounds. Find the weight (w) of the package.

Chapter 2: Answers

1) $d = -2.8$
2) $t = 9.2$
3) $n = -1\frac{9}{40}$
4) $u = 5\frac{2}{3}$
5) $p = 9\frac{1}{6}$
6) $h = 2.4$
7) $r = 7.5$
8) $x = -6\frac{5}{7}$
9) $d = 1.625$
10) $z = 10$
11) $t = \frac{4}{25}$
12) $u = 1$
13) $p = 6$
14) $h = 4.5$
15) $m = 3$
16) $r = 1\frac{3}{7}$

17)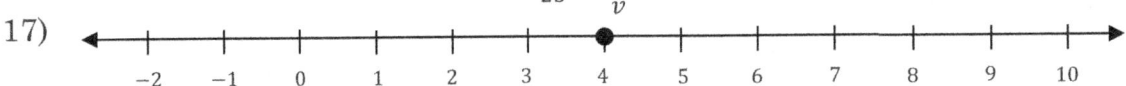

18)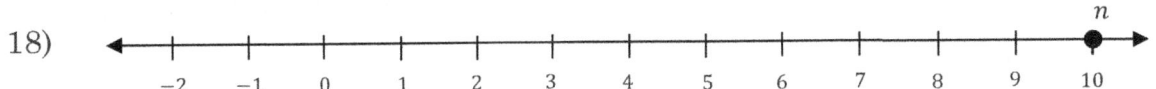

19)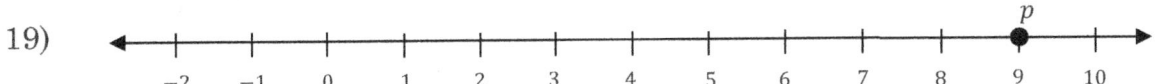

20)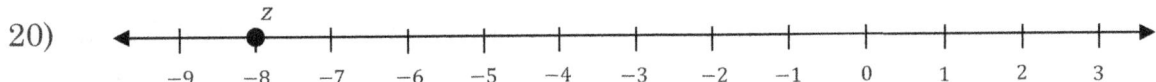

21)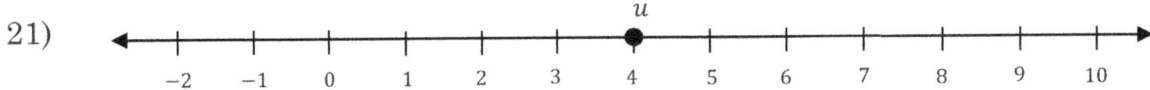

22)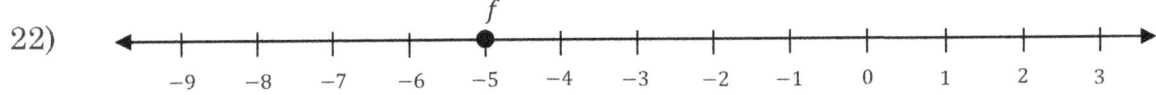

23)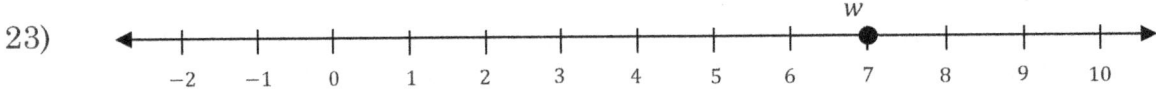

24)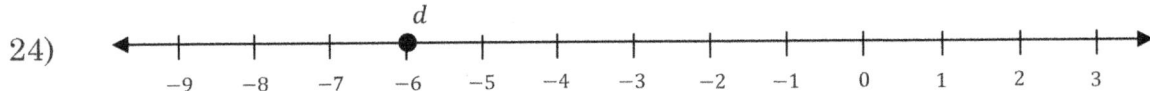

25)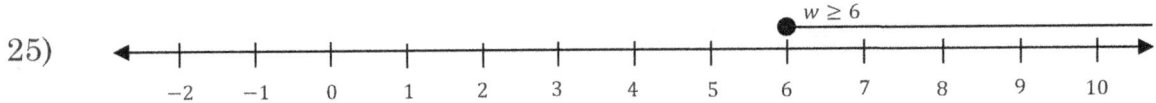

26)

27)

28)

29)

30)

31)

32)

33) −3
34) 6
35) −11
36) −5
37) −21
38) 12
39) 31
40) 32
41) 18
42) 42
43) $x + 27 = 65 \rightarrow x = 38$

44) $2.5x + 1.5 = 29 \rightarrow x = 11$
45) $5x = 75 \rightarrow x = 15 \, lb$
46) $16x = 20 \rightarrow x = 1.25\$$
47) $5x + 12 = 42 \rightarrow x = 6$
48) $\frac{3}{11}x = 12.30 \rightarrow x = 45.10\$$
49) $x + 30 = 47 \rightarrow x = 17 \, mi$
50) $x - 3 = 8 \rightarrow x = 11$
51) $5 \cdot p = 65 \rightarrow p = 13$
52) $\frac{b}{5} = 18 \rightarrow b = 90$
53) $c + 9 = 40 \rightarrow c = 31$
54) $w \cdot \frac{5}{8} = 43.75 \rightarrow w = 70$

CHAPTER
3 Inequalities

Math topics that you'll learn in this chapter:

- ☑ Write Inequalities from Number Lines
- ☑ Graphing Single–Variable Inequalities
- ☑ One-Step Inequalities
- ☑ Word Problems Involving One-step Inequalities

Write Inequalities from Number Lines

- In order to plot an inequality, like $x > 2$, on a number line, firstly draw a circle over the number (e.g., 2).

- Next, if the sign includes equal to ($\geq$ or $\leq$), fill in that circle. If the sign doesn't include equal to ($>$ or $<$), don't fill in the circle.

- Lastly, draw a line starting from the circle in the direction of the numbers which allows the inequality to be true.

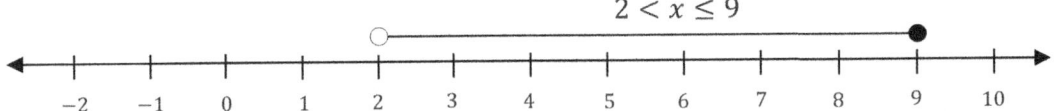

Examples:

Example 1. What inequality does this number line show?

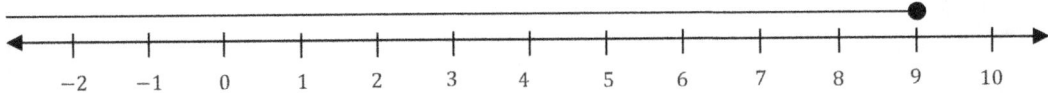

Solution: To write an inequality, the filled-in circle located on 9 shows that x can be equal to 9. And the line to the left indicates that x can be any number less than 9.

Since x can be any number equal and less than 9, the inequality is $x \leq 9$.

Example 2. What inequality does this number line show?

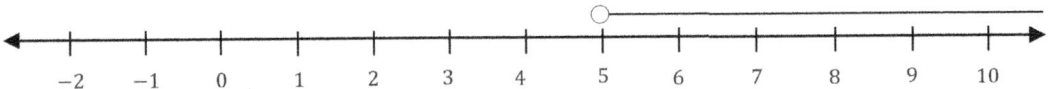

Solution: To write an inequality, the open circle located on 5 shows that x cannot be equal to 5. And the line to the right indicates that x can be any number more than 5.

Since x can be any number more than 5, the inequality is $x > 5$.

Graphing Single–Variable Inequalities

- An inequality compares two expressions using an inequality sign.
- Inequality signs are: "less than" <, "greater than" >, "less than or equal to" ≤, and "greater than or equal to" ≥.
- To graph a single–variable inequality, find the value of the inequality on the number line.
- For less than (<) or greater than (>) draw an open circle on the value of the variable. If there is an equal sign too, then use a filled circle.
- Draw an arrow to the right for greater or to the left for less than.

Examples:

Example 1. Draw a graph for this inequality. $x > 2$

Solution: Since the variable is greater than 2, then we need to find 2 in the number line and draw an open circle on it. Then, draw an arrow to the right.

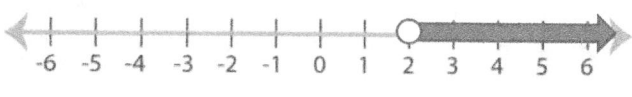

Example 2. Graph this inequality. $x \leq -3$.

Solution: Since the variable is less than or equal to -3, then we need to find -3 on the number line and draw a filled circle on it. Then, draw an arrow to the left.

One–Step Inequalities

- An inequality compares two expressions using an inequality sign.
- Inequality signs are: "less than" <, "greater than" >, "less than or equal to" ≤, and "greater than or equal to" ≥.
- You only need to perform one Math operation to solve the one-step inequalities.
- To solve one-step inequalities, find the inverse (opposite) operation is being performed.
- For dividing or multiplying both sides by negative numbers, flip the direction of the inequality sign.

Examples:

Example 1. Solve this inequality for x. $x + 5 \geq 4$

Solution: The inverse (opposite) operation of addition is subtraction. In this inequality, 5 is added to x. To isolate x we need to subtract 5 from both sides of the inequality.
Then: $x + 5 \geq 4 \rightarrow x + 5 - 5 \geq 4 - 5 \rightarrow x \geq -1$. The solution is: $x \geq -1$

Example 2. Solve the inequality. $x - 3 > -6$

Solution: 3 is subtracted from x. Add 3 to both sides.
$x - 3 > -6 \rightarrow x - 3 + 3 > -6 + 3 \rightarrow x > -3$

Example 3. Solve. $4x \leq -8$

Solution: 4 is multiplied to x. Divide both sides by 4.
Then: $4x \leq -8 \rightarrow \frac{4x}{4} \leq \frac{-8}{4} \rightarrow x \leq -2$

Example 4. Solve. $-3x \leq 6$

Solution: -3 is multiplied to x. Divide both sides by -3. Remember when dividing or multiplying both sides of an inequality by negative numbers, flip the direction of the inequality sign.
Then: $-3x \leq 6 \rightarrow \frac{-3x}{-3} \geq \frac{6}{-3} \rightarrow x \geq -2$

Word Problems Involving One-step Inequalities

- One-step inequalities are solved by dividing the same number into both sides of the equation.
- One-step inequalities are solved by multiplying the reciprocal coefficient of the term with a variable on both sides of the equation.
- You can solve word problems by becoming a detective and searching for clues in the form of keywords and phrases.
- Finding them helps you understand which operation and inequality symbols to use.
- Carefully read the text to understand what you are asked to solve in the problem.
- Write a number sentence then solve it in a single step.

Example:

Tyrone went to the grocery to buy 3 ice creams. He spent less than $15 in all to buy the ice cream. Let x represent how much each ice cream costs. This inequality describes the problem, $3x < 15$. Solve the inequality with algebra tiles. What is the price of each ice cream less than?

Solution: The expression $3x$ represents the total cost of the ice creams. That needs to be less than 15. The left side of the inequality is $3x$.

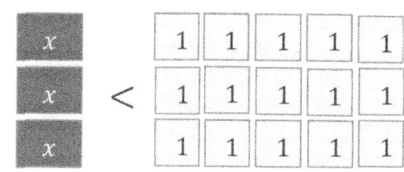

So, the left side of your answer should have 3, x —tiles. The right side of the inequality is 15. So, the right side of your answer should have 15, 1 —tiles. These algebra tiles model the inequality $3x < 15$.

And to solve the inequality for x, divide each side into 3 equal groups. Thus:

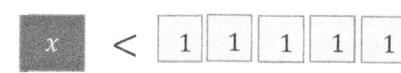

The solution to the inequality is $x < 5$. So, each ice cream cost less than $5.

Chapter 3: Practices

✎ **What inequalities do these number lines show?**

1)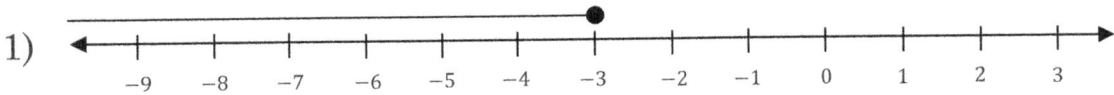

2)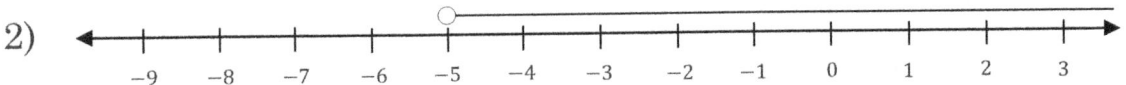

3)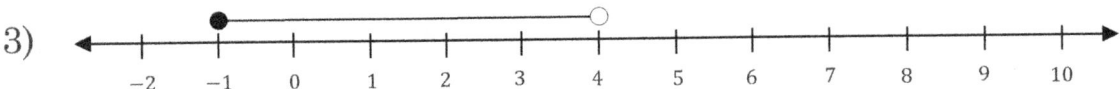

4)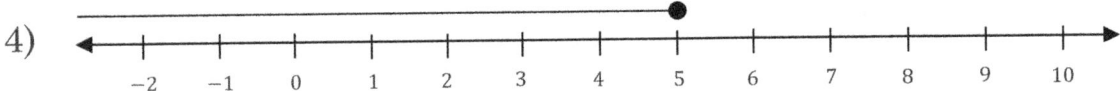

5)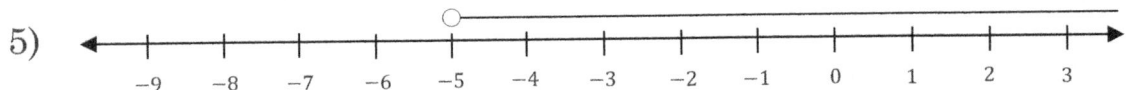

6)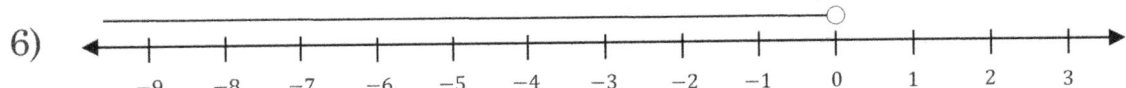

7)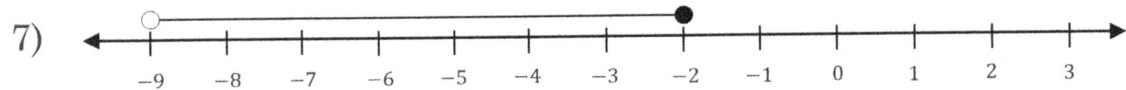

8)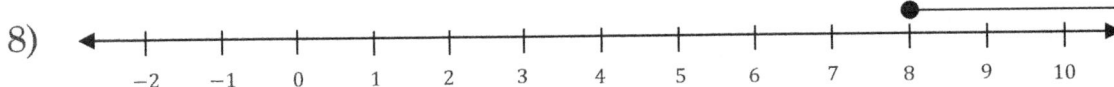

✎ **Draw a graph for each inequality.**

9) $x \leq -3$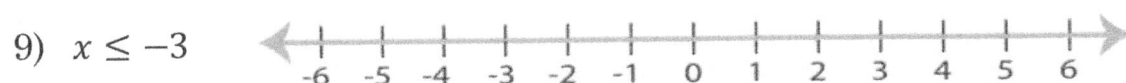

10) $x > -5$

◈ **Solve each inequality and graph it.**

11) $x - 2 \geq -2$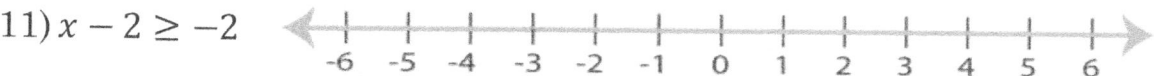

12) $2x - 3 < 9$

◈ **Solve the word problems.**

13) Kate sells muffins in boxes of 7. Depending on the type of muffins, a box can cost at most $21. Let x represent how much each muffin cost. This inequality describes the problem, $7x \leq 21$. Solve the inequality. And what is the price of each muffin at most?

14) A local restaurant has a parking lot with enough space for 28 cars. There are 7 cars in the parking lot right now. Let x represent how many more cars can park in the lot. This inequality describes the problem, $x + 7 \leq 28$. Solve the inequality. And how many more cars can park in the lot?

15) Daniel had $38 to spend at the museum. If the admission to the museum in each section is $5 and the rides cost the museum $8. Let x represent how many times Daniel can go to different sections. Write the inequality for it and solve it. So, what is the greatest number of sections that Daniel can go to?

16) Maria has $15. MP3 downloads cost $0.5 each. How many songs can she download and still have $3 left to spend? Write the inequality for it and solve it.

Chapter 3: Answers

1) $x \leq -3$

2) $x > -5$

3) $-1 \leq x < 4$

4) $x \leq 5$

5) $x > -5$

6) $x < 0$

7) $-9 < x \leq -2$

8) $x \geq 8$

9) $x \leq -3$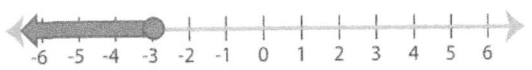

10) $x > -5$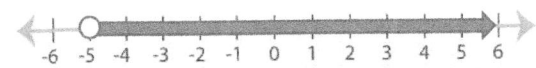

11) $x \geq 0$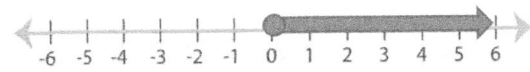

12) $x < 6$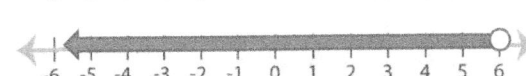

13) Each muffin costs at most $3.

14) It can park up to 21 cars in the lot.

15) $5x + 8 \leq 38$, can go to different sections up to 6 times.

16) $\frac{1}{2}x + 3 \leq 15$, she can download 24 songs.

Chapter 4: Variables and Equations

Math topics that you'll learn in this chapter:

- ☑ Independent and Dependent Variables in Tables and Graphs
- ☑ Independent and Dependent Variables in Word Problems
- ☑ Using Algebra Tiles to Model and Solve Equations
- ☑ Using Diagrams to Model and Solve Equations
- ☑ Evaluating One Variable

Independent and Dependent Variables in Tables and Graphs

- An independent variable is the one being controlled in the equation, and a dependent variable is one that changes because of that control.

x	y
3	$3 \div 3 = 1$
6	$6 \div 3 = 2$
9	$9 \div 3 = 3$
12	$12 \div 3 = 4$

- In the majority of data tables, the independent variable (the variable one is testing or changing consciously) is going to be in the left-hand column and the dependent variable(s) are going to be in the right-hand column of a table.

- The "independent" variable is put onto the $x-$axis (the bottom, horizontal one) and a "dependent" variable is put onto the $y-$axis (the left-hand side, vertical one).

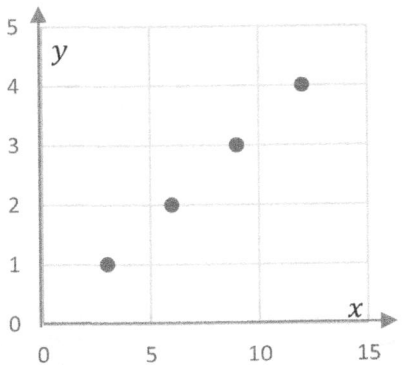

Example:

Max goes to the bakery store; he wants to order a chocolate-covered berry cake. The table shows the relationship between the pounds of chocolate-covered berry cake he orders, p, and the total cost, c. Which of the variables is independent and which is dependent? And write the relationship between the dependent variable and the independent.

p	c
1	$10
2	$20
3	$30
4	$40

Solution: According to the table, the number of pounds, p, of chocolate-covered berry cake that Max orders does not depend on the total cost. So, p is the independent variable. On the other side, the total cost, c, depends on how many pounds of chocolate-covered berry cake Max orders. So, c is the dependent variable.

Now, find the relationship between the dependent variable and the independent. According to table: $1 \times 10 = 10$, $2 \times 10 = 20$, $3 \times 10 = 30$, $4 \times 10 = 40$. So, $p \times 10 = c$. The dependent variable, c, is 10 times the independent variable, p.

Independent and Dependent Variables in Word Problems

- The variable whose value does not depend on the other variable is the independent variable. The variable whose value depends on the other variable is the dependent variable.

- When you go to a restaurant, the price of your order will determine how much taxes you pay.

- C = the price of your order, T = tax amount due

- Which of these variables are independent and which are dependent?

- Begin by discovering the dependent variable.

- Because the tax amount you owe is dependent on your order price, Thus, the tax amount (T) is a dependent variable.

- Since the order price isn't dependent on how much the taxes are, Hence, the order price (C) is an independent variable.

Example:

Ellen is baking cakes to sell at her bakery.

The number of cups of sugar she needs to use will affect how many the number of cakes she makes.
c = The number of cakes she makes.
s = The cups of sugar she needs to use.
Which of the variables is independent and which is dependent?

Solution: First, find the dependent variable. Since the number of cakes depends on how many cups of sugar to use, the number of cakes is the dependent variable. So, c is the dependent variable.

And since the number of cups of sugar she needs to use does not depend on how many cakes she makes; the cups of sugar are the independent variable. So, s is the independent variable.

Using Algebra Tiles to Model and Solve Equations

- Algebra tiles are mathematical manipulatives that let pupils understand better methods of algebraic thinking as well as algebraic concepts.

- How to model and solve the given equations using algebra tiles?

- Step 1: First we have to model the given equation using the above tiles.

- Step 2: Solve means finding the value of the variable. For that, we need to isolate the variable.

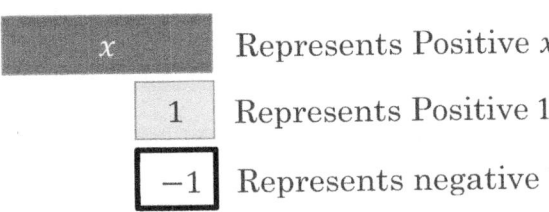

Examples:

Example 1. Show the equation $x + 5 = 8$, by using the algebra tiles.

Solution: Left side of the equation represent $x + 5$, which means 1 −tile of x and 5 −tiles of 1. And the right of the equation represents 8, which means 8 −tile of 1.

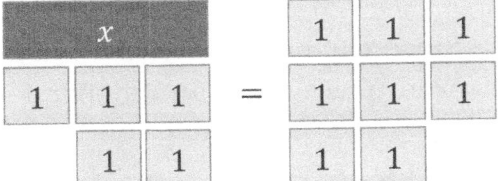

Now, to solve the equation, simplify the model and remove the tiles on the right side by the same tiles on the left side. That only the x tile remins on the left. So, the model shows $x = 3$.

Example 2. Show the equation $x - 2 = 5$, by using the algebra tiles.

Solution: Left side of the equation represent $x - 2$, which means 1 −tile of x and 2 −tiles of −1. And the right of the equation represents 5, which means 5 −tile of 1.

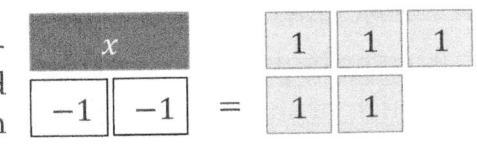

Now, to solve the equation, to remove the tiles on the left side, should add two tiles, 1, to the left and right side. Then simplify tiles of −1 in 1 on the left side but the tiles on the

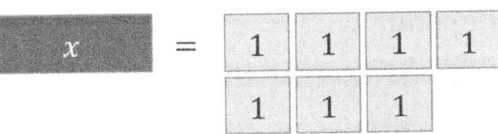

right side add together. Then only the x tile remins on the left. So, the model shows $x = 7$.

Using Diagrams to Model and Solve Equations

- Solve a system of linear equations VIA graphing:

  • Graph the 1st equation.

  • Graph the 2nd equation on the same rectangular coordinate system.

  • Ascertain if the lines are parallel, intersect, or are the same line.

  • Find the answer to the system.

  • Check the resolution for both equations.

$$a - 8 = 11$$

| 8 | 11 |

a

Examples:

Example 1. Which diagram represents the equation, $\frac{s}{4} = 8$?

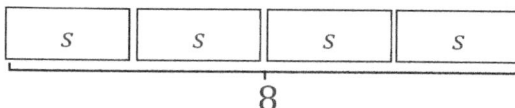

Solution: The equation says that if you have a number, s, and divide it by 4, it is equal to 8. Or if you have a number, s, it is equal to 4 times 8, $s = 4 \times 8$. So, x is included 4 times 8.

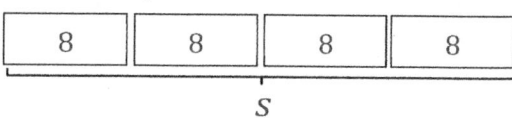

This diagram represents the equation. Now, solve for s. $s = 4 \times 8 \rightarrow s = 32$.

Example 2. Graph the diagram that represents the equation, $z - 12 = 5$.

Solution: The equation says that if you have a number, z, and subtract 12 from it, it is equal to 5. Or if you have a number, z, it is equal to the sum of 5 and 12, $z = 5 + 12$.

So, z is included in 5 and 12. And graph this.

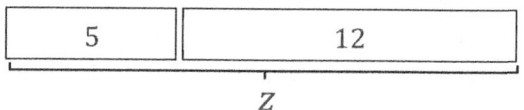

Now, solve for z. $z = 5 + 12 \rightarrow z = 17$.

Evaluating One Variable

- To evaluate one variable expressions, find the variable and substitute a number for that variable.

- Perform the arithmetic operations.

Examples:

Example 1. Calculate this expression for $x = 2$. $\quad 8 + 2x$

Solution: First, substitute 2 for x.

Then: $8 + 2x = 8 + 2(2)$

Now, use order of operation to find the answer: $8 + 2(2) = 8 + 4 = 12$

Example 2. Evaluate this expression for $x = -1$. $\quad 4x - 8$

Solution: First, substitute -1 for x.

Then: $4x - 8 = 4(-1) - 8$

Now, use order of operation to find the answer: $4(-1) - 8 = -4 - 8 = -12$

Example 3. Find the value of this expression when $x = 4$. $(16 - 5x)$

Solution: First, substitute 4 for x,

Then: $16 - 5x = 16 - 5(4) = 16 - 20 = -4$

Example 4. Solve this expression for $x = -3$. $\quad 15 + 7x$

Solution: Substitute -3 for x.

Then: $15 + 7x = 15 + 7(-3) = 15 - 21 = -6$

Chapter 4: Practices

✎ According to the graph and tables, determine independent and dependent variables. And write the relationship between the dependent and the independent variable.

1) There are phone plan charges for data usage. The graph shows the relationship between the number of gigabytes of data uses, d, and the total cost of the data, c, in dollars.

2) Meg drives a motorcycle. The graph shows the relationship between the time, t, in hours and distances, d, in kilometers.

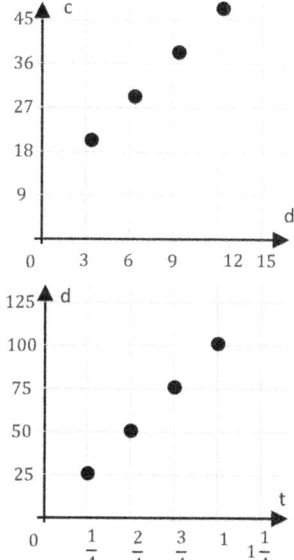

3) During summer, Elli practices swimming for the same number of hours each week. The table shows the relationship between the number of weeks that Elli goes to swimming practice, w, and the total number of hours that she practices, h.

w	h
1	2
2	4
3	6
4	8

4) Emma and her friends pack food in a box to be sent to the customers. The table shows the relationship between the weight of the food they pack, w, in pounds, and the total weight of the packed box, t.

w	t
1	4
2	5
3	6
4	7

✎ **According to the word problem, determine independent and dependent variables.**

5) Maureen manages the aviculture which produces many eggs. The more chickens that are kept in the aviculture, the more egg packs it produces.

   c = The number of chickens kept in the aviculture.

   p = The number of egg packs it produces.

6) Jack sorts the shelves of a grocery store. The more shelves the store has, the more packages of food can be sorted.

   s = The number of shelves in the store

   p = The number of packages

7) One summer day, Olivia is picking flowers in the meadow. The more time she spends in the meadow, the more flowers she picks.

   f = The number of flowers she picks.

   t = Time of picking

8) Charlotte runs for a few hours every noon. The more water she carries with her, the longer she can run.

   w = The amount of water she carries.

   t = Time of running

Calculate the equation.

9)

10)

11)

12)

13)

14)

15)

16)

Graph the diagram that represents the equation.

17) $d + 3 = 8$

18) $2f = 16$

19) $b - 8 = 5$

20) $\frac{k}{3} = 6$

21) $3x + 2 = 17$

22) $h - 4 = 15$

23) $\frac{a}{2} = -10$

24) $5p = 25$

✏️ **Evaluate each expression using the value given.**

25) $x = 4 \rightarrow 10 - x =$ ____

26) $x = 6 \rightarrow x + 8 =$ ____

27) $x = 3 \rightarrow 2x - 6 =$ ____

28) $x = 2 \rightarrow 10 - 4x =$ ____

29) $x = 7 \rightarrow 8x - 3 =$ ____

30) $x = 9 \rightarrow 20 - 2x =$ ____

31) $x = 5 \rightarrow 10x - 30 =$ ____

32) $x = -6 \rightarrow 5 - x =$ ____

33) $x = -3 \rightarrow 22 - 3x =$ ____

34) $x = -7 \rightarrow 10 - 9x =$ ____

35) $x = -10 \rightarrow 40 - 3x =$ ____

36) $x = -2 \rightarrow 20x - 5 =$ ____

37) $x = -5 \rightarrow -10x - 8 =$ ____

38) $x = -4 \rightarrow -1 - 4x =$ ____

Chapter 4: Answers

1) $d \times 3 = c$, d = independent, c = dependent
2) $t \times 100 = d$, t = independent, d = dependent
3) $w \times 2 = h$, w = independent, h = dependent
4) $w + 3 = t$, w = independent, t = dependent
5) c = independent, p = dependent
6) s = independent, p = dependent
7) f = independent, t = dependent
8) w = independent, t = dependent

9) $2x + 3 = 9 \rightarrow x = 3$
10) $2x + 1 = 9 \rightarrow x = 4$
11) $x + 5 = 7 \rightarrow x = 2$
12) $x + 4 = 6 \rightarrow x = 2$
13) $x + 8 = -5 \rightarrow x = -13$
14) $x - 4 = 7 \rightarrow x = 11$
15) $3x - 2 = 10 \rightarrow x = 4$
16) $x + 2 = -7 \rightarrow x = 9$

17)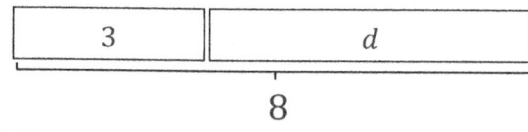

18)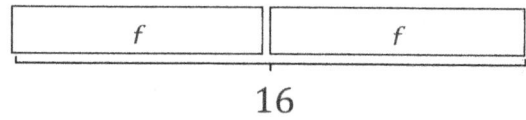

19)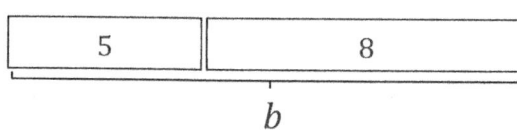

20)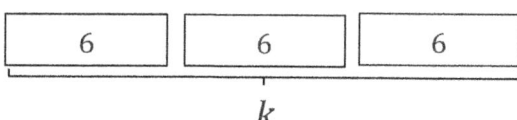

21)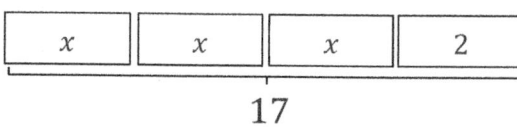

22)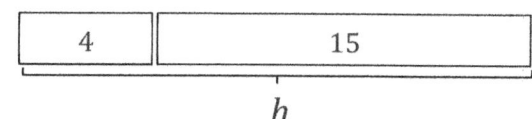

23)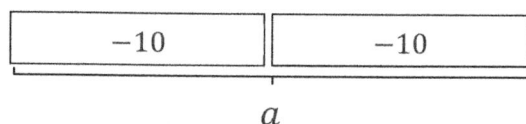

24)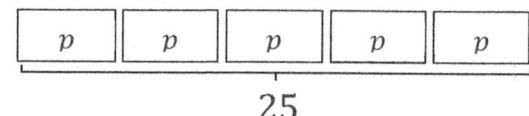

25) 6
26) 14
27) 0
28) 2
29) 53

30) 2
31) 20
32) 11
33) 31
34) 73

35) 70
36) −45
37) 42
38) 15

CHAPTER
5 Two-Variable Equation

Math topics that you'll learn in this chapter:

☑ Using a Table to Write down a Two-Variable Equation
☑ Complete a Table and Graph a Two-Variable Equation
☑ Evaluating Two Variables
☑ Solving Word problems by Finding Two-Variable Equation

Using a Table to Write down a Two-Variable Equation

- Write down a 2-variable equation from the given table.
- Firstly, you must look for the proper rule and after that, you just write it down on the table.
- In each of the table rows, the number appearing in the y column is 10 more than the one appearing in the x column. The equation is written thusly:

$$y = x + 8$$

x	y
3	11
4	12
5	13
6	14

Examples:

Example 1. Write the equation that represents the table.

w	h
1	7
2	8
3	9
4	10

Solution: First, determine the output and input columns. The left column, w, is input and the right column, h, is output. And can see relationships between w and h. Then find the rule that produces the number in the h column from the number in the w column in each row of the table, $1 + 6 = 7$, $2 + 6 = 8$, $3 + 6 = 9$, $4 + 6 = 10$.

Write the equation like this, $w + 6 = h$.

Example 2. Complete the equation:

$$d = \boxed{} \times h$$

h	d
6	48
7	56
8	64
9	72

Solution: First, determine the output and input columns. The left column, h, is input and the right column, d, is output. And can see relationships between h and d. Then find the rule that produces the number in the d column from the number in the h column in each row of the table, $6 \times 8 = 48$, $7 \times 8 = 56$, $8 \times 8 = 64$, $9 \times 8 = 72$.

Write the equation like this, $h \times 8 = d$ or $d = 8 \times h$.

Complete a Table and Graph a Two-Variable Equation

- Utilize the equation to finish the table: $y = x + 3$

x	0	2	4
y	3	5	5

- Firstly, utilize the equation $y = x + 3$ to finish the table. To figure out each y-value, add 3.

- Then, graph the equation. Begin by writing these values in the table as ordered pairs. $(0,3), (2,5), (4,7)$

- Draw a line that passes through these points.

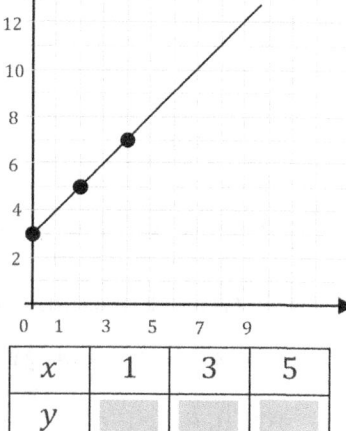

Examples:

Example 1. Complete the table by using the equation and graph the equation, $y = x + 6$.

x	1	3	5
y			

Solution: To find the y-value, put the value of x into the equation and calculate y. Now, graph the equation, by writing the values in the table as ordered pairs, $(1,7), (3,9), (5,11)$.

Then, draw a line that passes through determined points.

Example 2. Complete the table by using the equation and graph the equation, $y = 2x$.

x	0	1	3	5
y				

Solution: To find the y-value, put the value of x into the equation and calculate y. Now, graph the equation, by writing the values in the table as ordered pairs, $(0,0), (1,2), (3,6), (5,10)$.

Then, draw a line that passes through determined points.

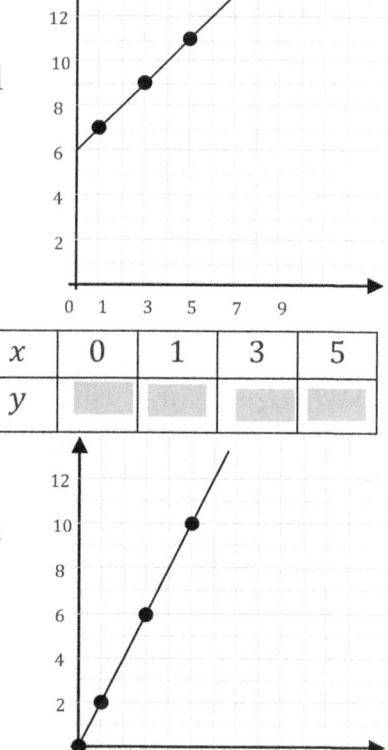

Evaluating Two Variables

- To evaluate an algebraic expression, substitute a number for each variable.
- Perform the arithmetic operations to find the value of the expression.

Examples:

Example 1. Calculate this expression for $a = 2$ and $b = -1$. $(4a - 3b)$

Solution: First, substitute 2 for a, and -1 for b.

Then: $4a - 3b = 4(2) - 3(-1)$

Now, use order of operation to find the answer: $4(2) - 3(-1) = 8 + 3 = 11$

Example 2. Evaluate this expression for $x = -2$ and $y = 2$. $(3x + 6y)$

Solution: Substitute -2 for x, and 2 for y.

Then: $3x + 6y = 3(-2) + 6(2) = -6 + 12 = 6$

Example 3. Find the value of this expression $2(6a - 5b)$, when $a = -1$ and $b = 4$.

Solution: Substitute -1 for a, and 4 for b.

Then: $2(6a - 5b) = 2(6(-1) - 5(4)) = 2(-6 - 20) = 2(-26) = -52$

Example 4. Evaluate this expression. $-7x - 2y$, $x = 4$, $y = -3$

Solution: Substitute 4 for x, and -3 for y and simplify.

Then: $-7x - 2y = -7(4) - 2(-3) = -28 + 6 = -22$

Solving Word problems by Finding Two-Variable Equation

- To solve word problems, we need to write a set of equations that represent the problem mathematically.
- Problem-solving strategy:

* Read the whole question. What are we asked to solve?

* Assign variables to the unknown quantity, for example, x and y.

* Translate the words into algebraic expressions by rewriting the given information in terms of the variable.

* Set up an equation or system of equations to solve for the variable.

$$y = mx + b$$

* Solve the equation algebraically using substitution.

* Check the solution.

Example:

A store has 24 permanent employees. It hires some temporary employees during busy times of the year. Let t represent the number of temporary employees and w represent the total number of employees. Find the value of w when $t = 11$.

Solution: First, look for relationships between the number of temporary employees, t, and the total number of employees, w.

In this relationship, t is the input, and w is the output. So, find w by adding 24 to t. Write the relationship as an equation, $w = t + 24$. Then, substitute 11 for t in the equation to find the w.

$$w = t + 24 \rightarrow w = 11 + 24 \rightarrow w = 35$$

When $t = 11$, $w = 35$.

Chapter 5: Practices

✎ **Complete the equation.**

1) $j = \underline{} \times k$

k	j
4	12
5	15
6	18
7	21

2) $m = u + \underline{}$

u	m
1	9
2	10
3	11
4	12

3) $s = t - \underline{}$

t	s
10	8
11	9
12	10
13	11

4) $l = \underline{} \times q$

q	l
1	11
2	22
3	33
4	44

5) $b = a - \underline{}$

a	b
3	−2
4	−1
5	0
6	1

6) $y = \underline{} \times x$

x	y
2	1
3	1.5
4	2
5	2.5

✎ **Complete the table and graph the equation.**

7) $y = x$

x	0	1		3	5
y					

8) $y = x + 2$

x	0	1	3	5
y				

9) $y = \frac{1}{2}x$

x	0	2	4	6
y				

10) $y = 3x$

x	1	2		4
y				

✏️ **Evaluate each expression using the values given.**

11) $x = 2, y = 1 \rightarrow 2x + 7y =$ _____

12) $a = 3, b = 5 \rightarrow 3a - 5b =$ _____

13) $x = 6, y = 2 \rightarrow 3x - 2y + 8 =$ _____

14) $a = -2, b = 3 \rightarrow -5a + 2b + 6 =$ _____

15) $x = -4, y = -3 \rightarrow -4x + 10 - 8y =$ _____

✏️ **Solve the relationships in the word problems.**

16) Car manufacturing produces 48 new cars each month. Let m represent the number of months and c represent the total number of cars produced. Find the number of cars when $m = 4$.

17) Jenny rides the train for 15 minutes every day. d represents the number of days and m represents the total number of minutes Jenny spends on the train. After a month how much time will she spend on the train?

18) Jessica has 50 biscuits in her kitchen. In the afternoon, she has several guests who eat 1 biscuit. Let b represent the number of biscuits left, and g represent the number of guests. Find the number of biscuits left when $g = 17$.

19) There are 9 cakes in a pack. Let p represent the number of packs and c represent the number of cakes. Find the number of cakes when $p = 3$.

Chapter 5: Answers

1) $j = 3 \times k$ 3) $s = t - 2$ 5) $b = a - 5$

2) $m = u + 8$ 4) $l = 11 \times q$ 6) $y = \frac{1}{2} \times x$

7)

x	0	1	3	5
y	0	1	3	5

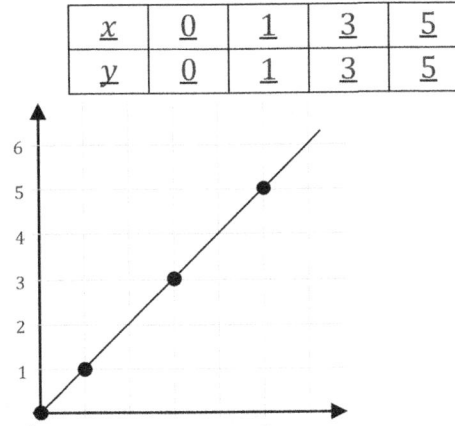

8)

x	0	1	3	5
y	2	3	5	7

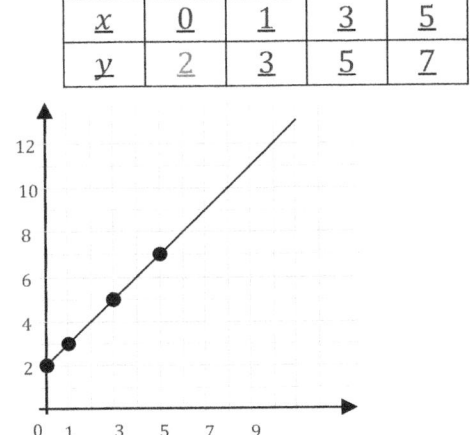

9)

x	0	2	4	6
y	0	1	2	3

10)

x	1	2	4
y	3	6	12

11) 11   14) 22   17) $m = 450$

12) −16   15) 50   18) $b = 33$

13) 22   16) $c = 192$ 19) $c = 27$

CHAPTER
6 Geometry and Solid Figures

Math topics that you'll learn in this chapter:

- ☑ Triangles
- ☑ Triangle Inequality
- ☑ Relationships Between Sides and Angles in a Triangle
- ☑ Definition of the Area of a Triangle
- ☑ Polygons
- ☑ Cubes
- ☑ Rectangle Prisms
- ☑ Definition of the Area of a Parallelogram
- ☑ Word Problems Involving Area of Quadrilaterals and Triangles
- ☑ Definition of the Area of a Trapezoid
- ☑ Finding Area of Compound Figures
- ☑ Finding Area Between Two Rectangles
- ☑ Finding Area Between Two Triangles
- ☑ Volume of Cubes and Rectangular Prisms: Word Problems

Triangles

- In any triangle, the sum of all angles is 180 degrees.
- Area of a triangle = $\frac{1}{2}$ (base × height)

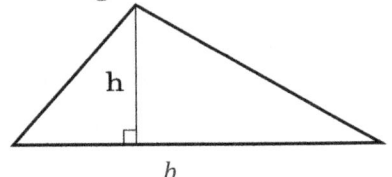

Examples:

Example 1. What is the area of this triangles?

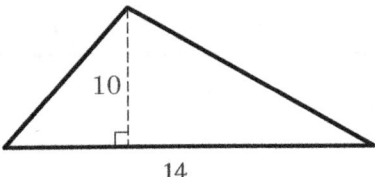

Solution: Use the area formula:
Area = $\frac{1}{2}$(base × height)
base = 14 and height = 10, Then:
Area = $\frac{1}{2}$(14 × 10) = $\frac{1}{2}$(140) = 70

Example 2. What is the area of this triangles?

Solution: Use the area formula:

Area = $\frac{1}{2}$(base × height)
base = 16 and height = 8; Area = $\frac{1}{2}$(16 × 8) = $\frac{128}{2}$ = 64

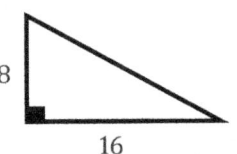

Example 3. What is the missing angle in this triangle?

Solution:
In any triangle, the sum of all angles is 180 degrees.
Let x be the missing angle.
Then: 55 + 80 + x = 180 → 135 + x = 180 →
x = 180 − 135 = 45
The missing angle is 45 degrees.

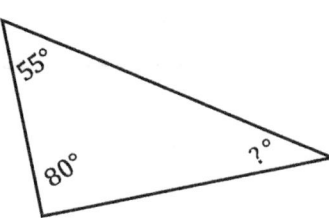

Triangle Inequality

- If the sum of any of the two sides is greater than the 3rd, then the difference between any of the two sides is going to be less than the 3rd.

- The sum of any of the two sides has to be higher than the 3rd side.

- The side which is opposite to a bigger angle will be the longest side of the triangle.

- To figure out if the 3 side lengths are a triangle, utilize the triangle inequality theorem, which declares that the sum of 2 sides of a triangle has to be larger than the 3rd side. Thus, you must add together each combination of the 2 sides to find out if it is larger than the 3rd side.

Examples:

Example 1. Can the sides of a triangle have the given lengths?

Lengths of a triangle: 7, 10 and 2

Solution: If $0 \leq a \leq b \leq c$, and $a + b > c$, then a, b, and c are the side of a triangle. Therefore, put the 3 numbers in order from smallest to largest, $a = 2$, $b = 7$, $c = 10$.

Now, $2 + 7$ is smaller than 10 and this statement, $a + b > c$ is not true for these lengths, $2 + 7 \ngtr 10$. So, these are not the side lengths of a triangle.

Example 2. Can the sides of a triangle have the given lengths?

Lengths of a triangle: 9, 9 and 12

Solution: If $0 \leq a \leq b \leq c$, and $a + b > c$, then a, b, and c are the side of a triangle. Therefore, put the 3 numbers in order from smallest to largest, $a = 9$, $b = 9$, $c = 12$.

Now, $9 + 9$ is larger than 12 and this statement, $a + b > c$ is true for these lengths, $9 + 9 > 12$. So, these are the side lengths of a triangle.

Relationships Between Sides and Angles in a Triangle

- Angle-Side Relationships: With triangles, the biggest side is opposite the biggest angle and vice versa and the smallest side is opposite the tiniest angle and vice versa.

- Isosceles triangle: A triangle that has 2 equal side lengths. The opposite angles of these congruent sides are similarly equal.

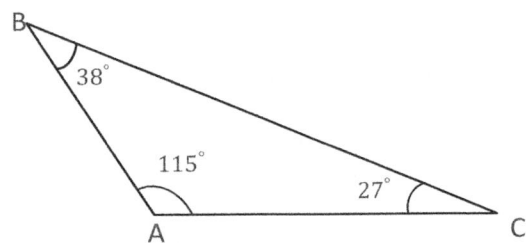

$115° > 38° > 27°$

$\angle A > \angle B > \angle C$; therefore, $\overline{BC} > \overline{AC} > \overline{AB}$

- In any triangle, the sum of the lengths of any 2 sides is more than the length of the 3rd side.

Examples:

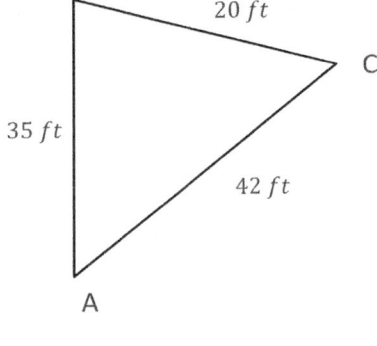

Example 1. Find the smallest angle of $\triangle ABC$.

Solution: Since $20 < 35 < 42$, $\overline{BC} < \overline{BA} < \overline{AC}$. And, their opposite angles are in the same order, from smallest to largest:

$$\angle A < \angle C < \angle B$$

So, the smallest angle is ∠A.

Example 2. Find the smallest side of $\triangle EFG$.

Solution: Since $40° < 51° < 89°$, $\angle G < \angle F < \angle E$. And, their opposite sides are in the same order, from smallest to largest: $\overline{EF} < \overline{EG} < \overline{GF}$

So, the smallest side is $\overline{EF}$.

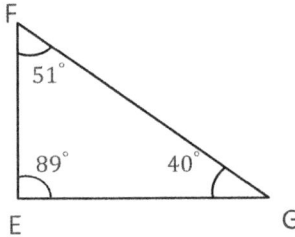

Definition of the Area of a Triangle

- The area of a triangle: $A = \frac{1}{2}(b \times h)$ square units. When b and h are the base and height of the triangle, correspondingly.

- The area of a triangle is described as the total space inhabited by the 3 sides of a triangle in a 2–dimensional plane. The basic formula for the area of a triangle is equal to half the product of its base and height, i.e., $A = \frac{1}{2} \times b \times h$.

Examples:

Example 1. Convert the following triangle into a rectangle by copying and forming. What is the area of the triangle?

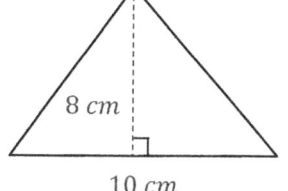

Solution: First, make a copy of the triangle, then cut the copy into two smaller triangles for making a rectangle. Rearrange the triangles. And finally, the area of this rectangle is 2 times larger than the area of the triangle.

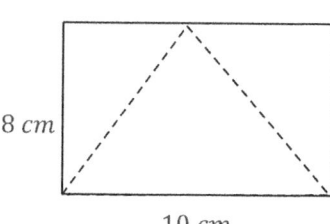

Now, to find the area of a triangle, find the area of the rectangle, its sides are 10 and 9 centimeters long. Multiply, $10 \times 8 = 80$. Since the area of a rectangle is 2 times larger than the area of the triangle. Thus, $\frac{1}{2} \times 80 = 40$.

So, the area of a triangle is equal to $40 \ cm^2$.

Example 2. What is the area of the triangle?

Solution: To find the area of a triangle, multiply, the base by the height, then multiply $\frac{1}{2}$ by the result. So, the area of the triangle is $15 \ in^2$.

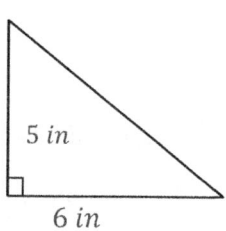

$$Area = base \times height \times \frac{1}{2} \rightarrow A = \frac{1}{2}(b \times h) \rightarrow A = \frac{1}{2}(5 \times 6) = 15$$

Polygons

- The perimeter of a square = 4 × side = 4s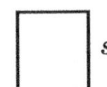

- The perimeter of a rectangle = 2(width + length)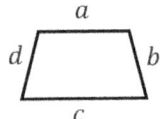

- The perimeter of trapezoid = a + b + c + d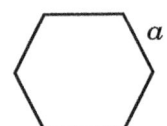

- The perimeter of a regular hexagon = 6a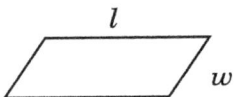

- The perimeter of a parallelogram = 2(l + w)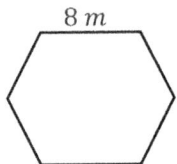

Examples:

Example 1. Find the perimeter of following regular hexagon.

Solution: Since the hexagon is regular, all sides are equal.

Then, the perimeter of the hexagon = 6 × (one side)

The perimeter of the hexagon = 6 × (one side) = 6 × 8 = 48 m

Example 2. Find the perimeter of following trapezoid.

Solution: The perimeter of a trapezoid = a + b + c + d

The perimeter of the trapezoid = 7 + 8 + 8 + 10 = 33 ft

Cubes

- A cube is a three-dimensional solid object bounded by six square sides.
- Volume is the measure of the amount of space inside of a solid figure, like a cube, ball, cylinder or pyramid.
- The volume of a cube = $(one\ side)^3$
- The surface area of a cube = $6 \times (one\ side)^2$

Examples:

Example 1. Find the volume and surface area of this cube.

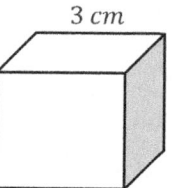

Solution: Use volume formula: $volume = (one\ side)^3$

Then: $volume = (one\ side)^3 = (3)^3 = 27\ cm^3$

Use surface area formula:

$surface\ area\ of\ a\ cube: 6(one\ side)^2 = 6(3)^2 = 6(9) = 54\ cm^2$

Example 2. Find the volume and surface area of this cube.

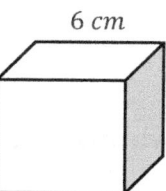

Solution: Use volume formula: $volume = (one\ side)^3$

Then: $volume = (one\ side)^3 = (6)^3 = 216\ cm^3$

Use surface area formula:

$surface\ area\ of\ a\ cube: 6(one\ side)^2 = 6(6)^2 = 6(36) = 216\ cm^2$

Example 3. Find the volume and surface area of this cube.

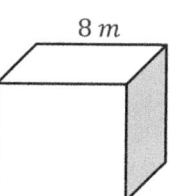

Solution: Use volume formula: $volume = (one\ side)^3$

Then: $volume = (one\ side)^3 = (8)^3 = 512\ m^3$

Use surface area formula:

$surface\ area\ of\ a\ cube: 6(one\ side)^2 = 6(8)^2 = 6(64) = 384\ m^2$

Rectangular Prisms

- A rectangular prism is a solid 3-dimensional object with six rectangular faces.

- The volume of a Rectangular prism = Length × Width × Height

$Volume = l \times w \times h$

$Surface\ area = 2 \times (wh + lw + lh)$

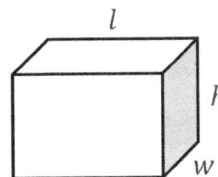

Examples:

Example 1. Find the volume and surface area of this rectangular prism.

Solution: Use volume formula: $Volume = l \times w \times h$

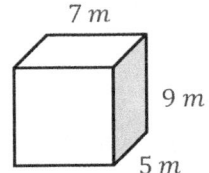

Then: $Volume = 7 \times 5 \times 9 = 315\ m^3$

Use surface area formula: $Surface\ area = 2 \times (wh + lw + lh)$

Then: $Surface\ area = 2 \times \big((5 \times 9) + (7 \times 5) + (7 \times 9)\big)$

$= 2 \times (45 + 35 + 63) = 2 \times (143) = 286\ m^2$

Example 2. Find the volume and surface area of this rectangular prism.

Solution: Use volume formula: $Volume = l \times w \times h$

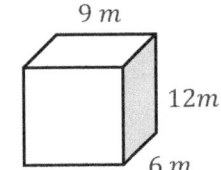

Then: $Volume = 9 \times 6 \times 12 = 648\ m^3$

Use surface area formula: $Surface\ area = 2 \times (wh + lw + lh)$

Then: $Surface\ area = 2 \times \big((6 \times 12) + (9 \times 6) + (9 \times 12)\big)$

$= 2 \times (72 + 54 + 108) = 2 \times (234) = 468\ m^2$

Definition of the Area of a Parallelogram

- The formula for determining the area of a parallelogram is base times height. This means $A = bh$, the same as the formula for the area of a rectangle.
- Parallelograms are quadrilaterals having 2 pairs of parallel sides.
- The opposite sides of the parallelogram are identical in length, and the opposite angles are identical in measure. Likewise, the interior angles on the same side of the transversal are supplementary.
- The sum of all the interior angles equals 360 degrees.

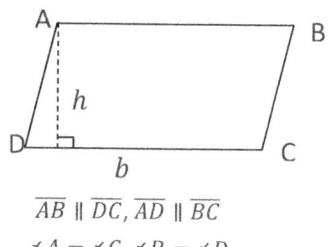

$\overline{AB} \parallel \overline{DC}, \overline{AD} \parallel \overline{BC}$
$\angle A = \angle C, \angle B = \angle D$

Examples:

Example 1. Convert the following parallelogram into a rectangle with the same area. And what is the area of the parallelogram?

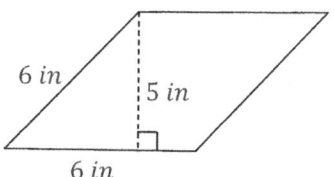

Solution: In this parallelogram is a base of 6 *in* and a height of 5 *in*. For converting to a rectangle, first, cut it into two pieces along the dashed line. Next, rearrange the pieces on the other side and put the pieces back together. And finally, this rectangle has the same area as the parallelogram.

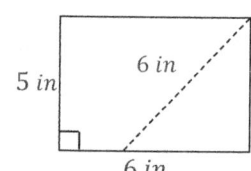

Now to find area of parallelogram, find the area of the rectangle, its sides are 5 and 6 inches long. Multiply, $5 \times 6 = 30$. Since, the area of rectangle is the same of the area of parallelogram.

So, the area of parallelogram is equal to 30.

Example 2. What is the area of the parallelogram?

Solution: To find the area of a parallelogram, multiply, the base by the height. So, the area of a parallelogram is $54\ cm^2$.

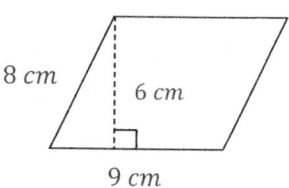

$$Area = base \times height \rightarrow A = b \times h \rightarrow A = 9 \times 6 = 54$$

Word Problems Involving Area of Quadrilaterals and Triangles

- You can solve word problems by becoming a detective and searching for clues in the form of keywords and phrases.
- Finding them helps you understand which operation to use.
- Carefully read the text to understand what you are asked to solve in the problem.
- Write a number sentence then solve it in a single step.

Examples:

Example 1. Fred and his buddies went to the opening of the brand-new community center in the park. The town's mayor unveiled a parallelogram-shaped decorative plaque at the park entrance which had the date of this special event. The bottom edge is nine inches long, and its area is 126 square inches.

What is the height of the plaque?

Solution: To determine the height of the plaque, first, write an equation to find the area of the parallelogram $A = b \times h$. And the area is 126 in^2 and the base is 9 in. So, $126 = 9 \times h$. Solve the equation:

$$126 = 9 \times h \rightarrow \frac{126}{9} = \frac{9h}{9} \rightarrow 14 = h$$

Thus, this plaque is 14 inches tall.

Example 2. Olivia likes to plant different flowers in her garden. She has a garden plot that is shaped like a square. Each side of the garden plot is 10 feet long. What is the area of the garden?

Solution: To determine the area of the garden. First, write an equation to find the area of the square, $A = S^2$. And the side is 10 ft. So, solve the equation:

$$A = S^2 \rightarrow A = 10^2 \rightarrow A = 100$$

Thus, this garden has 100 ft^2 areas.

Definition of the Area of a Trapezoid

- In order to determine the area of a trapezoid, multiply the sum of the bases (the parallel sides) by the height (the perpendicular distance between the bases), and after that divide by 2.

- Trapezoid Area Formula: Based on the trapezoid area formula, the area of a trapezoid is equal to half the product of the height and the sum of the two bases. Area=$\frac{1}{2}$×(Sum of parallel sides)×(perpendicular distance in between the parallel sides).

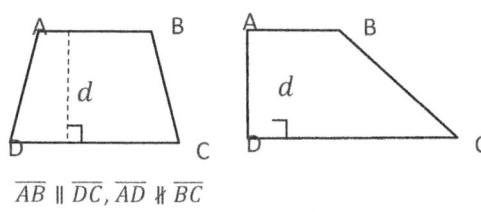

$\overline{AB} \parallel \overline{DC}, \overline{AD} \nparallel \overline{BC}$

$$A = \frac{1}{2} \times (\overline{AB} + \overline{DC}) \times (d)$$

Examples:

Example 1. Convert the following trapezoid into two triangles. What is the area of the trapezoid?

Solution: To convert the trapezoid into two triangles, we draw one of the diagonals of the trapezoid. And cut them. Now, to find the area of the trapezoid, find the area of the triangles, their bases are 8 and 4 yards long and its height is 5 yards. Calculate the area of two triangles, $\frac{1}{2} \times 8 \times 5 = 20$ and $\frac{1}{2} \times 4 \times 5 = 10$. Then add together $20 + 10 = 30$. Since the area of the trapezoid is equal to the two triangles made of it. Thus, $\frac{1}{2} \times (4 + 8) \times 5 = 30$.

So, the area of the trapezoid is equal to $30\ yd^2$.

Example 2. What is the area of the trapezoid?

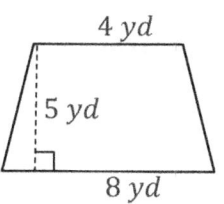

Solution: To find the area of a trapezoid, add the parallel sides, then multiply $\frac{1}{2}$ and the distance in between the parallel sides by the result. So, the area of the trapezoid is $60\ in^2$.

Finding Area of Compound Figures

- To figure out the area of compound shapes you have to divide the compound shape into basic shapes, then figure out the area of each of the basic shapes, and then they are added together.

- To figure out the area of irregular shapes, firstly, you must divide the irregular shape into regular shapes you are able to recognize like circles, rectangles, squares, triangles, etc. Afterward, figure out the area of these individual shapes and then add them to determine an area of irregular shapes.

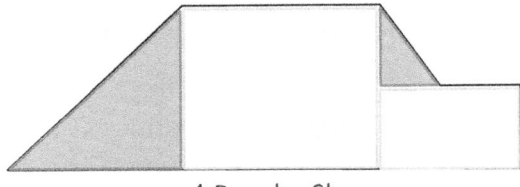

4 Regular Shapes

Examples:

Example 1. Calculate the area of the given shape.

Solution: Divide the figure into rectangles, and rename the shapes, A and B. Then calculate each rectangle. Area of rectangle A, $6 \times 4 = 24 \ m^2$. Area of rectangle B, $8 \times 10 = 80 \ m^2$.

Now, add the areas of two rectangles, $24 + 80 = 104 \ m^2$. So, the area is 104 square meters.

Example 2. What is the area of this figure?

Solution: Divide the figure into rectangle and triangle, and rename the shapes, A and B. Then calculate each rectangle. Area of rectangle A, $9 \times 4 = 36 \ cm^2$. Area of triangle B, $\frac{1}{2}(7 - 4) \times (9 - 3) = 9 \ cm^2$

Now, add the areas of two shapes A and B, $36 + 9 = 45 \ cm^2$. So, the area is 45 square centimeters.

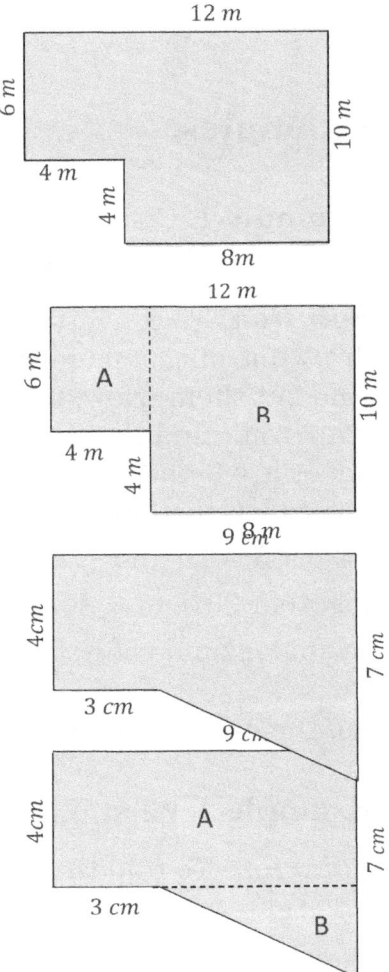

Finding Area Between Two Rectangles

- The area of a rectangle is provided by the formula: $A = l \times w$

- Step 1: Distinguish the length (l) and width (w) of the larger rectangle. Next, determine the area of the larger rectangle via utilizing the formula $A_B = l_B \times w_B$.

- Step 2: Distinguish the length (l) and width (w) of the lesser rectangle. Next, discover the area of the lesser rectangle via utilizing the formula $A_S = l_S \times w_S$.

- Step 3: Locate the area between the two rectangles by subtracting the area of the lesser rectangle from the area of the bigger rectangle.

Examples:

Example 1. What is the area of the shaded region?

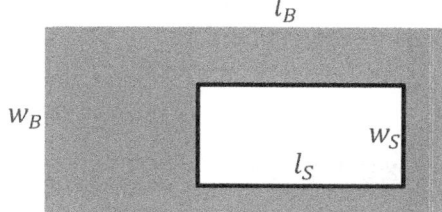

Solution: First, find the area of each rectangle. Then subtract the area of the inner rectangle from the area of the outer rectangle. The area of the inner rectangle, $5 \times 2 = 10 \ in^2$. The area of the outer rectangle, $9 \times 3.5 = 31.5 \ in^2$.

To find the shaded area, $31.5 - 10 = 21.5 \ in^2$.

So, the area of the shaded region is 21.5 square inches.

Example 2. What is the area of the shaded region?

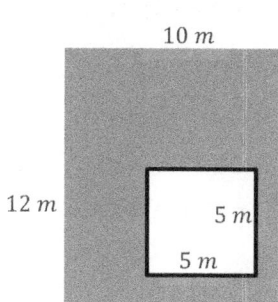

Solution: First, find the area of the rectangle and square. Then subtract the area of the inner square from the area of the outer rectangle. The area of the inner square is, $5 \times 5 = 25 \ m^2$. The area of the outer rectangle is, $12 \times 10 = 120 \ m^2$.

To find the shaded area, $120 - 25 = 95 \ m^2$.

So, the area of the shaded region is 95 square meters.

Finding Area Between Two Triangles

- $Area = \frac{1}{2} \times b \times h$, in which b is the length of the base of the triangle, and h is the height/altitude of the triangle.

- To locate the area of the shaded region, subtract the area of the inner shape from the area of the outer shape. Begin by discovering the area of the inner shape. Locate the base and height of the inner triangle.

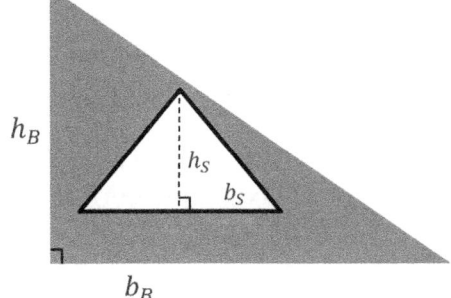

Examples:

Example 1. What is the area of the shaded region?

Solution: First, find the area of each triangle. Then subtract the area of the inner triangle from the area of the outer triangle. The area of the inner triangle, $\frac{1}{2} \times 11 \times 7 = 38.5 \; in^2$. The area of the outer triangle, $\frac{1}{2} \times 23 \times 16 = 184 \; in^2$.

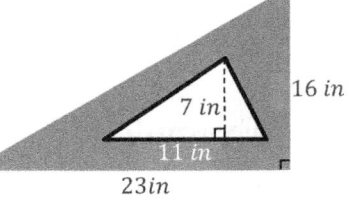

To find the shaded area $184 - 38.5 = 145.5 \; in^2$.

So, the area of the shaded region is 145.5 square inches.

Example 2. What is the area of the shaded region?

Solution: First, find the area of each triangle. Then subtract the area of the inner triangle from the area of the outer triangle. The area of the inner triangle, $\frac{1}{2} \times 4 \times 5 = 10 \; ft^2$. The area of the outer triangle, $\frac{1}{2} \times 18 \times 9 = 81 \; ft^2$.

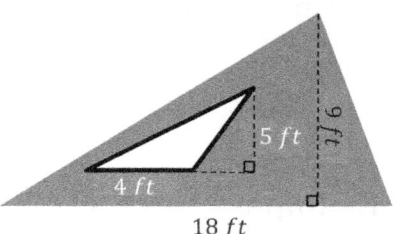

To find the shaded area, $81 - 10 = 71 \; ft^2$.

So, the area of the shaded region is 71 square feet.

Volume of Cubes and Rectangular Prisms: Word Problems

- You can solve word problems by becoming a detective and searching for clues in the form of keywords and phrases.
- Finding them helps you understand which operation to use.
- Carefully read the text to understand what you are asked to solve in the problem.
- Write a number sentence then solve it in a single step.

Examples:

Example 1. Lee purchased an aquarium shaped like a rectangular prism for her brand-new pet betta fish. This container can hold 1950 cubic inches of water. It's 15 inches long along with being 10 inches wide.

What is the height of the tank?

Solution: To figure out how tall the container, h, is, utilize the formula for the volume of a rectangular prism. $V = lwh$. Solve for $h, 1,950 = 15 \times 10 \times h \rightarrow \frac{1,950}{150} = \frac{150}{150} \times h \rightarrow 13 = h$

The tank's height is 13 inches.

Example 2. Meg bought a new pink dress for her sister's birthday party. She returned home with a box that was 30 inches long, 22 inches wide, and 5 inches tall.

What is the volume of the clothes box?

Solution: To find out the volume of the clothes box, V, is, utilize the formula for the volume of a rectangular prism. $V = lwh$. Solve for V.

$V = 30 \times 22 \times 5 \rightarrow V = 3,300\ in^3$

The clothes box is 3,300 cubic inches.

Chapter 6: Practices

✍ **Find the measure of the unknown angle in each triangle.**

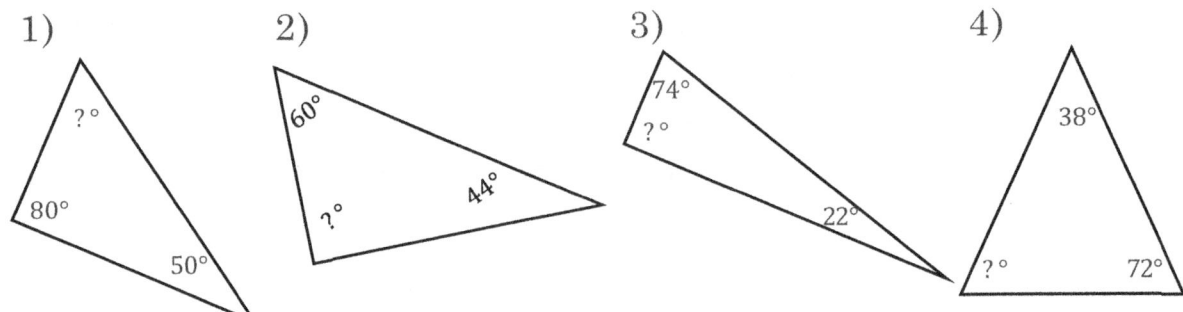

✍ **Find the area of each triangle.**

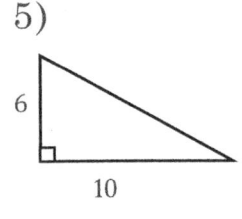 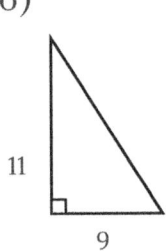 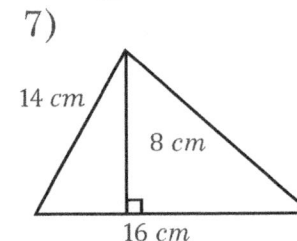 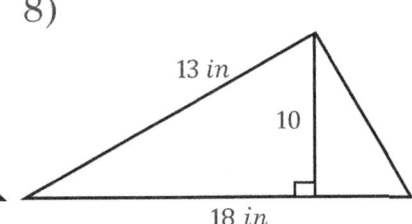

✍ **Which lengths of the given sides represent a triangle?**

9) $a = 4, b = 7, c = 11$ 13) $a = 2, b = 15, c = 17$

10) $a = 1, b = 5, c = 9$ 14) $a = 7, b = 7, c = 9$

11) $a = 5, b = 6, c = 8$ 15) $a = 3, b = 13, c = 13$

12) $a = 8, b = 10, c = 15$ 16) $a = 5, b = 8, c = 15$

✍ **Find the required side of the triangle.**

17) Smallest side   18) Smallest side

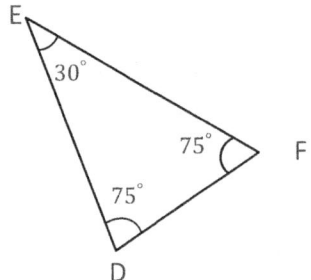 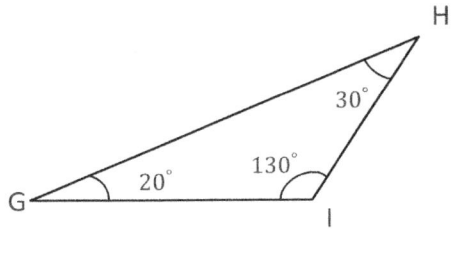

19) Largest side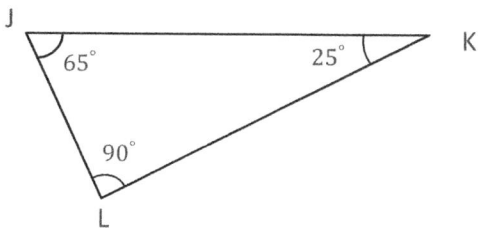

20) Largest side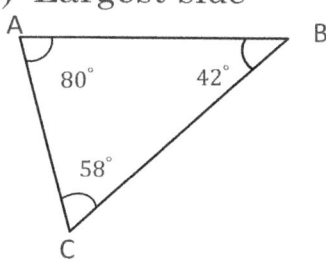

✎ **Find the required angle of the triangle.**

21) Largest angle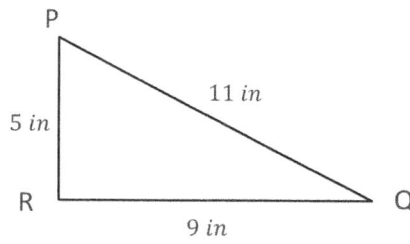

22) Smallest angle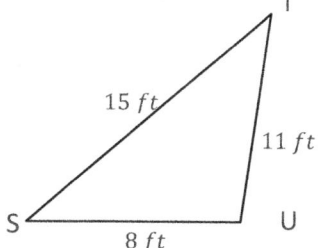

23) Smallest angle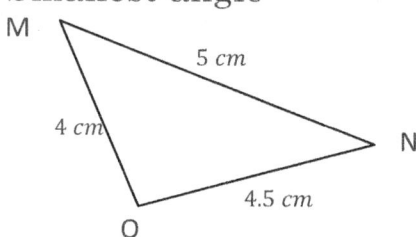

24) Largest angle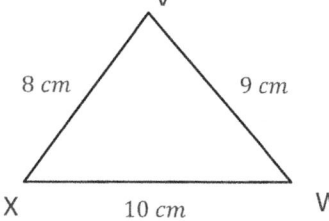

✎ **What is the area of the triangle?**

25)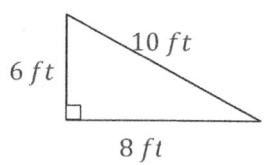

26)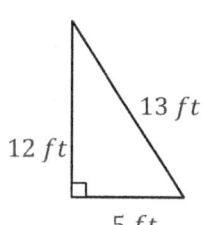

27)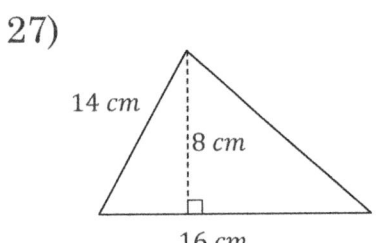

28)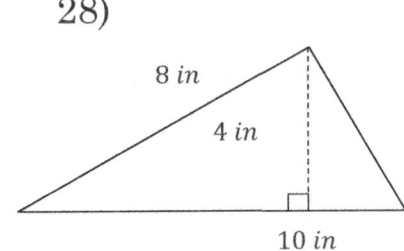

29)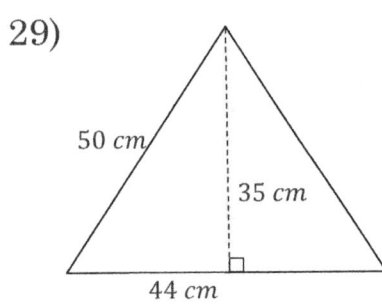

30)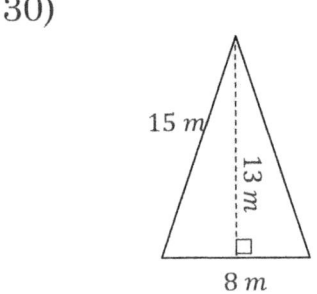

31)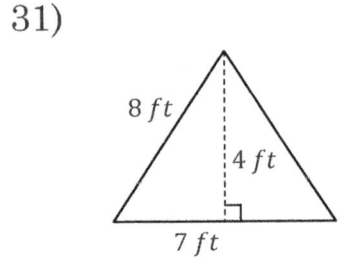

32)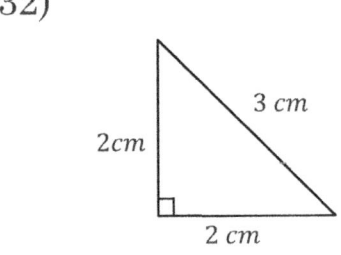

✏️ **Find the perimeter or circumference of each shape.**

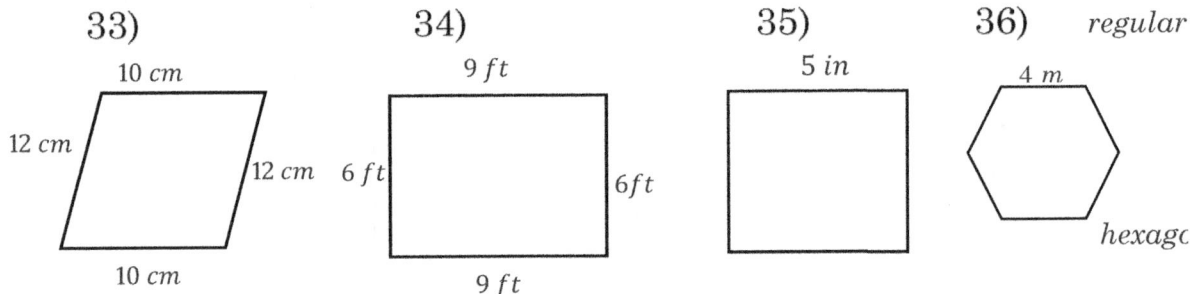

33) 10 cm, 12 cm, 12 cm, 10 cm

34) 9 ft, 6 ft, 6 ft, 9 ft

35) 5 in

36) regular 4 m hexagon

Chapter 6: Geometry and Solid Figures

🖋 **Find the volume of each cube.**

37)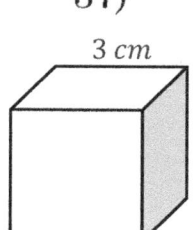
3 cm

38)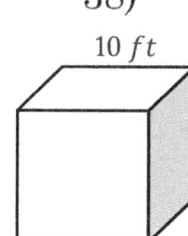
10 ft

39)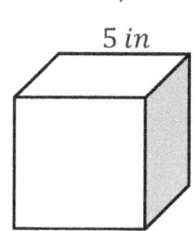
5 in

40)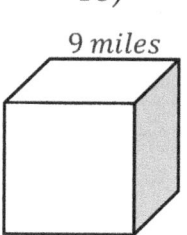
9 miles

🖋 **Find the volume of each Rectangular Prism.**

41)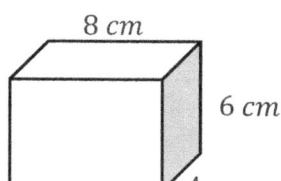
8 cm, 6 cm, 4 cm

42)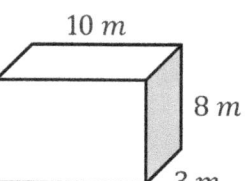
10 m, 8 m, 3 m

43)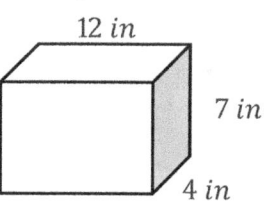
12 in, 7 in, 4 in

🖋 **What is the area of the parallelograms?**

44)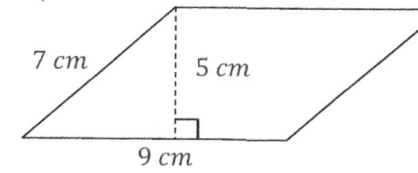
7 cm, 5 cm, 9 cm

45)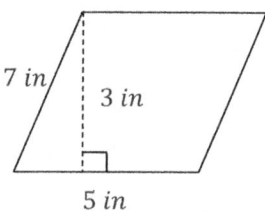
7 in, 3 in, 5 in

46)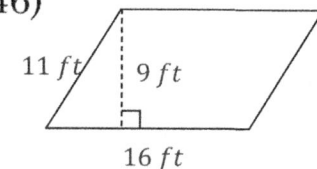
11 ft, 9 ft, 16 ft

47)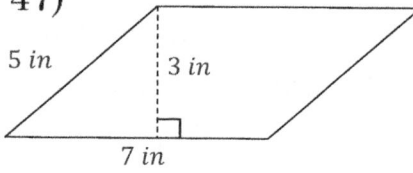
5 in, 3 in, 7 in

48)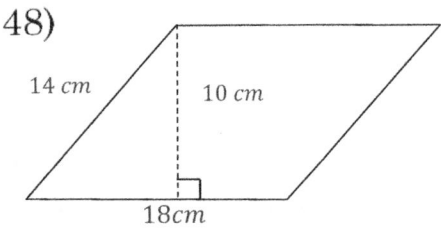

49)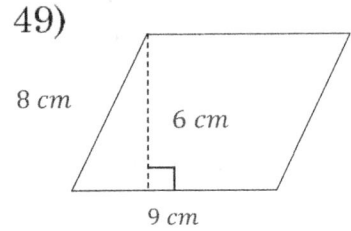

50)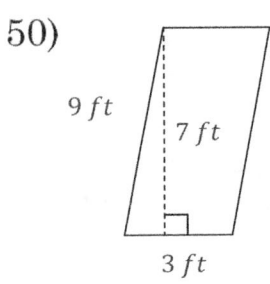

51)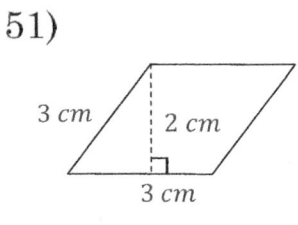

✍ **Solve the word problems.**

52) A trapezoid has an area of 60 cm^2 and its height is 6 cm and one base is 8 cm. What is the other base length?

53) There is a chess board, that is shaped like a square, and its sides are 16 inches long. What is the area of the chess board?

54) If a triangle has an area of 66 ft^2 and the length of the base is 12 ft, find the height.

55) A triangle has an area of 75 square inches and a height of 15 inches. What is the length of the triangle's base?

56) If a trapezoid has an area of 180 m^2 and its height is 12 m and one base is 20 m, find the other base length.

57) An advertising company made a banner for a construction company. The banner is shaped like a triangle with an area of 45 square feet. The banner is 5 feet tall. What is the length of the banner's base?

58) The area of a parallelogram is 625 ft^2 and its height is 25 ft. what is the base length?

59) The base of a parallelogram is 19 yards long, and its height is 13 yards. What is the area of the parallelogram?

✏ **What is the area of the trapezoids?**

60)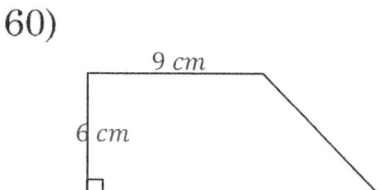

61)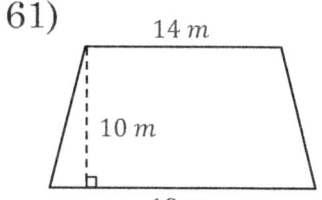

62)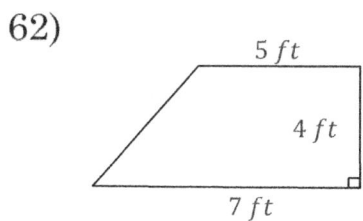

63)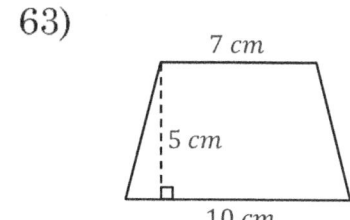

64)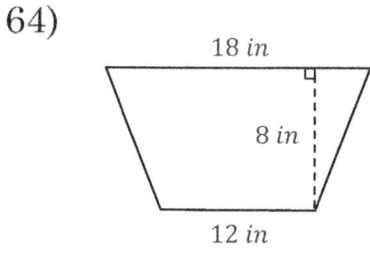

65)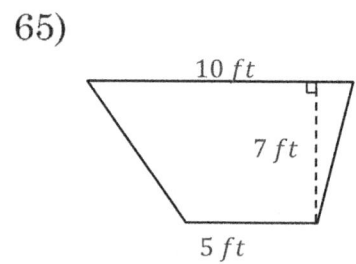

66)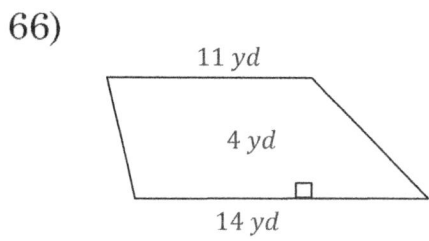

67)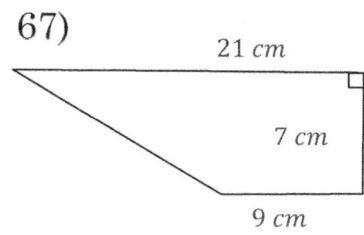

✏️ **Calculate the area of the given shapes.**

68)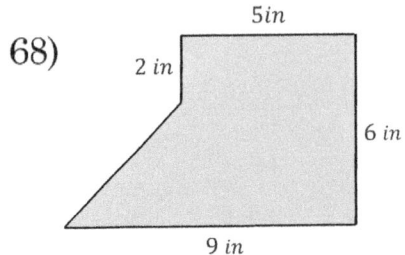

69)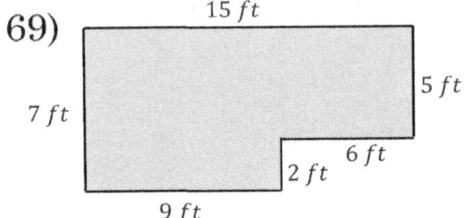

70)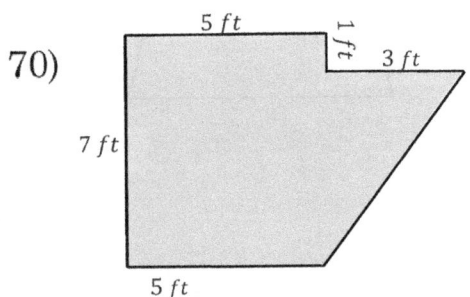

71)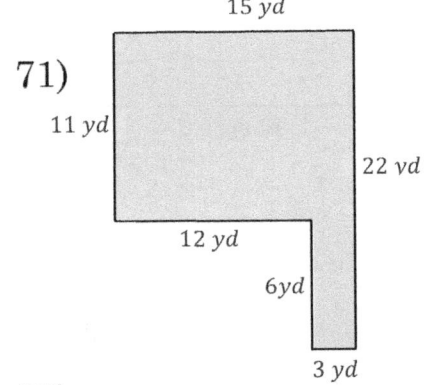

72)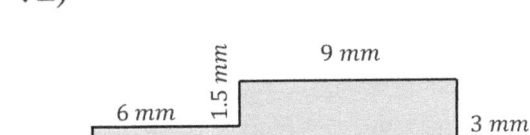

73)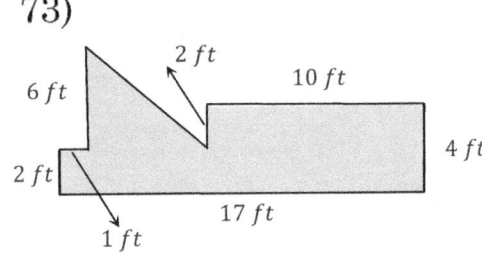

74)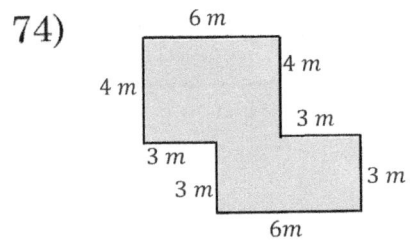

75)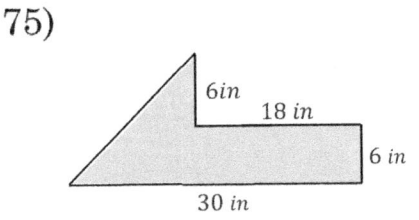

Calculate the shaded area of the given shapes.

76)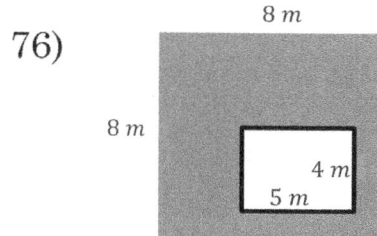

77)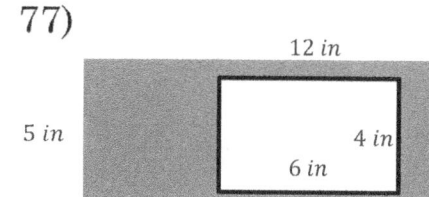

78)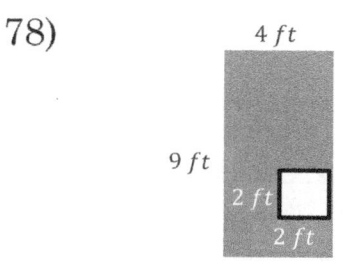

79)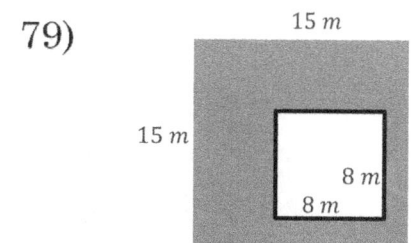

80)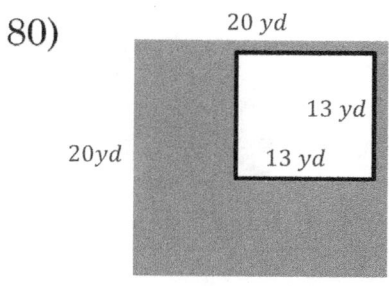

81)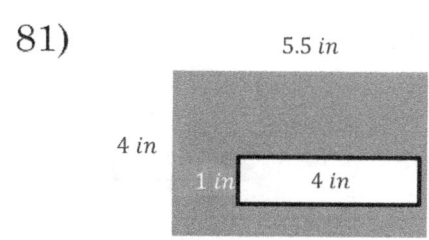

82)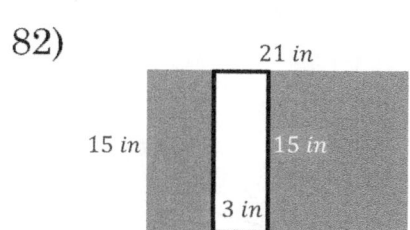

83)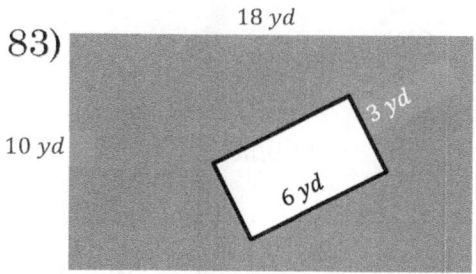

✎ **Calculate the shaded area of the given shapes.**

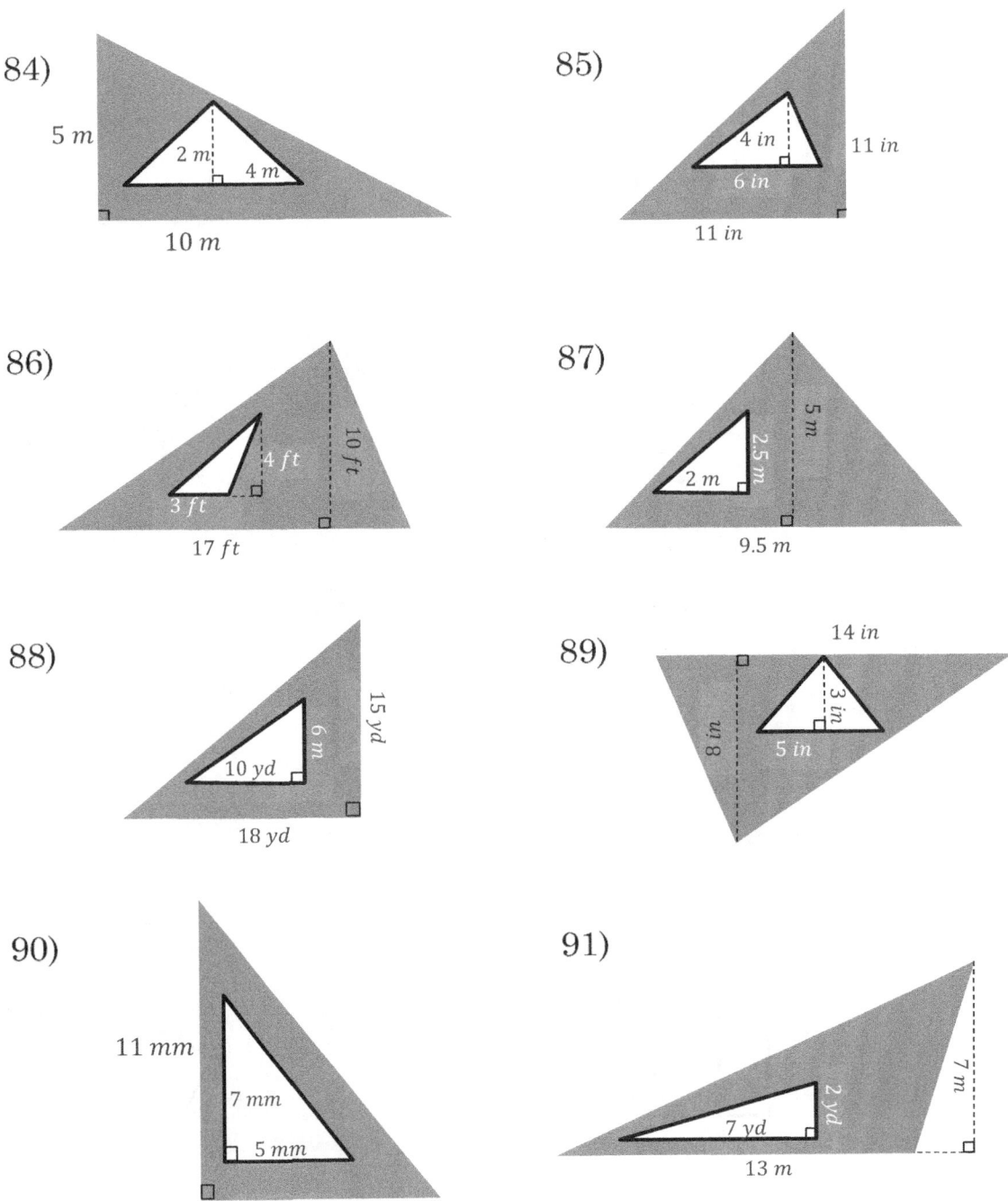

Chapter 6: Geometry and Solid Figures

✎ **Solve the word problems.**

92) There is the rectangular prism box for packing fruits that has a volume of 29700 cubic centimeters. The prism has a width of 30 centimeters and a height of 22 centimeters. What is the length of the box?

93) Employees of a company, to make happy the cancer children. They prepared some gifts such as toys and colored pencils and a cute notebook. They display the gifts in a glass case shaped like a rectangular prism. It has a length of 48 inches, a height of 19 inches, and a volume of 22800 cubic inches. What is the width of the prism?

94) There is a cube prism that has a volume of 125 cubic centimeters. The prism has a width of 5 centimeters. What is the length and height of the prism?

95) After visiting the zoo, Irma got her very own pet parrot. Irma bought a birdhouse shaped like a rectangular prism for her parrot to live in. The birdhouse is 20 inches long, 15 inches wide, and 37 inches tall. What is the volume of the birdhouse?

Chapter 6: Answers

1) 50
2) 76
3) 84
4) 70
5) 30
6) 49.5
7) $64\ cm^2$
8) $90\ in^2$
9) It is not a triangle.
10) It is not a triangle.
11) It is a triangle.
12) It is a triangle.
13) It is not a triangle.
14) It is a triangle.
15) It is a triangle.
16) It is not a triangle.
17) $\overline{DF}$ is the smallest.
18) $\overline{HI}$ is the smallest.
19) $\overline{JK}$ is the largest.
20) $\overline{BC}$ is the largest.
21) ∠R is the largest.
22) ∠T is the smallest.
23) ∠N is the smallest.
24) ∠V is the largest.
25) $24\ ft^2$
26) $30\ ft^2$
27) $64\ cm^2$
28) $20\ in^2$
29) $770\ cm^2$
30) $52\ m^2$
31) $14\ ft^2$
32) $2\ cm^2$
33) $44\ cm$
34) $30\ ft$
35) $20\ in$
36) $24\ m$
37) $27\ cm^3$
38) $1,000\ ft^3$
39) $125\ in^3$
40) $729\ mi^3$
41) $192\ cm^3$
42) $240\ m^3$
43) $336\ in^3$
44) $45\ cm^2$
45) $15\ in^2$
46) $144\ ft^2$
47) $21\ in^2$
48) $180\ cm^2$
49) $54\ cm^2$
50) $21\ ft^2$
51) $6\ cm^2$
52) $12\ cm$
53) $256\ in^2$
54) $11\ ft$
55) $10\ in$
56) $10\ m$
57) $18\ ft$
58) $25\ ft$
59) $247\ yd^2$
60) $63\ cm^2$
61) $160\ m^2$
62) $24\ ft^2$
63) $42.5\ cm^2$
64) $120\ in^2$
65) $52.5\ ft^2$
66) $50\ yd^2$
67) $105\ cm^2$
68) $38\ in^2$
69) $93\ ft^2$
70) $44\ ft^2$
71) $183\ yd^2$
72) $36\ mm^2$
73) $72\ ft^2$
74) $42\ m^2$
75) $180\ in^2$
76) $44\ m^2$
77) $36\ in^2$
78) $32\ ft^2$
79) $161\ m^2$
80) $231\ yd^2$
81) $18\ in^2$
82) $270\ in^2$
83) $162\ yd^2$
84) $21\ m^2$
85) $48.5\ in^2$
86) $79\ ft^2$
87) $21.25\ m^2$
88) $105\ yd^2$
89) $48.5\ in^2$
90) $26.5\ mm^2$
91) $38.5\ yd^2$
92) $45\ cm$
93) $25\ in$
94) $5\ cm$
95) $11100\ in^3$

CHAPTER 7: Ratios and Proportions

Math topics that you'll learn in this chapter:

- ☑ Write a Ratio
- ☑ Ratio Tables
- ☑ Using a Fraction to Write down a Ratio
- ☑ Matching a Model with a Ratio
- ☑ Word Problems Involving Writing a Ratio
- ☑ Finding Equivalent Ratio
- ☑ Word Problems Involving Comparing Ratio
- ☑ Word Problems Involving Equivalent Ratio
- ☑ Similarity and Ratios
- ☑ Equivalent Rates
- ☑ Word Problems Involving Comparing Rates
- ☑ Word Problems Involving Rates and Ratios
- ☑ Make a Graph of Ratios and Rates

Write a Ratio

- Ratios compare 2 quantities. They show us the number of times greater one quantity is than a different amount. The numbers in ratios are known as terms.

- Special kinds of ratios are unit rates, rates, measurement conversions, along with percentages.

- For instance, "The ratio of eyes to beaks in the zoo's birdhouse was 2:1 since for every two wings there's one beak".

Examples:

Example 1. What is the ratio of circles to squares?

Solution: First, count the number of circles. Write it down, 3. Then count, the number of squares. Write it down, 8. So, write as a ratio:

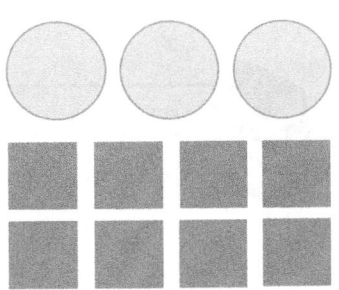

3:8

Example 2. What is the ratio of stars to triangles?

Solution: First, count the number of stars. Write it down, 9. Then count, the number of triangles. Write it down, 4. So, write as a ratio:

9:4

Ratio Tables

- Ratio tables are merely tables utilized to show a relationship in between 2 separate quantities.
- Ratio tables assist in visualizing relationships between the 2 separate quantities.
- In order to do a comparison of ratio tables, you must utilize either division or multiplication.

5	2
10	4
? = 15	6
20	? = 8
25	10

Examples:

Example 1. Complete the ratio table.

Solution: Start with the first row, $8:3$. Then write the ratio as a fraction, $\frac{8}{3}$. After it, multiply the numerator and the denominator by the same number to find an equivalent ratio. $\frac{8}{3} = \frac{8 \times 4}{3 \times 4} = \frac{32}{12}$, $\frac{8}{3} = \frac{8 \times 7}{3 \times 7} = \frac{56}{21}$.
Then write the answer in the table.

8	3
16	6
32	
48	18
	21

Example 2. Complete the ratio table.

Solution: Start with the first row, $2:9$. Then write the ratio as a fraction, $\frac{2}{9}$. After it, multiply the numerator and the denominator by the same number to find an equivalent ratio. $\frac{2}{9} = \frac{2 \times 5}{9 \times 5} = \frac{10}{45}$.

2	9
4	18
6	27
8	36
	45

Then write the answer in the table.

Using a Fraction to Write down a Ratio

- Ratios compare two amounts. They show the number of times greater one amount is than another amount.

- It's regarding part-to-part ratio, part-to-total ratio, the way to determine the various kinds of ratios, ratios, and fractions, simplify ratios, equivalent ratios, ratios, and percentages.

- For instance, $6:40 \rightarrow 3:20$ or $\frac{3}{20}$.

Examples:

Example 1. What is the ratio of circles to squares? Write the ratio as a fraction.

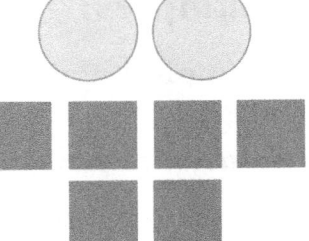

Solution: First, count the number of circles. Write it in the numerator, 2. Then count, the number of squares. Write it in the denominator, 6. So, write the ratio as a fraction:

$$\frac{2}{6}$$

Example 2. What is the ratio of stars to triangles? Write the ratio as a fraction.

Solution: First, count the number of stars. Write it in the numerator, 5. Then count, the number of triangles. Write it in the denominator, 4. So, write the ratio as a fraction:

$$\frac{5}{4}$$

Matching a Model with a Ratio

- There are several methods of representing a ratio.

- The most commonplace method of writing a ratio is doing so as a fraction, $\frac{2}{11}$.

- Write it utilizing the word "to," as in "2 to 11."

- Lastly, write down this ratio utilizing a colon in between the 2 numbers, 2:11.

- For instance, if there are 6 oranges as well as 16 lemons in the fruit bowl, then the ratio of oranges to lemons is 6 to 16 (so, 6:16, which is equivalent to a ratio of 3:8).

Examples:

Example 1. Which model (A or B) represents the ratio of 5 circles to 7 triangles?

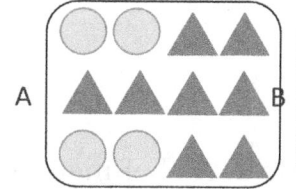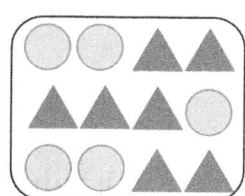

Solution: Count the number of circles and triangles in each model then compare with the given ratio. Model (A) has 4 circles and 8 triangles. It does not represent the ratio of 5 circles to 7 triangles. Model (B) has 5 circles and 7 triangles. It represents the ratio of 5 circles to 7 triangles.

Example 2. Which model (A or B) shows 3:5?

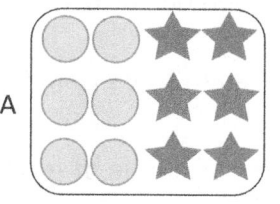

Solution: Count the number of each shape in each model then compare it with the given ratio. Model (A) has 6 circles and 6 stars. It does not represent the ratio of 3 to 5. Model (B) has 3 triangles and 5 stars. It represents the ratio of 3 to 5.

Word Problems Involving Writing a Ratio

- Ratios are a comparison of 2 numbers.

- A ratio can be written in several ways. You can write these using a colon (1: 5), utilizing the word "to" (1 to 5), or as a fraction: $\frac{1}{5}$.

Examples:

Example 1. Leo is reading the pasta with bacon and peas recipe. What is the ratio of pasta to bacon?

Pasta with bacon and peas recipe	
Pasta	8 oz.
Bacon	6 oz.
Onion	1
Frozen peas	1 cup
Parmesan	$\frac{1}{4}$ cup grated
Salt	$\frac{1}{4}$ tsp
Freshly cracked black pepper	$\frac{1}{4}$ tsp

Solution: First, write down pasta to bacon as a number relationship, 8 to 6. Then write as a ratio. 8: 6

Example 2. A chef made 18 bowls of soup that contained onion and 32 bowls of soup that contains garlic. What is the ratio of the number of soup bowls with onion to the number of soup bowls with garlic?

Solution: First, write numbers of bowls of onion soup and the numbers of bowls of garlic soup.

Numbers of bowls of onion soup = 18

Numbers of bowls of garlic soup = 32

Then, write the ratio, 18: 32.

Finding Equivalent Ratio

- Ratios are a comparison of 2 quantities.

- An equivalent ratio is a ratio that is identical whenever you do a comparison. You can compare 2 or more ratios with one another to find out if they are identical or not. For instance, $1:3$ and $2:6$ are equivalent weight ratios.

- Equivalent ratios have an identical value. To figure out if 2 ratios are equivalent weight, write them down as fractions. If these fractions are equal, then so are the ratios.

$$\frac{1}{3} = \frac{2}{6} \rightarrow \frac{1}{3} = \frac{1}{3}$$

Examples:

Example 1. Are the ratios $2:4$ and $3:6$ equivalent?

Solution: Convert a ratio as a fraction, $\frac{2}{4}$ and $\frac{3}{6}$. And you can compare the fractions using a common denominator. The denominators are 6 and 4. You can use 12 as the common denominator since 12 is a multiple of 4 and 6. $\frac{2}{4} = \frac{2 \times 3}{4 \times 3} = \frac{6}{12}$ and $\frac{3}{6} = \frac{3 \times 2}{6 \times 2} = \frac{6}{12}$. So, $\frac{2}{4}$ and $\frac{3}{6}$ are equal.

Therefore, ratios $2:4$ and $3:6$ are equivalent.

Example 2. Are the ratios $14:10$ and $2:1$ equivalent?

Solution: Convert a ratio as a fraction, $\frac{14}{10}$ and $\frac{2}{1}$. And you can compare the fractions using a common denominator. The denominators are 10 and 1. You can use 10 as the common denominator since 10 is a multiple of 1. $\frac{2}{1} = \frac{2 \times 10}{1 \times 10} = \frac{20}{10} \rightarrow \frac{20}{10} \neq \frac{14}{10}$. So, $\frac{14}{10}$ and $\frac{2}{1}$ are not equal.

Therefore, ratios $14:10$ and $2:1$ are not equivalent.

Word Problems Involving Comparing Ratio

Comparison of ratios can be done in two different and simple methods. Let us see both the methods below:

- *LCM* method of comparing ratios

  • First find the least common multiple (*LCM*) of the consequent and divide it by the consequents.

  • Multiply the quotient obtained with the ratios.

- Comparing ratios by cross multiplication method

  • Multiply the antecedent of the first ratio with the consequent of the second ratio and the consequent of the first ratio with the antecedent of the second ratio. For example - $8:9$ and $7:8$ according to this method we multiply the numbers. 8×8 and 9×7.

Examples:

Example 1. Megan and Jessika had smoothies for breakfast. Megan made her smoothie with 1 cup of melon and 5 cups of orange. Jessika made a giant smoothie with 2 cups of melon and 10 cups of orange. Did the smoothies have the same ratio of melon to orange?

Solution: The ratio of melon to oranges was for Megan, $\frac{1}{5}$. The ratio of melon to oranges was for Jessika, $\frac{2}{10}$. Simplify $\frac{2}{10}$ to $\frac{1}{5}$, the ratios are equal. $\frac{2}{10} = \frac{2 \div 2}{10 \div 2} = \frac{1}{5}$. So, the smoothies had the same ratio of melon to orange.

Example 2. Noah and Oliver each borrow some books from the library. Noah borrows 1 poetry book and 6 novels. Oliver borrows 3 poetry books and 8 novels. Did Noah and Oliver borrow the same ratio of poetry books to novels?

Solution: The ratio of poetry books to novels is for Noah, $\frac{1}{6}$. The ratio of poetry books to novels is for Oliver, $\frac{3}{8}$. Use cross multiplication: $\frac{1}{6} = \frac{3}{8} \rightarrow 1 \times 8 = 6 \times 3 \rightarrow 8 \neq 18$. So, Noah and Oliver did not borrow the same ratio of poetry books to novels.

Word Problems Involving Equivalent Ratio

- When a word problem expresses a ratio, follow these steps to find an equivalent ratio that solves the problem:
- Step 1: Identify the ratio given in the word problem.
- Step 2: One of the two values involved in the ratio will have a given value. Identify this value.
- Step 3: Divide the given value in step 2 by the corresponding value in the ratio from step 1.
- Step 4: Construct the equivalent ratio to the given ratio by multiplying both numbers in the original ratio by the number found in step 3.

Examples:

Example 1. Are these ratios equivalent? 8 full-time employees for every 18 part-time employees, 4 full-time employees for every 9 part-time employees.

Solution: For comparison: First, write the ratios as fractions: $\frac{8}{18}$ and $\frac{4}{9}$. And you can compare the fractions write a proportion. $\frac{8}{18} = \frac{4}{9}$. To understand that there is an equal relationship, use cross multiplication:

$$8 \times 9 = 18 \times 4 \rightarrow 72 = 72$$

So, the fractions are equivalent, so the ratios are equivalent.

Example 2. If a box contains red and blue balls in the ratio of 2 : 5 red to blue, how many red balls are there if 60 blue balls are in the box?

Solution: Write a proportion and solve. $\frac{2}{5} = \frac{x}{60}$

Use cross multiplication: $2 \times 60 = 5 \times x \Rightarrow 120 = 5x$

Divide to find x: $x = \frac{120}{5} \Rightarrow x = 24$

Similarity and Ratios

- Two figures are similar if they have the same shape.

- Two or more figures are similar if the corresponding angles are equal, and the corresponding sides are in proportion.

Examples:

Example 1. The following triangles are similar. What is the value of the unknown side?

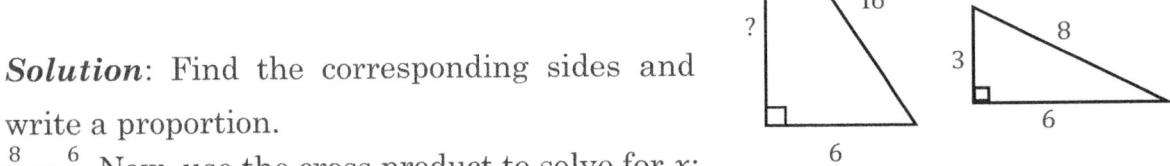

Solution: Find the corresponding sides and write a proportion.
$\frac{8}{16} = \frac{6}{x}$. Now, use the cross product to solve for x:
$\frac{8}{16} = \frac{6}{x} \to 8 \times x = 16 \times 6 \to 8x = 96$. Divide both sides by 8. Then: $8x = 96 \to x = \frac{96}{8} \to x = 12$

The missing side is 12.

Example 2. Two rectangles are similar. The first is 5 feet wide and 15 feet long. The second is 10 feet wide. What is the length of the second rectangle?

Solution: Let's put x for the length of the second rectangle. Since two rectangles are similar, their corresponding sides are in proportion. Write a proportion and solve for the missing number.
$\frac{5}{10} = \frac{15}{x} \to 5x = 10 \times 15 \to 5x = 150 \to x = \frac{150}{5} = 30$

The length of the second rectangle is 30 feet.

Equivalent rates

- Equivalent ratios will yield identical values.

- To see if 2 ratios are equivalent, write these down as fractions. If these fractions are equal, then so are the ratios.

- Equivalent ratios are ratios that are equal when compared. You can compare two or more ratios with each one another in order to check if they're equivalent or not.

- For instance, $1:5$ and $3:15$ both are equivalent ratios.

Examples:

Example 1. Complete the proportion and type in the blank box.

$$7 \text{ oranges on } 1 \text{ bowl} = \boxed{} \text{ 21 oranges on bowls}$$

Solution: Write the ratios as fractions $\frac{7}{1}$. Then write an equivalent fraction with 21 as the numerator. $\frac{7}{1} = \frac{7 \times 3}{1 \times 3} = \frac{21}{3}$.

So, 21 oranges on 3 bowls.

Example 2. Solve this proportion for x. $\frac{2}{4} = \frac{3}{x}$

Solution: Use cross multiplication: $\frac{2}{4} = \frac{3}{x} \Rightarrow 2 \times x = 3 \times 4 \Rightarrow 2x = 12$

Divide to find x: $x = \frac{12}{2} \rightarrow x = 6$

Word Problems Involving Comparing Rates

- Rates are a special type of ratio. They measure the amount one quantity or thing varies concerning the other.

- Rate word problems involve problems that deal with rates, time, distances, and water or wind current.

- Additional kinds of word problems utilizing systems of equations involve money word problems as well as age word problems.

Examples:

Example 1. At their school's book fair, Liam and Anne are both selling books. So far, Liam has sold 18 book volumes and has earned $31.50. Anne has sold 20 book volumes and has earned $34.00. Who is offering the better bargain?

Solution: Compare their unit prices. See which one charges less per book volume. Liam has sold 18 book volumes for a total of $31.50. Find the unit price, $\frac{31.50 \div 18}{18 \div 18} = \frac{1.75}{1}$.

Anne has sold 20 book volumes for a total of $34.00. Find the unit price, $\frac{34.00 \div 20}{20 \div 20} = \frac{1.70}{1}$.

$1.70 per book volume is less than $1.75 per book volume. So, Anne is offering a better bargain.

Example 2. Lucas's dog returns 13 ball throws per hour. William's dog returns 33 ball throws in 3 hours. Do the two dogs returns the ball at the same rate?

Solution: Compare the return times per unit of time. Lucas's dog returns 13 ball throws per hour. Find the return times per unit of time (hour), $\frac{13 \div 1}{1 \div 1} = \frac{13}{1}$. William's dog returns 33 ball throws in 3 hours. Find the return times per unit of time (hour), $\frac{33 \div 3}{3 \div 3} = \frac{11}{1}$.

11 returns per unit time is less than 13 returns per unit time. So, Lucas's dog is faster than William's dog at returning the ball.

Word Problems Involving Rates and Ratios

- Ratios are a comparison of 2 numbers.

- Rates are a special type of ratio. They measure the amount one quantity or thing varies concerning the other.

- Rate word problems involve problems which deal with rates, time, distances, and water or wind current.

- Additional kinds of word problems utilizing systems of equations involve money word problems as well as age word problems.

- To solve these types of word problems, follow these steps:

    - Identify the known ratio and the unknown ratio.

    - Set up the proportion.

    - Cross-multiply and solve.

    - Check the answer by plugging the result into the unknown ratio.

Example:

On weekday mornings, it takes William 60 minutes to hike 1.5 miles to his school. This Saturday, William will hike to the park to meet his friends. The park is 4 miles away from William's house. If he hikes at the same rate, how many minutes will it take William to get to the park?

Solution: It takes William 60 minutes to hike 1.5 miles. Write as a rate, $\frac{60\ minutes}{1.5\ miles}$. Divide the numerator and denominator by 1.5 to find the unit rate, $\frac{60\ minutes \div 1.5}{1.5\ miles \div 1.5} = \frac{40\ minutes}{1\ mile}$.

Now you need to find how many minutes it will take him to hike 4 miles at the same rate. Write a proportion:

$$\frac{40\ minutes}{1\ mile} = \frac{x\ minutes}{4\ miles} \rightarrow 40 \times 4 = 1 \times x \rightarrow x = 160\ minutes$$

It will take William 160 minutes to hike to the park.

Make a Graph of Ratios and Rates

- A ratio table gives a bunch of equivalent ratios.

- Find and organize equivalent ratios in a ratio table and generate a ratio table by using repeated addition or multiplication.

x	3	6	9	12
y	1	2	3	4

For a ratio of two quantities, use equivalent ratios to create ordered pairs of the form (first quantity, second quantity) and plot these ordered pairs in a coordinate plane and draw a line, starting at (0,0), through the points.

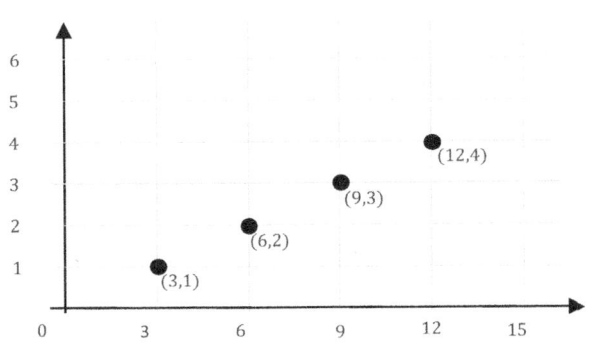

Example:

An airplane leaves Chicago and flies at a constant speed. The airplane flies 155 miles in 15 minutes. Complete the table. And make a graph.

minutes	15	30	45	60
miles flies	155			

Solution: The airplane flies 155 miles in 15 minutes. Write this as a rate. And use it to complete the table to find distances, $\frac{155 \ miles}{15 \ minutes}$.

$$\frac{155 \ mi \times 2}{15 \ min \times 2} = \frac{310 \ mi}{30 \ min}, \frac{155 \ mi \times 3}{15 \ min \times 3} = \frac{465 \ mi}{45 \ min} \text{ and } \frac{155 \ mi \times 4}{15 \ min \times 4} = \frac{620 \ mi}{60 \ min}$$

minutes	15	30	45	60
miles flies	155	310	465	620

Now, to graph data, write the pairs of numbers in the table as (x, y) ordered pairs. $x =$ minutes and $y =$ miles.

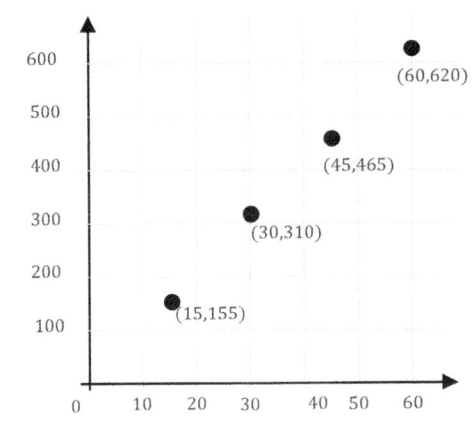

Chapter 7: Practices

✎ **What is the ratio of the given in each group to each other?**

1)

2) ⭐⭐⭐ ▪▪▪▪▪▪▪

3) ⭐⭐⭐ ●●

4) ▢▢▢▢▢ ●●

5) ▢▢▢▢ ★★★★★★★

6) ▢▢ ★★★

7) △△△△△△ ▪▪▪▪ △△

8) ▢▢▢▢ ▲▲▲▲▲

✎ **Complete the ratio table.**

9)

10	9
20	18
30	
40	36
50	45

10)

3	5
6	10
	15
12	20
15	25

11)

1	11
	22
3	33
4	44
5	55

12)

	7
24	14
36	21
48	28
60	35

13)

1	3
5	15
10	30
15	
20	60

14)

7	8
	24
42	48
63	72
84	96

15)

2	5
8	20
16	40
24	60
32	

16)

4	
12	39
26	78
36	117
48	156

✎ **According to the shapes, write down a ratio using a fraction.**

17)

18)

19)

20)

21)

22)

23)

24)

✎ Which model shows which ratio?

25) $\frac{2}{1}$

26) 6 : 3

27) $\frac{3}{4}$

28) 9 : 1

29) 1 to 3

30) 3 : 3

31) $\frac{2}{8}$

32) 5 to 7

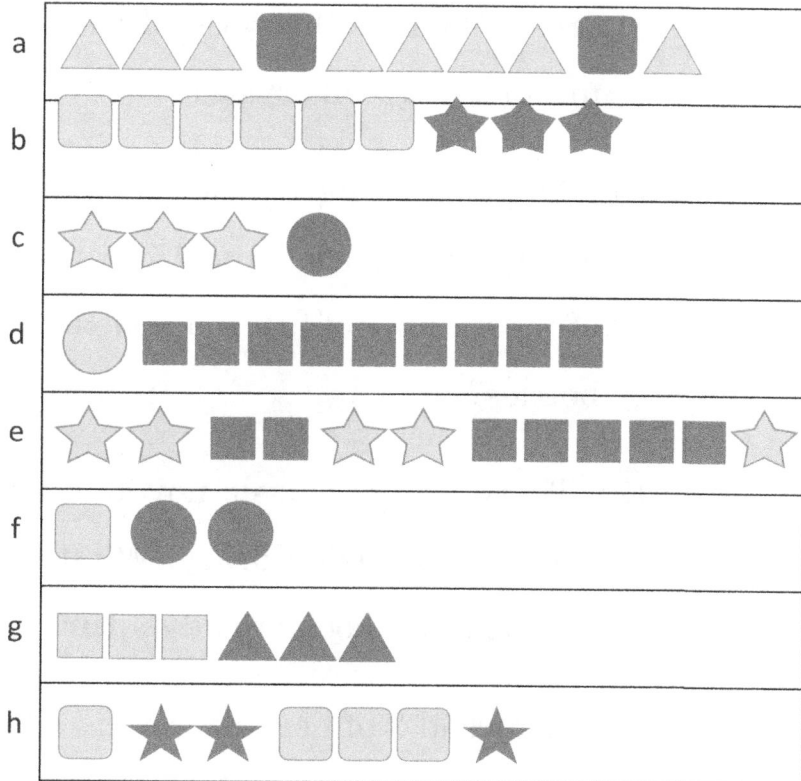

✏️ **The table shows the number of sold museum tickets per age category on a recent weekend. Write the ratios in question.**

33) The ratio of 5 − 15 to 36 − 45?

34) The ratio of 26 − 35 to 56 and up?

35) The ratio of 16 − 25 to 36 − 45?

36) The ratio of 46 − 55 to 16 − 25?

Age category	Number of sold ticket
5 − 15	88
16 − 25	28
26 − 35	19
36 − 45	16
46 − 55	5
56 and up	1

✏️ **Write the ratio.**

37) There are 45 green crystals and 15 red crystals on maria's dress. What is the ratio of the number of red crystals to the number of green crystals?

38) After spending a whole day in a restaurant, there are 90 empty soda bottles and 15 full soda bottles. What is the ratio of the number of full soda bottles to the number of empty soda bottles?

39) There are 12 classic novels books and 18 adventure novels books in Maria's library. What is the ratio of the number of classic novel books to adventure novel books?

40) Ava read 3 of her letters and has 8 of them left. What is the ratio of the number of reading letters to the unread letters?

Chapter 7: Ratios and Proportions

✎ Are the ratios equivalent?

41) $2:10$ and $4:20$

42) $1:2$ and $15:25$

43) $4:9$ and $40:81$

44) $6:11$ and $42:77$

45) $1:6$ and $8:48$

46) $5:6$ and $35:42$

47) $3:7$ and $27:72$

48) $2:5$ and $16:45$

✎ Solve

49) Ava's recipe for apple pie calls for 2 cups of chopped apple and 3 cups of flour. Mia's recipe calls for 3 cups of chopped apple and 5 cups of flour. Whose recipe makes stronger apple flavor?

50) There are two alloys A and B, both made up of carbon and iron. The ratio between carbon and iron in alloy (A) is $2\frac{1}{3}:4$. And the ratio between carbon and iron in the alloy (B) is $1\frac{1}{3}:1$. In which alloy do we have more carbon?

51) The price of 3 apples at the Quick market is $1.44. The price of 5 of the same apples at Walmart is $2.50. Which place is the better buy?

52) Rebecca works in a rehabilitation center. In the first month, she helped to rehabilitate 15 patients and 3 patients were discharged. In the second month, she helped to rehabilitate 22 patients and 9 patients were discharged. In which month has she been more successful in discharging patients?

✍ **Solve.**

53) Express ratios as a proportion. 180 miles on 9 gallons of gas, how many miles on 1 gallon of gas?

54) Bob has 12 red cards and 20 green cards. What is the ratio of Bob's red cards to his green cards?

55) At a party, 10 soft drinks are required for every 12 guests. If there are 252 guests, how many soft drinks are required?

56) In Jack's class, 18 of the students are tall and 10 are short. In Michael's class, 54 students are tall and 30 students are short. Are these ratios equivalent?

57) The bakers at a bakery can make 160 bagels in 4 hours. How many bagels can they bake in 16 hours?

58) You can buy 5 cans of green beans at a supermarket for $3.40. How much does it cost to buy 35 cans of green beans?

59) The ratio of boys to girls in a class is 2: 3. If there are 18 boys in the class, how many girls are in that class?

60) A free study club has 54 members, of which 24 are males and the rest are females. What is the ratio of females to males?

✍ **Solve each problem.**

61) Two rectangles are similar. The first is 8 *feet* wide and 32 *feet* long. The second is 12 *feet* wide. What is the length of the second rectangle? _____

62) Two rectangles are similar. One is 4.6 *meters* by 7 *meters*. The longer side of the second rectangle is 28 *meters*. What is the other side of the second rectangle? _____

Chapter 7: Ratios and Proportions

✎ Make the ratios equivalent.

63) $\frac{2}{4} = \frac{8}{x}$, $x = $ _____

64) $\frac{1}{2} = \frac{6}{x}$, $x = $ _____

65) $\frac{2}{3} = \frac{12}{x}$, $x = $ _____

66) $\frac{1}{4} = \frac{x}{20}$, $x = $ _____

67) $\frac{3}{4} = \frac{x}{8}$, $x = $ _____

68) $\frac{3}{4} = \frac{54}{x}$, $x = $ _____

69) $\frac{5}{8} = \frac{10}{x}$, $x = $ _____

70) $\frac{6}{9} = \frac{24}{x}$, $x = $ _____

✎ Solve

71) James is buying some cereal from the store. He finds a box of 8 frosted flakes for $5.00. And a box of 12 honey bunches of oats for $8.00. Which brand is the better value?

72) Which is the best value?

   10 pens that cost $8 or 5 pens that cost $2.50

73) Benjamin wants to learn to play the piano. His parents recommended two different music schools. Music school (A) charges $725 for 10 hours of lessons. Music school (B) offers 13 hours of lessons for $910. Which school offers the better deal?

74) Which is the best value?

   2 gallons of oil at $5.80 or 1.5 gallons of oil at $3.00

✎ Write a proportion. Then solve.

75) If books sell at 3 for $.75, how many books can be bought for $4.25?

76) If 12 sandwiches cost $60, what will 6 sandwiches cost?

77) If the rent of a room for 3 weeks is $550, how much rent is paid for 12 weeks?

78) If 5 scissors cost $160, how much would a dozen scissors cost?

79) How far will a car travel in 8 hours if it travels 45 miles in 1 hour?

80) A bus takes 1 hour to go 65 miles. How long will it take the bus to go 650 miles?

81) A plane like a Boeing 747 uses approximately 1 gallon of fuel every second. Over the course of a 1 and half hours (per hour is 3600 seconds) flight, how many gallons it might burn?

82) Leo drew a square with a perimeter of 50 inches. Since the ratio of the side length of a square to the square's perimeter is always 1 to 4. What is the side length of the square Leo drawing?

✎ Complete the table. And make a graph.

83) To make the dipping sauce, Daniel uses 7 cups of sour cream for every 3 cups of yogurt.

Cups of sour cream	7	14	21	28
Cups of yogurt	3	___	___	___

84) Kyle runs to exercise. He always runs 2 miles lengths at a slow pace for every 0.5 mile length at a fast pace.

Slow lengths	2	4	6	8
Fast lengths	0.5	___	___	___

85) Eli makes beaded earrings to sell at craft fairs. She uses 12 yellow beads for every 5 purple beads.

Yellow beads	12	24	36	48
Purple beads	5	___	___	___

86) James is planting in her field. He is planting 1 rows of strawberry plants for every 2 rows of raspberry plants.

Rows of strawberry plants	1	2	3	4
Rows of raspberry plants	2	___	___	___

Chapter 7: Answers

1) 2 : 5
2) 3 : 8
3) 3 : 2
4) 5 : 2
5) 5 : 6
6) 2 : 3
7) 8 : 4
8) 5 : 5
9) 27
10) 9
11) 2
12) 12
13) 45
14) 21
15) 80
16) 13
17) $\frac{9}{3}$
18) $\frac{7}{3}$
19) $\frac{3}{5}$
20) $\frac{2}{2}$
21) $\frac{1}{4}$
22) $\frac{5}{7}$
23) $\frac{2}{9}$
24) $\frac{4}{6}$
25) f
26) b
27) h
28) d
29) c
30) g
31) a
32) e
33) 88 : 16
34) 19 : 1
35) 28 : 16
36) 5 : 28
37) 15 : 45
38) 15 : 90
39) 12 : 18
40) 3 : 8
41) Yes
42) No
43) No
44) Yes
45) Yes
46) Yes
47) Yes
48) No
49) Ava's recipe
50) alloy (B)
51) Quick Market
52) 2nd month
53) 20
54) 3 : 5
55) 210
56) Yes
57) 640

Chapter 7: Ratios and Proportions

58) $23.80
59) 27
60) 5 : 4
61) 48 *meters*
62) 18.4 *meters*
63) 16
64) 12
65) 18
66) 5
67) 6

68) 72
69) 16
70) 36
71) Frosted flakes.
72) 10 pens are less value.
73) Music school (B)
74) 1.5 gallons are less value.
75) 17

76) 30
77) 2200
78) 384
79) 360
80) 10
81) 1.5
82) $\frac{25}{2}$

83) 6, 9, 12

84) 1, 1.5, 2

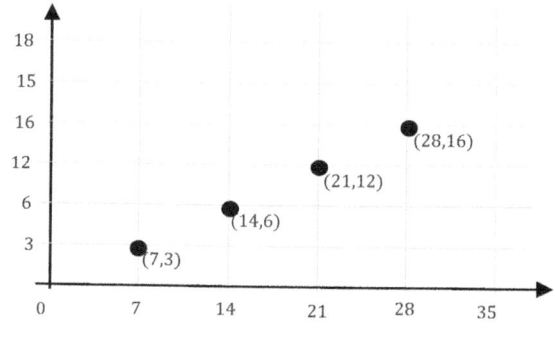

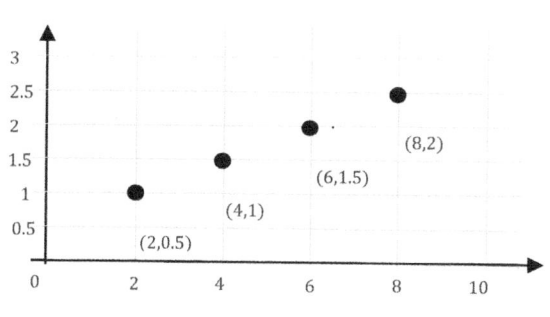

85) 10, 15, 20

86) 4, 6, 8

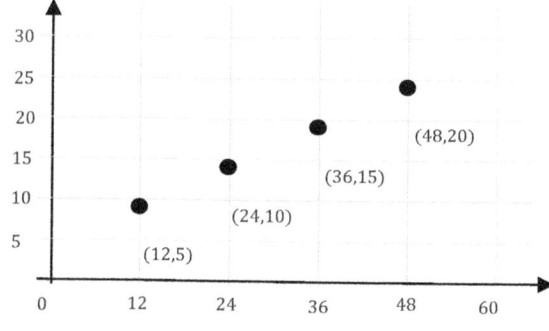

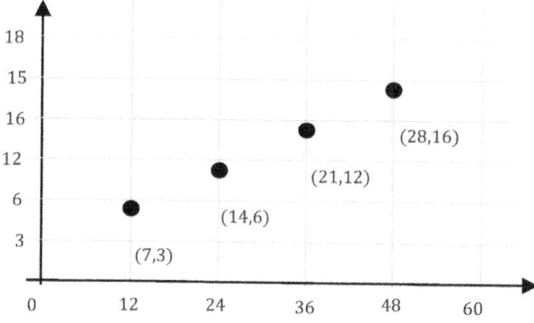

CHAPTER 8: Percentage

Math topics that you'll learn in this chapter:

- ☑ Representing Percentage
- ☑ Using Number Line to Graph Percentages
- ☑ Using Grid models to Represent Percent
- ☑ Using Strip Models to Explain Percent
- ☑ Using Grid Models to Solve Percentage Problems
- ☑ Using Strip Models to Solve Percentage Problems
- ☑ Word Problems of Determining Percentage of a Number
- ☑ Solving Percentage Word Problems
- ☑ Fractional and Decimal Percentages
- ☑ Using Grid Models to Convert Fractions to Percentages
- ☑ Word Problems: Comparing Percent and Fractions
- ☑ Word Problems: Conversion of Between Percent, Fractions, and Decimals
- ☑ Percent Problems

Representing Percentage

- In math, a percentage is a number or the ratio which may be expressed via a fraction of 100.

- If you have to compute the percent of a number, you divide it by the whole and then multiply this by 100.

- Therefore, the percentage means a part per each hundred. The hundred percent implies per 100.

- Hence, 1% represents $\frac{1}{100}$ or one-hundredths, and 9 percent signifies $\frac{9}{100}$ or nine-hundredths.

- Because percentages are merely the hundredth parts (which signifies they're FRACTIONS), you can simply write them down as fractions and decimals.

Examples:

Example 1. What percentage of the shape is shaded?

Solution: This shape is 100 parts, and 44 of the parts are shaded. Then write 44 out of 100 as a percentage:

44%

Example 2. What percentage of the shape is not shaded?

Solution: This shape is 100 parts, and 70 of the parts are shaded. And 30 of the part is empty. Then write 30 out of 100 as a percentage that is not shaded:

30%

Using Number Line to Graph Percentages

- To make 0.50; move 2 spaces to the right-hand side of 0. To make 0.75; move seven spaces to the right-hand side of 0. To make −0.25; move six spaces to the left-hand side of the 0.

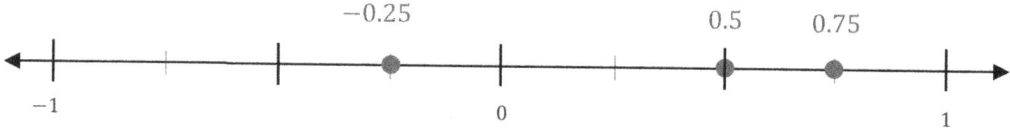

Each grid in graph is: 0.25

- To figure out a percentage, you must divide its value by the whole value and next you will multiply the result by 100.

$$Percentage\ formula = \left(\frac{Value}{Total\ value}\right) \times 100.$$

Examples:

Example 1. Graph $\frac{7}{8}$ on the number line. And write the percentage.

Solution: Divide the 100 by the denominator of the fraction to find out how much each part represents, $100\% \div 8 = 12.5\%$.

Label the number line, now finds 7 parts on the number line. And if using a formula, $\frac{7}{8} = \frac{7}{8} \times 100 = \frac{7}{8} \times \frac{100}{1} = 87.5\%$

Example 2. Graph 40% on the number line.

Solution: Write the 40% as a fraction, $\frac{2}{5}$. Then divide the 100 by the denominator of fraction to find out how much each part represents, $100\% \div 5 = 20\%$.

Label the number line, now finds 2 parts or 40% on the number line.

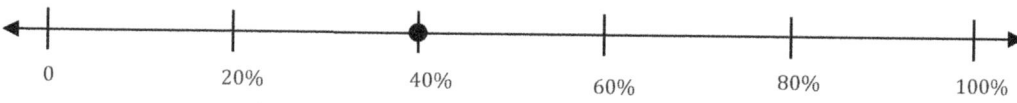

Using Grid models to Represent Percent

- The percentage is the rate per 100. You may utilize 10 × 10 grids to develop a percent.

- Write down 0.7 as 0.70, and that would be 70 hundredths. 70 hundredths are 70 percent. It is also possible to alter the decimal point 2 spaces to the right-hand side to obtain the percent equivalent.

- In order to transform a decimal into a percentage, multiply by 100 (merely move the decimal point two spaces to the right). For instance, $0.045 = 4.5\%$ and $2.85 = 285\%$.

- To obtain a percentage of a number, such as 20 percent of 70, merely multiply. For instance, $\left(\frac{20}{100}\right)(70) = 0.2 \times 70 = 14$.

- With any computation, the percent value must be changed in a number in fractional format via removing the percentage symbol and dividing it by 100.

Example:

Show 65% on the grade and write as a fraction and decimal.

Solution: To display 65% in the grid shape, shade 65 of the 100 squares.

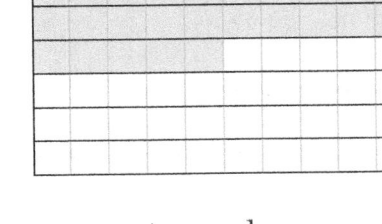

To write as a decimal and fraction. The grid shows that 65% is equivalent to $\frac{65}{100}$.

To write as a decimal:

$$65 \div 100 = 0.65$$

To write as a fraction in the simplest form: divide the numerator and denominator by 5:

$$\frac{65}{100} = \frac{65 \div 5}{100 \div 5} = \frac{13}{20}$$

Chapter 8: Percentage

Using Strip Models to Explain Percent

- It's a rectangular model utilized to display numerical relationships. It can be utilized to signify fractions or solve equations concerning operations.

Total number of cookies	
96 cookies	84 cookies
Total number of cookies in each	

Examples:

Example 1. Show the 75% using a strip model.

Solution: First, write 75% as a fraction. 75% means 75 parts out of 100, the same as $\frac{75}{100}$. Simplify fraction $\frac{3}{4}$. And now according to fraction, draw the strip model: shade 3 parts out of 4 total parts.

Example 2. Which model shows 25%?

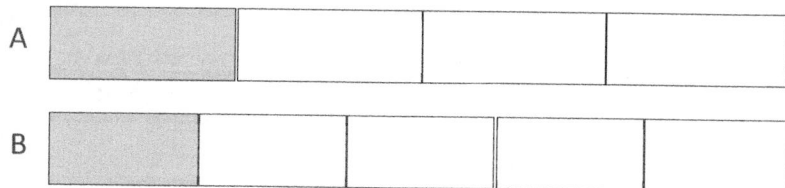

Solution: First, write 25% as a fraction. 25% means 25 parts out of 100, the same as $\frac{25}{100}$. Simplify fraction $\frac{1}{4}$. And now according to fraction, the strip model (A) shows 1 part out of 4 total parts.

Using Grid Models to Solve Percentage Problems

- A percentage compares a number to 100.

- So, the percentage of a number is a ratio in between that number and 100.

- For instance, 23 percent is the same as:

    $\frac{23}{100}$ (or) 23 to 100 (or) 23 : 100

    We will show you the way to utilize grids for modeling percentages.

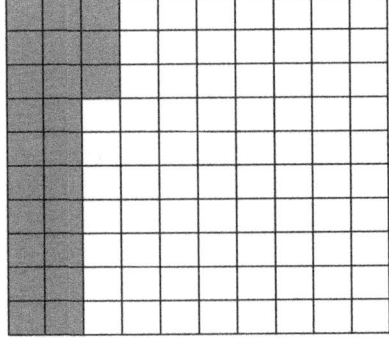

Example:

Anne was experimenting on mice in the laboratory. During experiments, 30% of the mice died, actually, the number of mice that died is 6. Shade the grid to show the mice that died. How many mice were there in total?

Solution: The grid has 100 squares. Since 30% of the mice died, shade 30 of the 100 squares in the grid.

The 30 shaded squares represent the 6 dead mice. But the whole grid represents the total number of pens. So, find the number of dead mice that each row of squares represents. Since 3 shaded rows represent 6 dead mice, you can divide, $6 \div 3 = 2$.

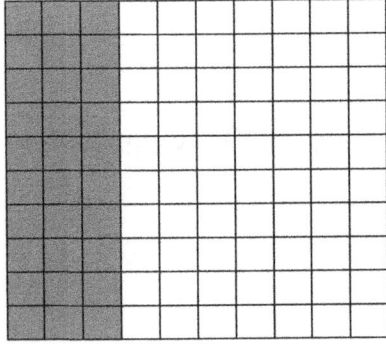

Each row represents 2 mice. Now, multiply 10 rows in 2 mice.

$$10 \times 2 = 20$$

So, there were 20 mice in her experiment.

Using Strip Models to Solve Percentage Problems

- For solving a problem, you must use a formula.

$$Part \div whole = percentage$$

- We will show you the way to utilize Strip Models to Solve Percentage Problems.

Examples:

Example 1. The motel has 125 rooms. If 25 of them are empty, what percentage of them are empty? Use strip model to show.

Solution: Total rooms are 125 and empty rooms are 25. Since 25 is $\frac{1}{5}$ of 125,

0%	20%	40%	60%	80%	100%
25	50	75	100	125	

divide strips model into 5 parts. Then divide 100% by 5 to find the percent of each part of 125. So, 25 empty rooms are equal to 20%.

Example 2. 70% of the 30 dishes on the shelves have a blue flower print. How many of the dishes on the shelves have a blue flower print? Use strip model to show.

Solution: The total percentage of dishes is 30 and blue flower print dishes are 70%. Since 70% is $\frac{7}{10}$ of 100%, divide the strip model into 10 parts. Then divide 30 by 10 to find a number of each part of the percentage, $30 \div 10 = 3$. To find 70% of the blue flower print dishes, multiply the 7 parts of the strip model by 3 in each part, $7 \times 3 = 21$. So, there are 21 blue flower print dishes.

0%	10%	20%	30%	40%	50%	60%	70%	80%	90%	100%
	3	6	9	12	15	18	21	24	27	30

Word Problems of Determining Percentage of a Number

- Percentages have no dimension. Hence it is called a dimensionless number. If we say, 50% of a number, then it means 50 percent of its whole.

- Problems involving percent have any three quantities to work with: the percent, the amount, and the base.

    - The percent has the percent symbol (%) or the word "percent."
    - The base is the whole amount.
    - The amount is the number that relates to the percent. It is always part of the whole.

Examples:

Example 1. At the store, Anne bought a package of needles. She got 25 needles in all. 25 of the needles were large. What percentage of the needles were large?

Solution: 100% of 25 is 25, to check this by doing the math. 25 is a part of the whole number 25. Let x represent the percent of the part. So, write a proportion for x, $\frac{25}{25} = \frac{x}{100} \rightarrow 25 \times 100 = 25x \rightarrow 2500 = 25x \rightarrow 2500 \div 100 = x \rightarrow 25 = x$.

100% of the needles were large.

Example 2. A veterinarian examined chickens in aviculture to see if they were infected with a virus. 66 out of 88 chickens were infected with the virus. What percentage of chickens were infected?

Solution: 66 is a part of the number 88. To find a percent of 66 of 88, first, let x represents the percent. So, write a proportion for x, $\frac{66}{88} = \frac{x}{100} \rightarrow 66 \times 100 = 88x \rightarrow 6600 = 88x \rightarrow 6600 \div 88 = x \rightarrow 75 = x$.

75% of chickens were infected with the virus.

Solving Percentage Word Problems

- Percent problems can be solved by writing equations. An equation uses an equal sign (=) to show that two mathematical expressions have the same value.

- Percents are fractions, and just like fractions, when finding a percent (or fraction, or portion) of another amount, you multiply.

- The percent of the base is the amount.

The Percentage of the Base is the Amount.

$$Percent \times Base = Amount$$

Examples:

Example 1. A home appliance store has 45 employees. 20% of the employees work part-time. How many part-time employees does the home appliance store have?

Solution: To find 20% of 45. First, determine x instead of the unknown part. And write a proportion for x, $\frac{45}{x} = \frac{100}{20} \to 45 \times 20 = 100x \to 900 = 100x \to 900 \div 100 = x \to 9 = x$.

The home appliance store has 9 part-time employees.

Example 2. Leo bought 25 fresh fruits, and after a week, 16% of the fruits spoiled. How many fruits are spoiled?

Solution: To find 16% of 25. First, determine x instead of the unknown part. And write a proportion for x, $\frac{25}{x} = \frac{100}{16} \to 25 \times 16 = 100x \to 400 = 100x \to 400 \div 100 = x \to 4 = x$.

4 fruits were spoiled after a week.

EffortlessMath.com

Fractional and Decimal Percentages

- A percentage in mathematics is a number or ratio which can be represented as a fraction of 100. The symbol (%) is used to denote the percentage.

- Similarly, the percentage is sometimes denoted by the abbreviation 'pct.' For example, we can express 50 percent as 50% or 50 pct.

- Percentages are written inform whole numbers, fractions, or decimals. For example, 5%, 20%, 0.8%, 0.35%, $\frac{5}{6}$% etc. are all percentages.

- Example:

percentage	fraction	decimal
60 percent	$\frac{60 \div 10}{100 \div 10} = \frac{60}{10}$	0.6

- To get from a percentage right to a decimal merely move the decimal two spaces to the left-hand side.

Examples:

Example 1. Complete: 72.5% of 40 ☐

Solution: The whole is 40. And 72.5% is a part of 40. Let x represent the part. Then write a proportion for x and solve it, $\frac{x}{40} = \frac{72.5}{100} \rightarrow 100x = 72.5 \times 40 \rightarrow 100x = 2900 \rightarrow x = 2900 \div 100 \rightarrow x = 29$.

So, 72.5% of 40 is 29.

Example 2. Complete: $32\frac{1}{2}$% of 120 ☐

Solution: The whole is 120. And $32\frac{1}{2}$% is a part of 120, which is 32.5%. Let x represent the part. Then write a proportion for x and solve it, $\frac{x}{120} = \frac{32.5}{100} \rightarrow 100x = 32.5 \times 120 \rightarrow 100x = 3900 \rightarrow x = 3900 \div 100 \rightarrow x = 39$.

So, 32.5% of 120 is 39.

Using Grid Models to Convert Fractions to Percentages

- Utilizing models, like 10 × 10 grids, will assist you in understanding the way percentages, fractions, and decimals, fractions are related.

- If the total is lower than 1 whole, you have to have one 10 × 10 grid.

- If the total is larger than 1 whole, you have to have more than a single grid.

- 2 steps to change a fraction into a percentage:

  - According to the fraction, shade a fraction of the 100 squares in the grid. Multiply to find how many squares to shade: $\frac{3}{5}$

  - There is a number of shaded squares out of a total of 100 squares. So, percent of the grid is shaded: 60%

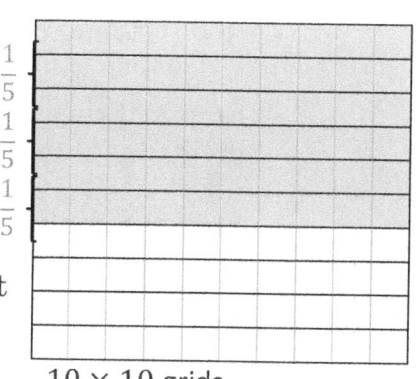

10 × 10 grids

Example:

Shade $\frac{3}{10}$ of the grid model. And write the percentage.

Solution: To display $\frac{3}{10}$ in the 100 squares of the grid model, multiply to find how many squares to shade:

$\frac{3}{10} \times 100 = \frac{3}{10} \times \frac{100}{1} = \frac{300}{10} = 30$

Shade 30 of the 100 squares.

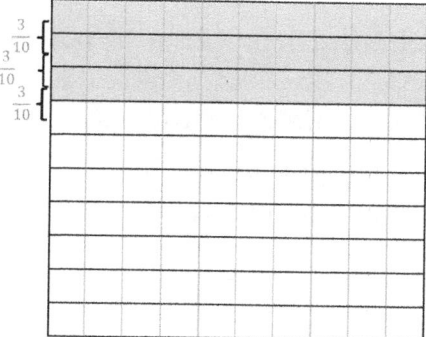

Count the shaded squares. And there are 30 shaded squares out of a total of 100 squares. So, write 30%.

Word Problems: Comparing Percent and Fractions

- The percentage of the whole number is calculated by dividing the value by the total value and then multiplying by 100. The percentage is nothing but "per 100".

$$Percentage = (\frac{Value}{Total\ Value}) \times 100$$

- Follow the below-provided steps to convert between a percentage and a fraction:

    • Step 1: Write the given percent divided by 100. That means $\frac{percent}{100}$.

    • Step 2: If the given number is not a whole number, then multiply and divide by 10 for every number after the decimal point.

    • Step 3: Simplify the fraction.

Examples:

Example 1. John and Leo are trying to finish their homework before their favorite TV show starts. John finishes $\frac{5}{8}$ of his homework. Leo finishes 45% of his homework. Who finishes a greater percentage of his homework in time?

Solution: Firstly, write a fraction as a decimal. And then convert to a percentage, $\frac{5}{8} = 0.625 = 62.5\%$. Now compare the percentages, $62.5\% > 45\%$.
John finishes a greater percentage of his homework in time.

Example 2. In the hotel, the manager wants to hire a crew that includes an equal number of women and men. After a week, 75% of the required number of women crew members have been hired, and $\frac{3}{5}$ of the required number of men. Which member of the crew has the largest now?

Solution: Firstly, write a fraction as a decimal. And then convert to a percentage, $\frac{3}{5} = 0.60 = 60\%$. Now compare the percentages, $60\% < 75\%$. Members of the women's crew are the largest now.

Word Problems: conversion of Percent, Fractions, and Decimals

- A decimal is a different way to represent a fraction. Some decimals have whole number parts and fractional parts, while others have only fractional parts. Examples of decimals include 2.5, 0.83, and 0.042.

- Here is how to change a decimal to a percent:

  - Percent means per hundred, so multiply the decimal by 100.
  - Add a % sign.

- For example, convert $\frac{1}{5}$ to decimal and percent:

  - Set $\frac{1}{5}$ as a decimal, which is 0.2.
  - Set $\frac{1}{5}$ as a percentage, which is 20%.

Examples:

Example 1. Leo is helping his dad clean out the basement. He finds a bolt that is $\frac{2}{5}$ of a foot in diameter.

Write $\frac{2}{5}$ of a foot as a decimal. And write $\frac{2}{5}$ of a foot as a percent.

Solution: To write as a decimal, divide 2 by 5, $2 \div 5 = 0.4$. To write as a percent, multiply $\frac{2}{5}$ in 100, $\frac{2}{5} \times 100 = \frac{2}{5} \times \frac{100}{1} = \frac{200}{5} = 40$.

$\frac{2}{5}$ is equal to 0.4 and 40%.

Example 2. Bob is painting his kitchen. He uses 25% of a gallon.

Write 25% of a gallon as a fraction. And write 25% of a gallon as a decimal.

Solution: 25% is 25 parts out of 100. So, it will be as a fraction, $25\% = \frac{25}{100}$. And simplify $\frac{25}{100} = \frac{25 \div 25}{100 \div 25} = \frac{1}{4}$.

To write 25% as a decimal, divide 25 by 100. $25 \div 100 = 0.25$.

Percent Problems

- Percent is a ratio of a number and 100. It always has the same denominator, 100. The percent symbol is "%".
- Percent means "per 100". So, 20% is $\frac{20}{100}$.
- In each percent problem, we are looking for the base, or the part or the percent.
- Use these equations to find each missing section in a percent problem:
  - ❖ Base = Part ÷ Percent
  - ❖ Part = Percent × Base
  - ❖ Percent = Part ÷ Base

Examples:

Example 1. What is 20% of 40?

Solution: In this problem, we have the percent (20%) and the base (40) and we are looking for the "part". Use this formula: $Part = Percent \times Base$.
Then: $Part = 20\% \times 40 = \frac{20}{100} \times 40 = 0.20 \times 40 = 8$. The answer: 20% of 40 is 8.

Example 2. 25 is what percent of 500?

Solution: In this problem, we are looking for the percent. Use this equation: $Percent = Part \div Base \rightarrow Percent = 25 \div 500 = 0.05 = 5\%$.
Then: 25 is 5 percent of 500.

Example 3. 80 is 20 percent of what number?

Solution: In this problem, we are looking for the base. Use this equation:
$Base = Part \div Percent \rightarrow Base = 80 \div 20\% = 80 \div 0.20 = 400$
Then: 80 is 20 percent of 400.

Chapter 8: Practices

✎ What percentage of the shape is shaded?

1)

2)

3)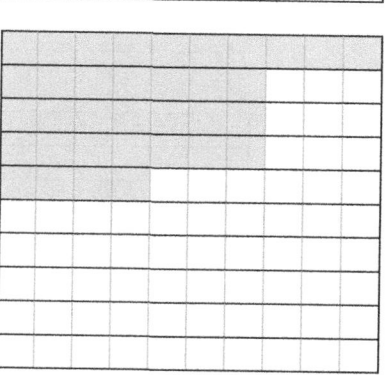

4)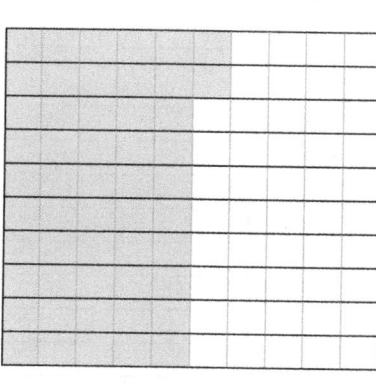

5)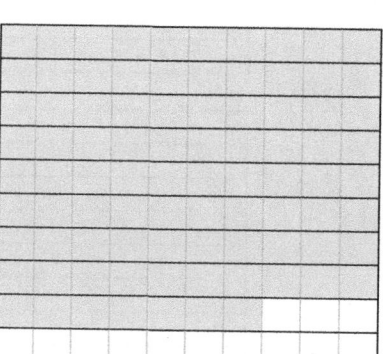

6)

✎ Graph the percentage on the number line.

7) 90%

8) $\frac{2}{8}$%

9) $66\frac{2}{3}$%

10) $\frac{1}{10}$%

11) $28\frac{4}{7}$%

12) $\frac{3}{4}$%

13) $\frac{1}{5}$%

14) 50%

🖊 **What percentage of the shape is shaded? Write as a decimal and fraction, too.**

15)

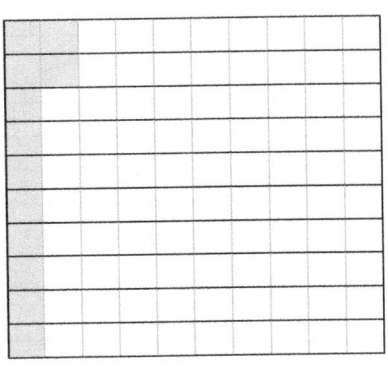

16)

17)

18)

19)

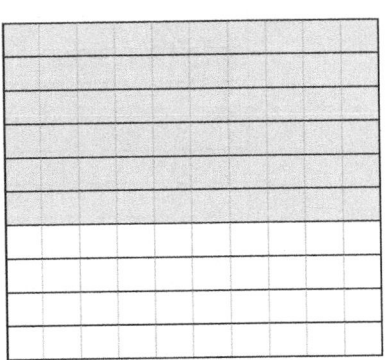

20)

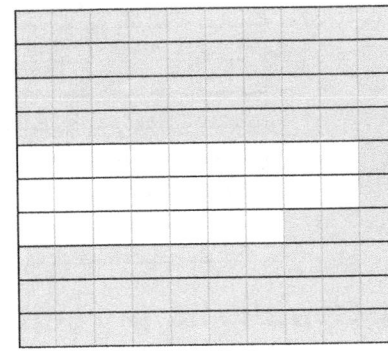

✎ **Which models show percentages? Attention one of the models is redundant.**

21) 70%

22) 35%

23) 75%

24) 60%

25) 12.5%

26) 50%

27) 40%

28) 65%

✎ **Solve the word problem by the grid model.**

29) Maria bakes bread. 15% of them were burned and the number of burned bread is 21. Shade the grid to show the burned bread. And how many breads were there in total?

30) In the library, there are 90 books on the shelves. 60% of those books are old. Shade the grid to show the percentage of books that are old. And how many books are old?

31) 3 of the 12 bears at the zoo were born in the wild. Shade the grid to show the fraction of the bears that were born in the wild. What percent of the bears were born in the wild?

32) In a box of muffins, 15 of the muffins are with the nuts core. That is 20% of the muffins in the box. Shade the grid to show the percent of muffins that are with the nuts core. How many muffins are in the box?

✒ **Solve and use strip model to show.**

33) Jones filled 40% of the 3 liters pot with water to cook the soup. How many liters of water did he put in the pot?

34) Frank bought a new coat at a discount. He paid just $120, but its cost was $150. What percentage of the cost did he pay?

35) An artist's color palette contained 320 grams of paint, which she used for 1 month, and now her color pallet is 80 grams. What percentage of colors are left?

36) Louis has 15 books from the library, and 40% of them are about the economy. How many of the books are about the economy?

✒ **Solve each percent word problem.**

37) A cinema has 240 seats. 144 seats were sold for the current movie. What percent of seats are sold?

38) There are 48 employees in the company. On a certain day, 36 were present. What percent showed up for work?

39) There are 35 students in a class and 7 of them are girls. What percent are girls?

40) The Royals softball team played 75 games and won 60 of them. What percent of the games did they win?

41) A shirt was originally priced at $48. It went on sale for $38.40. What was the percentage that the shirt was discounted?

42) A bank is offering a simple interest on a savings account. If you deposit $7,500, you will earn $525 interest in two years. What percentage is this offering?

43) Isabella has a new beaded necklace. 5 out of the 25 beads on the necklace are pink. What percentage of beads on Isabella's necklace are pink?

44) There are 18 boys and 46 girls in the class. 8 students do not take the bus to school. What percentage of students do not take the bus to school?

✎ Solve the percent word problem.

45) A new car, valued at $28,000, depreciates at 9% per year. What is the value of the car one year after purchase?

46) A metal bar weighs 24 ounces. 15% of the bar is gold. How many ounces of gold are in the bar?

47) A crew is made up of 12 women; the rest are men. If 20% of the crew are women, how many people are in the crew?

48) The price of a pair of shoes increases by 18% from $25. How much has the price increased?

49) At a coffee shop, the price of a cup of coffee was $1.50. In the new year, there is a 20% price increase in the cost of coffee. What is the new price of a cup of coffee?

50) 14% is cut from a 20 *cm* board. How much is the reduction in length?

51) In a class, the number of new students is 30%. In total, there are 40 students. What is the number of new students?

52) Students voted to appoint a new representative. 80% of the 40 votes were in favor of the new representative. How many votes were in favor?

✏ **Find the percent of the number.**

53) $12\frac{1}{4}\%$ of 20

54) 17% of 232

55) 55% of 160

56) $40\frac{1}{8}\%$ of 80

57) 77% of 300

58) $33\frac{1}{4}$ of 120

59) $62\frac{1}{2}\%$ of 40

60) 25% of 812

✏ **According to the fraction shade, write the grid model as a percentage.**

61) $\frac{3}{5}$

62) $\frac{2}{8}$

63) $\frac{1}{5}$

64) $\frac{4}{10}$

65) $\frac{3}{10}$

66) $\frac{3}{4}$

✏ **Write a proportion. Then solve.**

67) Adams owns 69% of the restaurants in Adams. In Lincoln, Frank owns $\frac{2}{3}$ of the restaurant. Who owns a greater percentage of restaurants in his area?

68) Last night Carol drove 35% of the way to the next state. Then rests for a while and today she drives $\frac{1}{2}$ of the way. Which day did she drive the most?

69) Yesterday, Susan read 10% of her novel book and Beti read $\frac{1}{8}$ of her novel book. Who read a greater percentage of her book?

70) So far, Mason has completed 82% of his school project. Jacob has finished $\frac{7}{10}$ of his school project. Who has finished a greater percentage of his school project?

✎ Write as a fraction and decimal.

71) In a school, 60% of the students were taken on a trip.

72) Jenny spent 30% of her money to buy a new bag.

73) In a camp, 40% of the tents have blue fabrics.

74) Farmer Johnson plants corn in 75% of his fields.

✎ Write as a decimal and percent.

75) One ounce is equal to $\frac{1}{16}$ pound.

76) In a park, $\frac{7}{8}$ of the flowers are pink.

77) Sarah used $\frac{3}{8}$ of her pen.

78) Jack has traveled $\frac{7}{10}$ of the way to reach the city.

✎ Solve each problem.

79) What is 15% of 60? ____

80) What is 55% of 800? ____

81) What is 22% of 120? ____

82) What is 18% of 40? ____

83) 90 is what percent of 200? ____%

84) 30 is what percent of 150? ____%

85) 14 is what percent of 250? ____%

86) 60 is what percent of 300? ____%

87) 30 is 120 percent of what number? ____

88) 120 is 20 percent of what number? ____

89) 15 is 5 percent of what number? ____

90) 22 is 20% of what number? ____

Chapter 8: Answers

1) 71%

2) 25%

3) 35%

4) 52%

5) 87%

6) 18%

7)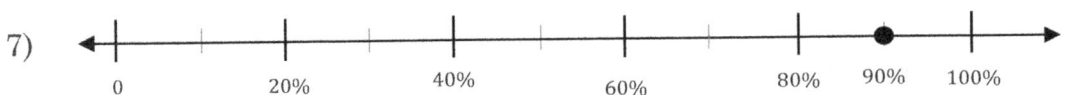

8)

9)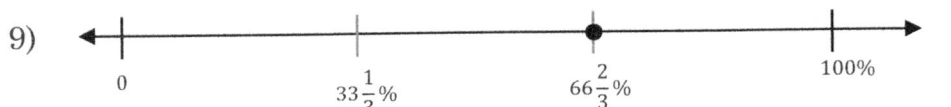

10)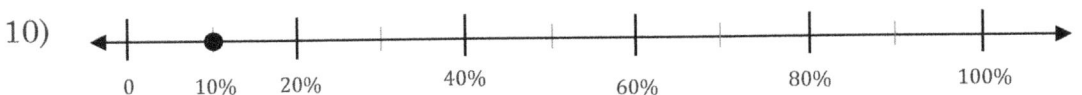

11)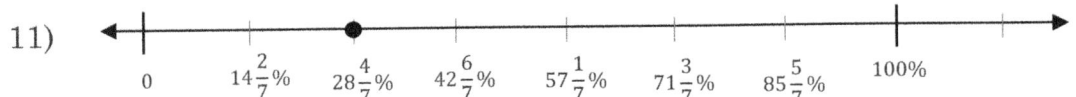

12)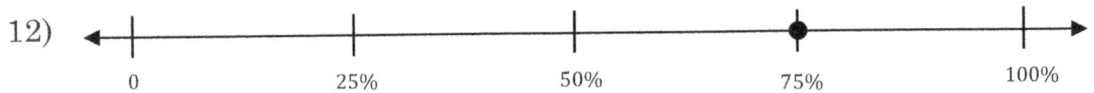

13)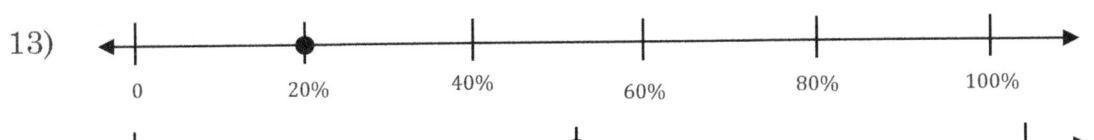

14)

15) $12\%, 0.12, \frac{3}{25}$

16) $44\%, 0.44, \frac{11}{25}$

17) $36\%, 0.36, \frac{9}{25}$

18) $50\%, 0.50, \frac{1}{2}$

19) $60\%, 0.60, \frac{6}{10}$

20) $75\%, 0.75, \frac{3}{4}$

21) c

22) h

23) e

24) f

25) a

26) d

27) i

28) b

29) 140

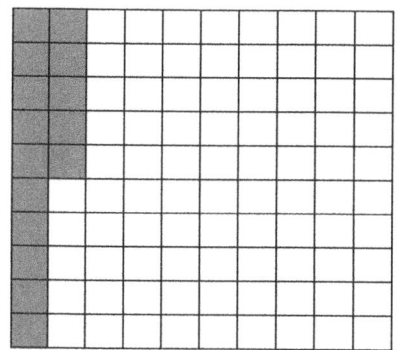

30) 54

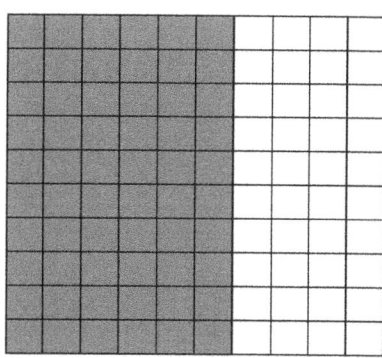

31) 25

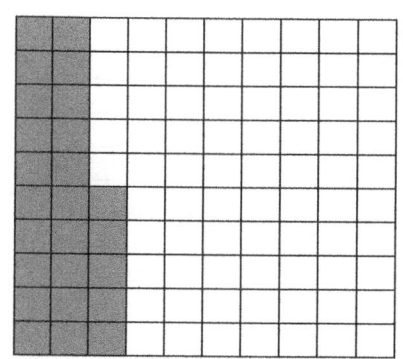

32) 75

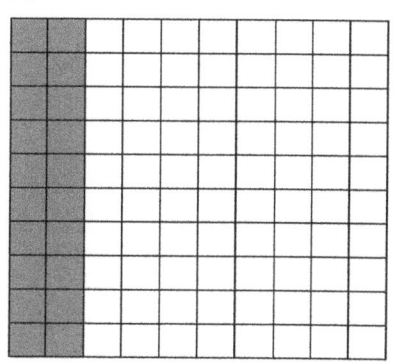

33) 1.2

0%	20%	40%	60%	80%	100%
0.6	1.2	1.8	2.4	3	

34) 80%

0%	20%	40%	60%	80%	100%
$30	$60	$90	$120	$150	

35) 25%

0%	25%	50%	75%	100%
$80	$160	$240	$320	

36) 6

0%	20%	40%	60%	80%	100%
3	6	9	12	15	

37) 60%
38) 75%
39) 20%
40) 80%
41) 20%
42) 3.5%
43) 20%
44) 12.5%
45) $25,480
46) 3.6 *oz*

47) 60
48) 4.5
49) $1.80
50) 2.8
51) 12
52) 32
53) 2.45
54) 39.44

55) 88
56) 32.10
57) 231
58) 39.90
59) 25
60) 203

61) 60%

62) 25%

63) 20%

64) 40%

65) 30%

66) 75%

67) Adams owns greater.

68) Today she drives the most.

69) Beti read to a greater percentage.

70) Mason has finished a greater.

71) $\frac{3}{5}$ and 0.6

72) $\frac{3}{10}$ and 0.3

73) $\frac{2}{5}$ and 0.4

74) $\frac{3}{4}$ and 0.75

75) 0.0625 and 6.25%

76) 0.875 and 87.5%

77) 0.375 and 37.5%

78) 0.7 and 70%

79) 9

80) 440

81) 26.4

82) 7.2

83) 45%

84) 20%

85) 5.6%

86) 20%

87) 25

88) 600

89) 300

90) 110

CHAPTER 9: Measurement System

Math topics that you'll learn in this chapter:

- ☑ Mixed Customary Units Operations
- ☑ Mixed Numbers and Fractions Customary Unit Conversions
- ☑ Using Proportions to Convert Traditional and Metric Units
- ☑ Compare the Temperatures Above and Below Zero

Mixed Customary Units Operations

- In mathematics, the traditional system may be described as a set of weights and measures utilized for measuring length, weight, capacity, and temperature. Lengths and distances in the traditional system will be measured in inches, feet, yards, and miles.

- In order to convert between traditional units, use these rules:

    - In order to convert from a bigger unit to a lesser smaller unit, you multiply.

    - In order to convert from a lesser unit to a bigger unit, you divide.

Examples:

Example 1. Compare. Select >, <, or = to make the sentence true.

8,715 pounds ☐ 7 tons 190 pounds

Solution: First, convert both sides to the smallest unit (pounds). Since the left side is the pounds unit. And now, the right side needs to convert to the pounds. Convert 7 tons to pounds, $7 \times 2{,}000 = 14{,}000$. Then, add 190 pounds, $14{,}000 + 190 = 14{,}190$. So, 8715 is smaller than 14190.

8,715 pounds < 7 tons 190 pounds.

Example 2. Convert.

14,960 yards = ☐ mile ☐ yards

Solution: There are 1760 yards in a mile. So, to convert yards to miles, divide the number of yards by 1760. Then, divide, $14{,}960 \div 1{,}760 = 8.5$ miles

There are 8 miles, and 880 ($1760 \div 2 = 880$) yards left over. $14{,}960 = 8mi\ 880yd$

Mixed Numbers and Fractions Customary Unit Conversions

- Unit conversions express the identical property as a different unit of measurement.

- Whenever you need to do a conversion, the proper conversion factor to an equal value has to be utilized.

- For instance, in order to convert inches to feet, the proper conversion value is 12 inches equal 1 foot. In order to convert minutes to hours, the appropriate conversion value is 60 minutes equals 1 hour.

Examples:

Example 1. Convert. Simplify and write as a fraction or whole or mixed number.

___ Inches = $\frac{1}{4}$ of a foot.

Solution: To find out how many inches are in $\frac{1}{4}$ of a foot, multiply a larger unit by a smaller unit and cancel common factors:

$$\frac{1}{4} \times 12 = \frac{1}{4} \times \frac{12}{1} = \frac{1 \times 3}{1 \times 1} = 3$$

So, 3 Inches = $\frac{1}{4}$ of a foot.

Example 2. Convert. Simplify and write as a fraction or whole or mixed number.

3 teaspoons = ___ tablespoons.

Solution: Divide a smaller unit into a larger unit and cancel common factors:

$$3 \div 3 = 1$$

So, 3 teaspoons = 1 tablespoons.

Using Proportions to Convert Traditional and Metric Units

- It's possible to convert any measuring unit to a different kind by multiplying it via a quite special ratio (or ratios) that equals one. You may form these special ratios from the conversion factors.
- For instance, $1ft = 12\ in$ are a conversion factor and the ratios $\frac{1ft}{12in}$ and $\frac{12in}{1ft}$ can be written from it, in which both equal 1.

Examples:

Example 1. Which proportion could you use to convert 60 cups to quarts?

$$\frac{4\ cups}{1\ quart} = \frac{60\ cups}{?\ quarts} \qquad \frac{4\ cups}{1\ quart} = \frac{?\ quarts}{60\ cups}$$

Solution: In the first, write a unit rate that shows the relation between cups and per quart. Then, write another rate with the numbers in the problem. To match the unit rate, the unit is in the numerator in the same form and in the denominator as well, $\frac{4\ cups}{1\ quart} = \frac{60\ cups}{?quarts}$. And use this proportion to convert. To get from 4 to 60, multiply by 15.

$$\frac{4\ cups \times 15}{1\ quart \times 15} = \frac{60\ cups}{15 quarts}$$

So, $60 cups = 15 quarts$.

Example 2. Write proportion to convert 3 inches to feet.

Solution: Write a unit rate that shows the relation between feet and per inch. Then, write another rate with the numbers in the problem. To match the unit rate, the unit is in numerator the same form and in the denominator as well, $\frac{1\ feet}{12\ inches} = \frac{?feet}{3inches}$. And use this proportion to convert. To get from 12 to 3, divide by 4.

$$\frac{1\ feet \div 4}{12\ inches \div 4} = \frac{\frac{1}{4} feet}{3 inches}$$

So, $3\ inches = \frac{1}{4}\ feet$ or $0.25\ feet$.

Compare the Temperatures Above and Below Zero

- You can show the temperature changes via a number line.

- A number line has negative numbers to the left of 0 as well as positive numbers to the right of 0. That signifies the numbers beyond the right-hand side are always larger than the ones on the left-hand side.

- For the conditions of the temperature, the ones that are the coldest (the lower number) are on the left-hand side, as well as the warmest temperatures (the higher numbers) are on the right-hand side.

- You can now put down these temperatures from the coldest to the warmest as: $-7, -6, -2, -1, 0, 3,$ and 5.

Examples:

Example 1. At $4:00$ *AM* the temperature was 14 degrees Celsius. At $4:00$ *PM* the temperature was 20 degrees Celsius. Did the temperature rise or fall?

Solution: 20 degrees Celsius is warmer than 14 degrees Celsius. So, the temperature rose.

Example 2. The temperature in Chicago was $18°F$. The temperature in Houston was $12°F$. Was Chicago hotter or colder than Houston?

Solution: 18 degrees Fahrenheit is hotter than 14 degrees Fahrenheit. So, Chicago was hotter than Houston.

Chapter 9: Practices

✎ Compare.

1) 6 quarts 2 pint ☐ 15 pint

2) 8,355 yd ☐ 3 mi 1,555 yd

3) 3 kg ☐ 3,500 g

4) 80 inches ☐ 2.03 meter

✎ Convert

5) 10 feet = ___ m

6) 15 cm = ___ m

7) 0.5 kg = ___ g

8) 10 mi = ___ ft

✎ Add and subtract.

9) 1,840 lb + 878 lb = ☐ T ☐ lb

10) 2 lb 5 oz + 3 lb 10 oz = ☐ lb ☐ oz

11) 4 mi 170 yd − 1 mi 1,200 yd = ☐ mi ☐ yd

12) 7 m 40 cm − 5 m 80 cm = ☐ m ☐ cm

✎ Convert. Simplify and write as a fraction or whole or mixed number.

13) 8 yd = ___ in

14) ___ ounce = $\frac{1}{12}$ lb

15) 15,000 lb = ___ t

16) 8 quarts = ___ gallon

17) ___ ft = $\frac{2}{5}$ mi

18) ___ mi = 440 yd

19) 0.07 kg = ___ g

20) 46 ft = ___ yd

✍ Write proportion to convert traditional and metric units.

21) 9 inches to yards
22) 3 mile to ft
23) 2500 gram to kilogram
24) 352 yard to mile
25) 660 feet to mile
26) 10 quarts to cups
27) 6 gallons to quarts
28) 700 meters to kilometers
29) 30 pints to quarts
30) 150 milligrams to gram
31) 9 pints to cups
32) 100 millimeters to meters
33) 18 feet to yards
34) 10 cups to pints
35) 5 yard to feet
36) 250 centimeters to meters

✍ Solve.

37) There are low temperatures (in Celsius) for five days in summer:

Wednesday	Thursday	Friday	Saturday	Sunday
5	0	−3	−4	−2

Arrange them in order from coldest to warmest.

38) On the first day of autumn, the high temperature in Sophia's city was 15 degrees below zero (in °C), and the second day the high temperature was 23 degrees below zero (in °C). Which day was hotter?

39) The highest temperature ever recorded on earth was 56°C. The highest temperature on Mars is around minus 158°C. Which is the coldest? Write an inequality.

40) Jake recorded a temperature of 31 degrees Celsius, and Emma recorded a temperature of 25 degrees Celsius. Did Emma record a temperature that was warmer or cooler?

Chapter 9: Answers

1) <

2) >

3) <

4) =

5) $3.05 m$

6) $0.15 m$

7) $500 g$

8) $52800 ft$

9) $1 T\ 232\ lb$

10) $5\ lb\ 15\ oz$

11) $2\ mi\ 730\ yd$

12) $1\ m\ 60\ cm$

13) $288\ in$

14) $1\frac{1}{3} oz$

15) $7\frac{1}{2} t$

16) $2 gal$

17) $2112\ ft$

18) $\frac{1}{4} mi$

19) $70 g$

20) $15\frac{1}{3} yd$

21) $\frac{1\ yd}{36\ in} = \frac{0.25\ yd}{9\ in}$

22) $\frac{1\ mile}{5280\ ft} = \frac{3\ mile}{15840\ ft}$

23) $\frac{1\ kg}{1000\ g} = \frac{2.5\ kg}{2500\ g}$

24) $\frac{1\ mile}{1760\ yd} = \frac{0.2\ mile}{352\ yd}$

25) $\frac{1\ mile}{5280\ ft} = \frac{0.125\ mile}{660\ ft}$

26) $\frac{1\ qt}{4\ c} = \frac{10\ qt}{40\ c}$

27) $\frac{1\ gal}{4\ qt} = \frac{6\ gal}{24\ qt}$

28) $\frac{1\ km}{1000\ m} = \frac{0.7\ km}{700\ m}$

29) $\frac{1\ qt}{2\ pt} = \frac{15\ qt}{30\ pt}$

30) $\frac{1\ g}{10\ mg} = \frac{15\ g}{150\ mg}$

31) $\frac{1\ pt}{2\ c} = \frac{9\ pt}{18\ c}$

32) $\frac{1\ m}{1000\ mm} = \frac{0.1\ m}{100\ mm}$

33) $\frac{1\ yd}{3\ feet} = \frac{6\ yd}{18\ feet}$

34) $\frac{2\ c}{1\ pt} = \frac{10\ c}{5\ pt}$

35) $\frac{1\ yd}{3\ ft} = \frac{5\ yd}{15\ ft}$

36) $\frac{1\ m}{100\ cm} = \frac{2.5 m}{250\ cm}$

37) $-4 < -3 < -2 < 0 < 5$

38) First day

39) $56 > -158$

40) cooler

CHAPTER
10 Statistics and Data Analysis

Math topics that you'll learn in this chapter:

- ☑ Pie Graph
- ☑ Graph The Line Plot
- ☑ Distributions in Line Plot
- ☑ Relative Frequency Tables
- ☑ Frequency Charts
- ☑ Mean, Median, Mode, and Range of the Given Data
- ☑ Interpreting Charts to find mean, median, mode, and range
- ☑ Finding an Outlier
- ☑ Finding Range, Quartiles, and Interquartile Range
- ☑ Interpreting Categorical Data
- ☑ Identifying Statistical Questions
- ☑ Completing a Table and Making a Graph: Word Problems

Pie Graph

- A Pie Graph (Pie Chart) is a circle chart divided into sectors, each sector represents the relative size of each value.
- Pie charts represent a snapshot of how a group is broken down into smaller pieces.

Examples:

A library has 750 books that include Mathematics, Physics, Chemistry, English and History. Use the following graph to answer the questions.

Example 1. What is the number of Mathematics books?

Solution: Number of total books = 750

Percent of Mathematics books = 28%

Then, the number of Mathematics books: $28\% \times 750 = 0.28 \times 750 = 210$

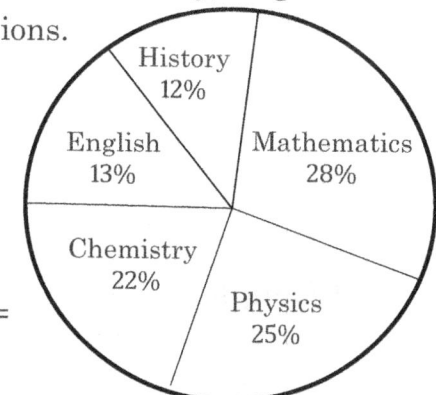

Example 2. What is the number of History books?

Solution: Number of total books = 750

Percent of History books = 12%

Then: $0.12 \times 750 = 90$

Example 3. What is the number of Chemistry books in the library?

Solution: Number of total books = 750

Percent of Chemistry books = 22%

Then: $0.22 \times 750 = 165$

Graph The Line Plot

- Draw a number line that encloses all the values included in the data set.
- Put an × (or dot) over each data value on this number line.
- If a value happens over one time in a data set, put an × over this number for each of the times it happens.
- An instance of a line plot is a plot illustrating the number of pupils who like the colors pink, green, purple, red, and blue.
- These colors will be values on the x-axis, along with the number of pupils liking each of these colors gets illustrated over the values as ×s.

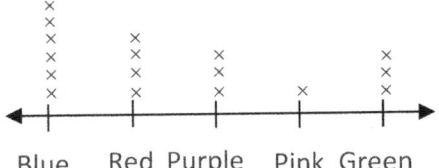

Examples:

Example 1. A researcher working for a research company surveyed people about sleeping habits. Use the data to graph the line plot.

Sleeping time:

23, 22, 22, 22, 23, 24, 1, 23, 24, 22, 23, 23, 1, 2, 24, 23, 22, 23, 23

Solution: First, count how many times each set number appears in the list. 22 appear 5 times in the list, 23 appear 8 times, 24 appear 3 times, 1 appears 2 times, 2 appears 1 time. Then graph it on the line plot.

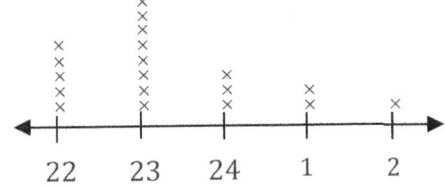

Example 2. The following data shows the daily sales of kilograms of apples in a store. Use the data to graph the line plot.

15 kg, 20 kg, 13 kg, 20 kg, 18 kg, 18 kg, 13 kg, 13 kg, 15 kg, 18 kg, 15 kg, 13 kg, 15 kg, 13 kg, 13 kg, 15 kg, 15 kg, 18 kg, 15 kg, 13 kg.

Solution: First, count how many times each set of numbers appears in the list.

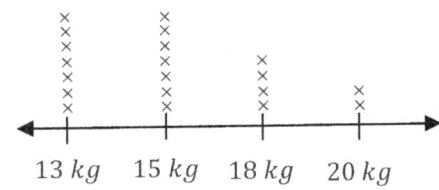

13 appears 7 times in the list, 15 appears 7 times, 18 appears 4 times, 20 appears 2 times. Then graph it on the line plot.

Distributions in Line Plot

- Step one: Compute the data set's range.
- To compute the data set's range, firstly you must determine the greatest data value as well as the least of the data values. Therefore, you subtract the smallest data value from the biggest data value.

$$Range = greatest\ value - smallest\ value$$

- Step two: Utilize the range for describing the distribution.

Example:

What does the line plot show?

Solution: Look at the line plot. The smallest number is 10 and the greatest is 45.

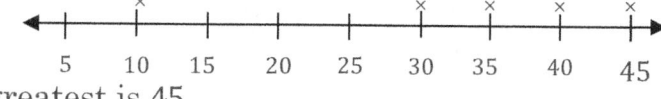

The column for 30 has the most ×s. So, there is a peak at 30, that is the mode of this data.

There are no ×s in the columns for 15 to 25. So, there is a gap from 15 to 25.

The data has a cluster from 30 to 45. There is a group of ×s in the columns for 30 and 45. Every column has at least one ×, and the columns are next to one another.

There is an × in the column for 10, and it is far away from the rest of the ×s. So, there is an outlier at 10 pieces.

The data is skewed right. The left and right sides of the distribution are not mirrored images. So, the distribution is roughly asymmetric.

The leftmost column with an × is 10. The rightmost column with an × is 45. So, the data is spread out from 10 to 45.

The number of ×s to the left of 35 is almost the same as the number to the right. So, the center of the data is at 35.

Relative Frequency Tables

- Frequency tables are tables that list items as well as show the number of times these items happen.
- Frequency is signified by the English alphabet 'f'.
- Relative frequency is:

$$\text{Relative Frequency} = \frac{\text{Subgroup frequency}}{\text{Total frequency}} = \frac{f}{n}$$

- Producing a frequency table:
    - Step one: Draw 3 columns. The 1st column holds the data values in rising order (from lowest to highest).
    - Step two: The 2nd column holds the number of times the data value happens utilizing tally marks. Count for each row in the table. Utilize tally marks for calculating.
    - Step three: Calculate the number of tally marks for each of the data values and put it in the 3rd column.

Example:

Deb wants to subscribe to a plan for education. This plan has weekly hours for different courses. Math 7 hours, chemistry 5 hours, physics 5 hours, and earth science 3 hours. Complete the relative frequency table for the data.

Education plan				
Courses	Math	Chemistry	Physics	Earth science
Relative frequency	___%	___%	___%	___%

Solution: First, find the total number of hours plan, $7 + 5 + 5 + 3 = 20$. Write the relative frequency of each course as a fraction with a denominator of 20. Then write as a percent.

Math course: $\frac{7}{20} = \frac{7 \times 5}{20 \times 5} = \frac{35}{100} = 35\%$

Chemistry course: $\frac{5}{20} = \frac{5 \times 5}{20 \times 5} = \frac{25}{100} = 25\%$

Physics course: $\frac{5}{20} = \frac{5 \times 5}{20 \times 5} = \frac{25}{100} = 25\%$

Earth science course: $\frac{3}{20} = \frac{3 \times 5}{20 \times 5} = \frac{15}{100} = 15\%$

Chapter 10: Statistics and Data Analysis

Frequency Charts

- Any table illustrating the frequencies of the values of one or more of the variables in a data set.

- Frequency tables are created whenever the accumulated data values get placed in ascending order of magnitude together with their parallel frequencies.

- You must count these frequencies in order to create a frequency distribution table.

- The primary reason to make this kind of table is to illustrate how many times the value happens.

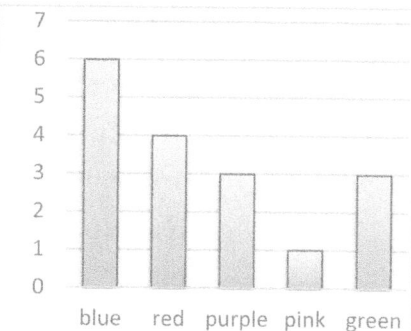

Color	Frequency
blue	6
red	4
purple	3
pink	1
green	3

Examples:

Example 1. A student counted the number of hours that spend on each of her tests. Use the data to complete the frequency chart below.

Hours per test: 1:45, 1:20, 3:00, 2:45, 2:33, 3:12, 1:48, 1:57, 2:28, 2:49, 4:00, 3:10, 4:05, 2:55, 2:11, 3:30, 2:08, 4:16, 3:55, 3:27.

Number of hours	Number of tests
1 – 1:59	4
2 – 2:59	7
3 – 3:59	
4 – 4:59	3

Solution: The blank row is for 3 – 3:59. Count the number of 3 – 3:59. So, there are **6** hours between 3:00 and 3:59.

Example 2. In the neonatal unit of a hospital, weighed all the newborn babies that were born on the same day. Use the data to complete the frequency chart below.

Babies weight: 7.5 lb, 5.7 lb, 6 lb, 5.8 lb, 6.3 lb, 5.3 lb, 8.1 lb, 7.8 lb, 8 lb, 6.6 lb, 7.3 lb, 5.7 lb, 7 lb, 6.7 lb, 5.9 lb, 7.1 lb.

Babies weight	Number of weights
5 – 5.9 lb	5
6 – 6.9 lb	
7 – 7.9 lb	5
8 – 8.9 lb	2

Solution: The blank row is for 6 – 6.9 lb. Count the number of 6 – 6.9 lb. So, there are **4** weights between 6 and 6.9 lb.

Mean, Median, Mode, and Range of the Given Data

- **Mean:** $\frac{\text{sum of the data}}{\text{total number of data entires}}$
- **Mode:** the value in the list that appears most often
- **Median:** is the middle number of a group of numbers arranged in order by size.
- **Range:** the difference of the largest value and smallest value in the list

Examples:

Example 1. What is the mode of these numbers? $5, 6, 8, 6, 8, 5, 3, 5$

Solution: Mode: the value in the list that appears most often.

Therefore, the mode is number 5. There are three number 5 in the data.

Example 2. What is the median of these numbers? $6, 11, 15, 10, 17, 20, 7$

Solution: Write the numbers in order: $6, 7, 10, 11, 15, 17, 20$

The median is the number in the middle. Therefore, the median is 11.

Example 3. What is the mean of these numbers? $7, 2, 3, 2, 4, 8, 7, 5$

Solution: Mean: $\frac{\text{sum of the data}}{\text{total number of data entires}} = \frac{7+2+3+2+4+8+7+5}{8} = \frac{38}{8} = 4.75$

Example 4. What is the range in this list? $3, 7, 12, 6, 15, 20, 8$

Solution: Range is the difference of the largest value and smallest value in the list. The largest value is 20 and the smallest value is 3.

Then: $20 - 3 = 17$

Interpreting Charts to find mean, median, mode, and range

These 4 measures are the median, mean, range, and mode.

- Mean stands for the average. The mean is determined via the addition of the numbers, and after that, you divide via the number of numbers in a group.

- The median is the middle number of a data set whenever put in order from the lowest to the highest. To determine a median place all the numbers in greatest to smallest order or vice versa, then chose the middle number.

- Mode is the number that happens the most. To discover the mode in an easy fashion, place your numbers in order from lowest to highest then calculate the number of times each of the numbers happens. Whichever one happens the most will be your mode.

- Range is the difference between the greatest and smallest values. To discover the range, firstly place all numbers in order. After that subtract the smallest number from the biggest.

Example:

Jake paid attention to how many pages of books he read in the past 7 days. What is the range, mean, median, and mode of the number of pages?

Day	Number of pages
Saturday	14
Sunday	27
Monday	33
Tuesday	13
Wednesday	13
Thursday	27
Friday	13

Solution: To find the range, first find the greatest number, 33. Next find the latest number, 13. Subtract the least number from the greatest number, $33 - 13 = 20$. The range is 20.

To find the mean, count how many numbers are in the group. 10. Then add all of them together, $14 + 27 + 33 + 13 + 13 + 27 + 13 = 140$. Now divide the result by the number of numbers, $140 \div 10 = 14$. The mean is 14.

To find mode, count how many times each number appears. And The number that appears most often (3 times) is 13. The mode is 13.

To find the median, arrange the numbers from least to greatest. Then, find the number in the middle. 13, 13, 13, 14, 27, 27, 33. The number in the middle is 14. The median is 14.

Finding an Outlier

- To discover an outlier, find a value that is either a lot bigger or a lot littler than the rest.

- One may transform extreme data points into *z* scores which illustrate the number of standard deviations away they are from the mean.

- Should the value be a high or low enough *z* score, you can call it an outlier.

- An outlier is an extreme value in a data set that is either much larger or much smaller than all the other values.

Examples:

Example 1. Select the outlier in the data set.

28, 44, 48, 25, 30, 33, 7, 39, 53, 44, 25, 33, 44, 28, 33

Solution: First, find the much larger or much smaller value in the data set. The value 7 is an outlier because it is much smaller than all other values.

Example 2. Select the outlier in the data set.

4, 4, 8, 5, 1, 3, 7, 9, 3, 4, 5, 3, 4, 8, 33, 7, 9, 3, 4, 5,

Solution: First, find the much larger or much smaller value in the data set. The value 33 is an outlier because it is much larger than all other values.

Finding Range, Quartiles, and Interquartile Range

- To determine IQR, you first subtract the 1st quartile from the 3rd quartile.

- The interquartile range denotes the middle half, or middle 50 percent, of the data. The lesser the IQR is for a dataset, the nearer the middle half of the data will be to the median.

- IQR illustrates the middle 50 percent of values whenever it is ordered from lesser to greater.

- To determine the interquartile range (IQR), firstly determine the median (middle value) of the lower and upper half of your data.

- These values will be quartile 1 (Q_1) and quartile 3 (Q_3). IQR is the difference between Q_3 and Q_1.

Examples:

Example 1. What is the range of the data set?

28, 48, 25, 30, 39, 53, 44, 25, 33, 42

Solution: First, find the greatest and the least number, 53 and 25. Next, subtract the least number from the greatest number, $53 - 25 = 28$.

The range is 28.

Example 2. Based on the data of example, 1, find the quartiles, then find the interquartile range.

Solution: First order the data from least to greatest. To find the quartiles, divide a data set into quarters, or four parts. Split the data into a lower half and an upper half. Next, find Q_1, the median of the lower half. And find Q_3, the median of the upper half.

Lower half	Upper half
25, 25, 28, 30, 33	39, 42, 44, 48,
Q_1	Q_3

$$Q_2 = \frac{38 + 39}{2} = 38.5$$

$Q_1 = 28$, $Q_2 = 38.5$, $Q_3 = 44$

Now, to find IQR subtract Q_1 from Q_3, $44 - 28 = 16$. So, interquartile range is 16.

Interpreting Categorical Data

- Categorical data gets analyzed utilizing mode and median distributions, whereas nominal data gets analyzed with mode and ordinal data utilizes both.

- Ordinal data can additionally get analyzed utilizing linear trends, univariate statistics, classification methods, bivariate statistics, and regression applications.

- To interpret categorical data:

  • First, we need to organize the data in order from least to greatest. We are given the following data set.

  • Second, we need to create a frequency table using the given information. The constructed frequency table should look like the following figure.

  • Last, we will use this information to create a histogram of frequencies.

Example:

Emma went to the shop and bought 11 cucumbers, 5 oranges, 7 bananas, 2 coconuts, and 9 melons. What is the mean, mode, and median of her purchase?

Solution: To find the mean, count how many numbers are in the group, 5. Then add all of the fruits together. Then divide the result by the number of numbers.

$$mean = \frac{2 + 5 + 7 + 9 + 11}{5} = \frac{34}{5} = 6.8$$

The mean is 6.8.

To find mode, find which fruits Emma bought the most, 2, 5, 7, 9, 11. Emma bought 11 cucumbers, which is more than any other. So, cucumber is the mode.

To find the median, arrange the numbers of fruits from least to greatest. Then, find the number in the middle. 2, 5, 7, 9, 11. The number in the middle is 7. The median is the bananas.

Identifying Statistical Questions

- Statistical questions are those you can answer via accumulating data and where there is variability in the data.

- This is not the same as a question that foresees a deterministic answer. For instance, "What amount of minutes do 6th-grade pupils typically spend on doing homework every week?" is a statistical question.

- Therefore, statistical questions are those you can answer via gathering data that varies.

Examples:

Example 1. Is the following a statistical question?

How much money does Eva spend on clothes in a typical month?

Solution: This question can be answered by recording how much money Eva spends on clothes every month. The amount of money she spends probably varies from month to month.

So, this is a statistical question.

Example 2. Is the following a statistical question?

What are your sister's favorite songs?

Solution: This question can be answered by a single piece of data. In fact, there is no varied data.

So, this is not a statistical question.

Completing a Table and Making a Graph: Word Problems

- You can solve word problems by becoming a detective and searching for clues in the form of keywords and phrases.
- Carefully read the text to understand what you are asked to solve in the problem.
- Write a number sentence then solve it in a single step.

Examples:

Example 1. Complete the table. And graph the data from the table.

Nights	Total drops
1	
2	
3	
4	

Sue adores her brand-new scented-oil diffuser. She places five drops of lavender oil in the diffuser every night and it helps her go to sleep.

Solution: Figure out the total drops of lavender oil utilized after one night:1 = 5, two nights: 2 = 10, three nights: 3 = 15, and four nights: 4 = 20.

Utilize the table to write down ordered pairs of numbers. For each pair, write down the number of nights first and then the total number of drops second, (1,5), (2,10), (3,15), (4,20). Then, graph the ordered pairs. Begin with the first pair, (1,5).

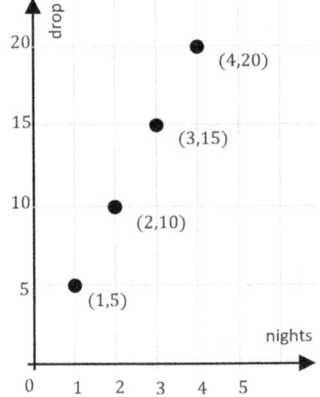

Example 2. Complete the table. And graph the data from the table.

Nights	Total drops
1	
2	
3	
4	

Riley works at the burger restaurant. Riley must be able to assemble 2 burgers per minute.

Solution: Figure out the total burger after one minute:1 = 2. After two minutes: 2 = 4, three minutes: 3 = 6 and four minutes: 4 = 8.

Utilize the table to write down ordered pairs of numbers. For each pair, write down the number of minutes first and then the total number of burgers, (1,2), (2,4), (3,6), (4,8).
Then, graph the ordered pairs. Begin with the first pair, (1,2).

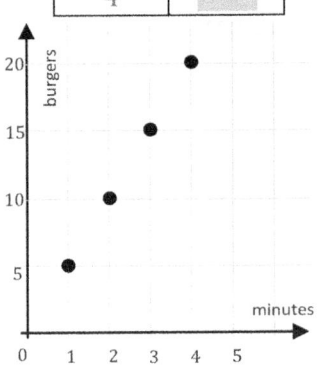

Chapter 10: Practices

✏ **The circle graph below shows all Bob's expenses for last month. Bob spent $790 on his Rent last month.**

1) How much did Bob's total expenses last month? _____

2) How much did Bob spend for foods last month? _____

3) How much did Bob spend for his bills last month? _____

4) How much did Bob spend on his car last month? _____

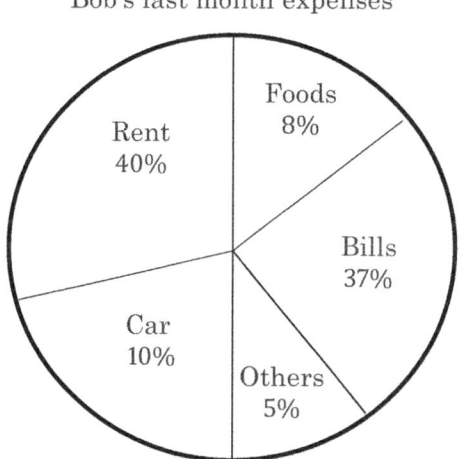

Bob's last month expenses

✏ **Use the data to graph the line plot.**

5) The following data is about the number of customers of a restaurant each day.

   210, 200, 190, 240, 210, 210, 210, 190, 190, 200, 150, 210, 200, 190

6) The following data is about the daily low temperatures.

   13°C, 10°C, 11°C, 10°C, 15°C, 10°C, 14°C, 11°C, 15°C, 15°C, 10°C, 11°C, 13°C, 15°C.

7) The following data is about the number of sales of a new shoe model each week.

   5, 25, 20, 25, 15, 30, 30, 15, 15, 20, 30, 35, 25, 20, 30, 15, 15

8) Sarah is knitting scarves, and every week, she takes a number of knitted scarves to the shop for sale. The following data is about the weekly scarf sales.

10, 10, 11, 12, 10, 9, 11, 12, 5, 10, 15, 10, 11, 12, 11, 15, 9, 15, 12, 11

✎ **Select all the statements that describe the distribution of the data.**

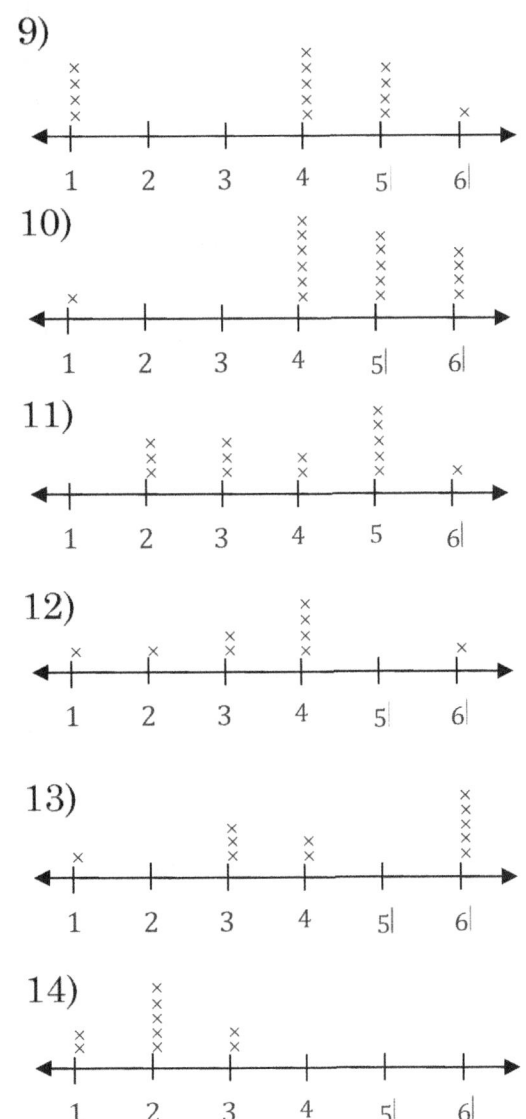

a	The data has a peak at 4.
b	The data has a cluster from 1 to 3.
c	There is a gap from 2 to 3.
d	The data is spread out from 1 to 3.
e	The data has a cluster from 1 to 4.
f	The least number is 2 and the greatest is 6.
g	There is an outlier at 1 piece.
h	The data has a peak at 2.
i	The data has a cluster from 4 to 6.
j	The data is spread out from 2 to 6.
k	The distribution is roughly symmetric.
l	The least number is 2 and the greatest is 3.
m	There is an outlier at 6 pieces.
n	The data is spread out from 1 to 6.
o	The data has a cluster from 3 to 4.
p	The data is skewed left.
q	The data has a peak at 6.

✏ Complete the relative frequency table for the data.

15) Maria bakes cupcakes with various flavors. 5 lemon, 8 coffee, 9 carrots, and 3 red velvet.

16) Eva went to the bakery and bought some bread such as 3 challah bread, 5 yeast bread and 2 pieces of focaccia.

17) During a month, the maximum air temperature was as follows, nine days 33°C, twelve days 31°C, three days 27°C and six days 29°C.

18) In a cafe, the number of orders for coffee cups is recorded. The number of cups ordered in the last 10 days is as follows, 40 − 49 cups in three days, 50 − 59 cups in two days, 30 − 39 cups in four days, and 20 − 29 cups in one day.

✏ Use the data and draw the frequency chart.

19) Every day, Maria bakes various cakes for a cafe. The following data is about the various cakes baked daily.

    3, 7, 5, 4, 7, 4, 7, 3, 7, 4, 3, 7, 5, 3, 5, 7, 4, 5, 3, 7, 7, 4, 3, 7, 3, 7, 5, 7, 4, 5.

20) Eva went to the shop and bought fruits such as 4 apples, 6 peaches, 3 bananas, 5 pineapples, and 8 melons.

21) The following data is about the daily high temperatures.

23°C, 25°C, 22°C, 23°C, 25°C, 26°C, 24°C, 25°C, 25°C, 23°C, 22°C, 23°C, 23°C, 22°C.

22) The following data is about the number of soft drink bottles that are drunk in a restaurant per day.

235, 137, 111, 127, 130, 230, 250, 187, 270, 220, 243, 135, 129, 222, 177, 164, 205, 238, 229, 292, 182, 254, 216,

Find the values of the Given Data.

23) 6, 11, 5, 3, 6

Mode: _____   Range: _____
Mean: _____   Median: _____

24) 4, 9, 1, 9, 6, 7

Mode: _____   Range: _____
Mean: _____   Median: _____

25) 10, 3, 6, 10, 4, 15

Mode: _____   Range: _____
Mean: _____   Median: _____

26) 12, 4, 8, 9, 3, 12, 15

Mode: _____   Range: _____
Mean: _____   Median: _____

A boutique kept a record of how many clothes it sold each day.

Day	Number of clothes
Monday	25
Tuesday	40
Wednesday	29
Thursday	38
Friday	26
Saturday	35
Sunday	38

27) What is the median of the number of clothes?

28) What is the range of the number of clothes?

29) What is the mode of the number of clothes?

30) What is the mean of the number of clothes?

✍ Leo looked at the download manager history on his computer to find out how many he had download songs in the past 8 days.

31) What is the mode of the number of songs?

32) What is the mean of the number of songs?

33) What is the median of the number of songs?

34) What is the range of the number of songs?

Day	Number of songs
1st	9
2nd	5
3rd	5
4th	8
5th	5
6th	9
7th	5
8th	2

✍ Select the outlier in the data set.

35) 14, 24, 34, 44, 54, 24, 44, 54, 14, 24, 94

36) 150, 163, 134, 184, 151, 128, 143, 175, 70, 151, 134

37) 17, 27, 30, 35, 44, 34, 29, 335, 55, 27, 84

38) 1, 4, 3, 2, 5, 9, 1, 3, 4, 2, 1

39) 93, 94, 93, 92, 25, 90, 91, 97, 98, 103, 99

40) 55, 50, 53, 51, 57, 59, 11, 53, 49, 60, 61

41) 1001, 1004, 1003, 1002, 1005, 1009, 250, 1010, 1004

42) 2, 14, 17, 12, 18, 19, 20, 22, 13, 20, 17

✍ What is the range?

43) 6, 4, 8, 11, 2

44) 5, 7, 3, 12, 7, 10, 6, 9, 4

45) 10, 10, 6, 7, 10, 7, 13, 15

46) 8, 7, 4, 7, 5, 4, 12, 7

✎ **In the data set below:**

14, 24, 34, 44, 54, 24, 44, 54, 14, 24, 94

47) What is the lower quartile, Q_1?

48) What is the upper quartile, Q_3?

49) What is the range?

50) What is the interquartile range?

✎ **Solve.**

51) In a javelin throw competition, five athletes score 56, 40, 56, 59, and 65 meters. What are their mean and mode?

52) Bob has 12 black pens, 14 red pens, 15 green pens, 24 blue pens, and 3 boxes of yellow pens. If the mean and median are 16 and 15 respectively, what is the number of yellow pens in each box?

53) At a petting zoo, there were 3 goats, 8 sheep, 5 llamas, 16 ponies, and 9 pigs. Pick the mode of this data set. There may be more than one.

54) Julia planted some seeds in her garden. The flowers that grew included 12 roses, 8 azaleas, 5 sunflowers, 3 orchids, 12 lilies, and 9 violets. Pick the mode of this data set. There may be more than one. And what is the median?

Chapter 10: Statistics and Data Analysis

✎ **Determine whether the following questions are statistical or not.**

55) How often is a typical employee at your company absent?

56) How many hours of sleep do babies get per night?

57) What day is your parents' wedding anniversary?

58) How much does Jason spend on his car each month?

59) How much are ticket sales in each football match?

60) How heavy are rhinos?

61) In what year did Bob become a graduate of college?

62) How much did the museum make on opening day this year?

✎ **Complete the table and graph the equation.**

63) Timothy was late to collect apples from the garden. By the time he arrived, his friend Zack had already collected 3 packages. Timothy collected the rest of the apples with Zack.

Packages of Timothy	Packages of Zack
1	
2	
3	
4	

64) Anne knits 6 gloves in a month. She plans to knit more gloves this month.

Number of months	Total gloves
1	
2	
3	
4	

65) Olivia swims for 2 hours each day over the summer.

Number of days	Total hours
1	
2	
3	
4	

66) At the market, watermelon cost $2 per 3 pounds.

Weight of watermelon	price
3	
6	
9	
12	

Chapter 10: Answers

1) $1,975

2) $158

3) $730.75

4) $197.50

5)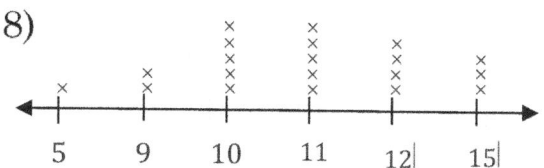

6)

7)

8)

9) a, c, g, i, n

10) a, c, g, i, n

11) f, j, k

12) a, e, m, n, p

13) n, o, q

14) b, d, h, k, , p

15)

Maria's cupcakes				
Various flavors	lemon	coffee	carrot	red velvet
Relative frequency	20%	40%	36%	12%

16)

Eva's breads			
Breads	Challah	Yeast	Focaccia
Relative frequency	30%	50%	20%

17)

Maximum air temperature during a month				
Temperature	33°C	31°C	29°C	27°C
Relative frequency	30%	40%	20%	10%

18)

Number of cups ordered				
Cup of coffee range	50 – 59	40 – 49	30 – 39	20 – 29
Relative frequency	20%	30%	40%	10%

19)

Various cakes	Number of days
3	7
4	6
5	6
7	11

20)

Fruits	Number of weights
Apple	4
Peaches	6
Banana	3
Pineapple	5
Melon	8

21)

Temperatures	Number of days
22°C	3
23°C	5
24°C	1
25°C	4
26°C	1

22)

Number of bottles	Number of days
100 − 149	6
150 − 199	4
200 − 249	9
250 − 299	4

23) Mode: 6, Range: 8, Mean: 6.2, Median: 6
24) Mode: 9, Range: 8, Mean: 6, Median: 6.5
25) Mode: 10, Range: 12, Mean: 8, Median: 8
26) Mode: 12, Range: 12, Mean: 9, Median: 9
27) 35
28) 15
29) 38
30) 33
31) 5
32) 6
33) 5
34) 7
35) 94
36) 70
37) 335
38) 9
39) 25
40) 11
41) 250
42) 2
43) 9
44) 9
45) 9
46) 8
47) 24
48) 54
49) 80
50) 30
51) mean= 55.2, mode= 56
52) 5
53) 16 ponies
54) mode= 12 roses and 12 lilies, median= 8.1
55) This is a statistical question.
56) This is a statistical question.
57) This is **not** a statistical question.
58) This is a statistical question.
59) This is a statistical question.
60) This is a statistical question.
61) This is **not** a statistical question.
62) This is **not** a statistical question.

63)

Packages of Timothy	Packages of Zack
1	4
2	5
3	6
4	7

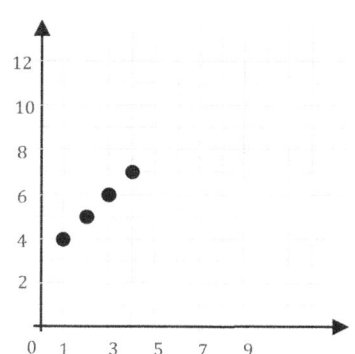

64)

Number of months	Total gloves
1	6
2	12
3	18
4	24

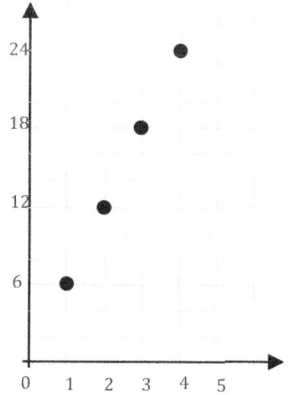

65)

Number of days	Total hours
1	2
2	4
3	6
4	8

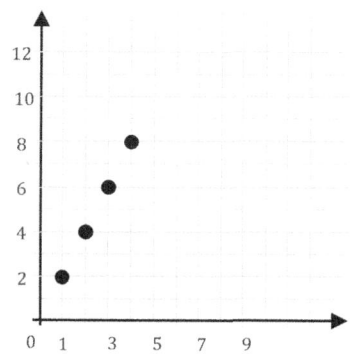

66)

Weight of watermelon	price
3	2
6	4
9	6
12	8

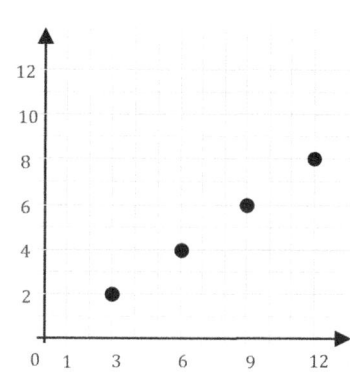

Chapter 11
Fundamentals of Computations

Math topics that you'll learn in this chapter:

- ☑ Additive and multiplicative relationships
- ☑ Properties of Addition
- ☑ Using Area Models and the Distributive Property to Multiply
- ☑ Reciprocals

Additive and multiplicative relationships

- Whenever additive identity is added to a number, it yields the original number. Likewise, when multiplicative identity gets multiplied by any number, it yields the original number.

- Additive relationships imply you must add the IDENTICAL number to any x-value to get the resultant y-value.

- Multiplicative relationships imply you must multiply any x-value times the IDENTICAL number to yield the subsequent y-value.

Examples:

Example 1. Which table shows an additive relationship?

a	
x	y
1	3
2	4
3	5
4	6

b	
x	y
1	4
2	8
3	12
4	16

Solution: Firstly, find relationships of x and y in tables. Table (a): $1 + 2 = 3$, $2 + 2 = 4$, $3 + 2 = 5$, $4 + 2 = 6$, then $x + 2 = y$. So, table (a) shows an additive relationship.

But table (b): $1 \times 4 = 4$, $2 \times 4 = 8$, $3 \times 4 = 12$, $4 \times 2 = 8$, then $x \times 4 = y$. So, table (b) shows a multiplicative relationship.

Example 2. What relationship (additive/ multiplicative) do the following equations show?

$b = 2a$ and $k = 7 + y$

Solution: Look at equations:

$k = 7 + y$: To find k add 7 to y. So, this equation shows an additive relationship.

$b = 2a$: To find b, multiply a by 2. This equation shows a multiplicative relationship.

Properties of addition

- The four properties of addition:

  - Commutative property.
  - Associative property.
  - Distributive property.
  - Additive identity property.

- In mathematics, the associative and commutative properties are laws utilized for addition and multiplication that always exist.

  - The associative property declares it's possible to re-group numbers and end up with the same answer.
  - The commutative property asserts it's possible to move numbers around and still get the same answer.

Examples:

Example 1. Which property of addition is shown in the equation below?
$$f + (a + b) = (f + a) + b$$

Solution: If add a and b (as a group), then add f to the result is equivalent to another expression that says if add f and a (as a group), then add b to the result. So, this is the associative property of addition.

Example 2. Write the equivalent of the following expression according to the commutative property of addition.
$$8 + a = ?$$

Solution: The commutative property shows that you can add numbers in any order and get the same sum. So, $8 + a = a + 8$.

Using Area Models and the Distributive Property to Multiply

- Area models are shown as rectangular diagrams or models utilized for division and multiplication problems.

  - To multiply two-digit numbers, using the area model, follow the given steps:

  - Draw a 2 × 2 grid.

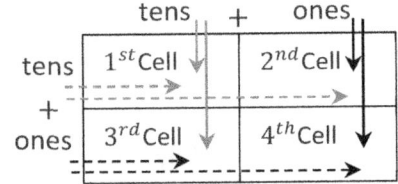

  - Write the terms of one of the multiplicands on the top of the grid.

  - On the left of the grid, write the terms of the other multiplicand.

  - Write the products of the number on the cells.

  - Finally, add all the partial products to get the final product.

$1^{st} Cell + 2^{nd} Cell + 3^{rd} Cell + 4^{th} Cell = 2 - digit$ number $\times 2 - digit$ number

Examples:

Example 1. Use the area model to multiply, $4(3a + 5)$.

Solution: 4 is the first factor with one digit. And $(3a + 5)$ is the second factor that has 2 digits. Then, draw the model. This area model shows the partial products:

Actually, use the distributive property and find the part of the model: $4 \times 3a = 12a$ and $4 \times 5 = 20$.

Now, add the partial products to find the product, $4(3a + 5) = 12a + 20$

Example 2. Use the area model to multiply, 121×25.

Solution: 121 is the first factor with three digits. And 25 is the second factor that has 2 digits. Then, draw the model. This area model shows the partial products:

Now, add the partial products to find the product:

$$121 \times 25 = 2,000 + 500 + 400 + 100 + 20 + 5$$

$$121 \times 25 = 3,025$$

Reciprocals

- A number's reciprocal is 1 divided by the number.

- Reciprocals define something which is identical on both sides. For instance, the number 5's is 1 divided by 5, thus written as $\frac{1}{5}$.

- Reciprocals additionally are a number taken to the power of -1. Therefore, $\frac{1}{7}$ is identical to 7 to the power of -1.

- A reciprocal is similarly merely shown as the reverse of a value or a number. Thus, whenever they are multiplied, they end up equal.

$$\frac{1}{2} \times \frac{2}{1} = \frac{2}{2} = 1$$

Examples:

Example 1. Write the reciprocal of $\frac{3}{15}$:

Solution: If you changed the numerator and the denominator, then the reciprocal of the numbers is obtained: $\frac{3}{15} \to \frac{15}{3} = 5$

Example 2. Write the reciprocal of 8:

Solution: First, place the whole number over the 1 as $\frac{8}{1}$. Then change the numerator and the denominator. Then, the reciprocal of the numbers is obtained: $\frac{8}{1} \to \frac{1}{8}$

Chapter 11: Practices

✎ **What relationship (additive/ multiplicative) do the following equations show?**

1) $a = 3 + b$

2) $m = 8h$

3) $y = x + 8$

4) $z = \frac{1}{2}k$

✎ **What relationship (additive/ multiplicative) do the following tables show?**

5)

x	1	2	3	4
y	5	10	15	20

6)

x	0	2	4	6
y	0	6	12	18

7)

x	0	3	6	9
y	5	8	11	14

8)

x	0	3	5	7
y	1	4	6	8

✎ **Which property of addition is shown in the equations below?**

9) $(s + t) + 5 = s + (t + 5)$

10) $5 = 5 + 0$

11) $7 + 2 = 2 + 7$

12) $5(a + b) = 5a + 5b$

13) $t + 5 + s = s + t + 5$

14) $a + c + 0 = c + a$

15) $8 + (1 + 5) = (8 + 1) + 5$

16) $2(3 + 7) = 6 + 14$

Chapter 11: Fundamentals of Computations

✎ Use the area model to multiply.

17) $5(3 + 9g + 2)$

18) $14 \times 12a$

19) $13(2x + 5y)$

20) $11(4a + 6)$

21) $40s \times 17$

22) 25×25

23) $805(1 + 5d)$

24) 115×333

✎ Write the reciprocal of each number.

25) $\frac{5}{2}$

26) -2

27) 6

28) $\frac{77}{50}$

29) -3

30) $\frac{1}{20}$

31) -4

32) $-\frac{1}{2}$

Chapter 11: Answers

1) additive

2) multiplicative

3) additive

4) multiplicative

5) multiplicative

6) multiplicative

7) additive

8) additive

9) Associative

10) Identity

11) Commutative

12) Distributive

13) Commutative

14) Identity and Commutative

15) Associative

16) Distributive

17) $25 + 45g$

	3 +	9g +	2
5	15	45g	10

18) $168a$

	$10a$ +	$2a$
10 +	$100a$	$20a$
4	$40a$	$8a$

19) $26x + 65y$

	$2x$ +	$5y$
10 +	$20x$	$50y$
3	$6x$	$15y$

20) $44a + 66$

	$4a$ +	6
10 +	$40a$	60
1	$4a$	6

21) $680s$

	10 +	7
$40s$ +	$400s$	$280s$
$0s$	$0s$	$0s$

22) 625

	20 +	5
20 +	400	100
5	100	25

23) $805 + 4,025d$

	1	+ 5d
800 +	800	4,000d
00 +	0	0
5	5	25d

24) $38,295$

	300	+ 30	+ 3
100 +	30,000	3,000	300
10 +	3,000	300	30
5	1,500	150	15

25) $\dfrac{2}{5}$

26) $-\dfrac{1}{2}$

27) $\dfrac{1}{6}$

28) $\dfrac{50}{77}$

29) $-\dfrac{1}{3}$

30) 20

31) $-\dfrac{1}{4}$

32) -2

CHAPTER 12
Operations of Fraction, Decimal, and Mixed Numbers

Math topics that you'll learn in this chapter:

- ☑ Scaling Whole Numbers by Fractions
- ☑ Using Models to Divide Whole Numbers by Unit Fractions
- ☑ Dividing Fractions by Whole Numbers in Recipes
- ☑ Using Models to Multiply Two Fractions
- ☑ Multiplying and Dividing Fractions
- ☑ Word Problem for Explaining Fractions as Division
- ☑ Word Problem of Dividing Fractions
- ☑ Multiplication and Division of Decimals by Powers of Ten
- ☑ Estimate Products of Mixed Numbers
- ☑ Scaling by Fractions and Mixed Numbers
- ☑ Multiplying Mixed Numbers
- ☑ Dividing Mixed Numbers
- ☑ Word Problem of Multiplying Mixed Numbers
- ☑ Multiplying and Dividing Decimals
- ☑ Multiplying Three Rational Numbers, and Whole Numbers

187

Scaling whole numbers by fractions

- For scaling whole numbers by fractions, we must convert the number into an upside-down format.

- If you know this concept, you can figure out if your answer is reasonable:

  • Whenever a fraction is multiplied by a fraction that is LESS THAN ONE WHOLE, its size gets scaled down.

  • Whenever a fraction is multiplied by a fraction that is LARGER THAN ONE WHOLE, its size gets scaled up.

Examples:

Example 1. Is this inequality correct? $3 \times \frac{2}{5} < 3$

Solution: Multiplying a whole number by a fraction less than 1 the answer will be less than the whole number. Since, $\frac{2}{5}$ is smaller than 1, multiplying by $\frac{2}{5}$ makes the value of the whole number smaller. Then, $3 \times \frac{2}{5} < 3$

Example 2. Which expression is greater? 7 or $7 \times \frac{9}{4}$

Solution: Multiplying a whole number by a fraction greater than 1 the answer will be greater. Since, $\frac{9}{4}$ is greater than 1, multiplying by $\frac{9}{4}$ makes the value of the whole number greater. Then, $7 \times \frac{9}{4} > 7$

Using Models to Divide Whole Numbers by Unit Fractions

- A fraction is a number with a denominator and a nominator.
- For instance, this is the whole number of 5 and a fraction of $\frac{2}{7}$
- So, you wish to solve $5 \div \frac{2}{7} = ?$
- First, place the whole number over the 1 as $\frac{5}{1}$.
- After that, flip the 5 so it becomes the denominator and the one becomes the nominator, so it appears as $\frac{1}{5}$.
- Then multiply these numbers: $5 \times \frac{7}{2} = \frac{35}{2}$

Examples:

Example 1. Divide $1 \div \frac{1}{3}$. Use the models to help you.

Solution: First, model the whole number 1. Then model $\frac{1}{3}$ and see how many fraction pieces make up 1. To make 1 it takes 3 of the fraction pieces. So, $1 \div \frac{1}{3} = 3$.

Example 2. Divide $3 \div \frac{1}{2}$. Use the models to help you.

Solution: First, model the whole number 3. Then model $\frac{1}{2}$ and see how many fraction pieces make up 3. To make 3 it takes 2 of the fraction pieces. So, $3 \div \frac{1}{2} = 6$.

Dividing fractions by whole numbers in recipes

- The first step you must do is change the whole numbers to fractions.
- Firstly put 1 for the denominator of the whole number. Next reverse the numerator and denominator.
- Then, multiply the 2 numerators. Next, multiply the 2 denominators. Lastly, simplify the fractions if you need to.

Examples:

Strawberry cake
$2\frac{1}{5}$ cups sugar
$3\frac{3}{5}$ cups flour
$\frac{3}{5}$ cup mashed strawberry
$1\frac{1}{3}$ cup milk
$\frac{1}{3}$ cup vegetable oil
$1\frac{1}{3}$ teaspoons vanilla
$\frac{3}{5}$ teaspoon cinnamon
1 teaspoon baking powder
4 eggs

Example 1. What quantity of milk would you need to make a quarter recipe?

Solution: The recipe calls for $1\frac{1}{3}$ of a cup of milk. To cut the recipe into quarters, divided $1\frac{1}{3}$ cups by 4. Write 4 as an improper fraction. And convert $1\frac{1}{3}$ as an improper fraction, too, $\frac{4}{3} \div \frac{4}{1}$. You must turn this from a division problem into a multiplication problem by multiplying by the reciprocal.

So, $\frac{4}{3} \div \frac{4}{1} = \frac{4}{3} \times \frac{1}{4} = \frac{4}{12} = \frac{1}{3}$.

You would need $\frac{1}{3}$ of a cup of milk.

Example 2. According to example 1: What quantity of strawberry would you need to make a half recipe?

Solution: The recipe calls for $\frac{3}{5}$ of a cup of mashed strawberry. To cut the recipe in a half, divide $\frac{3}{5}$ cups by 2. Write 2 as an improper fraction, $\frac{3}{5} \div \frac{2}{1}$. You must turn this from a division problem into a multiplication problem by multiplying by the reciprocal.

So, $\frac{3}{5} \div \frac{2}{1} = \frac{3}{5} \times \frac{1}{2} = \frac{3}{10}$.

You would need $\frac{3}{10}$ of a cup of mashed strawberry.

Using Models to Multiply Two Fractions

- Use area models to show a visual depiction of the product of 2 fractions.

  - Draw a rectangle. The denominator in the first factor represents how many columns to draw, and the numerator represents how many columns to shade: $\frac{1}{2}$

  - The denominator in the second factor represents how many rows to draw, and the numerator represents how many rows to shade: $\frac{1}{2} \times \frac{1}{4}$

  - The numerator for the product is the number of parts that were shaded twice. The denominator for the product is the number of total parts in the rectangle: $\frac{1}{2} \times \frac{1}{4} = \frac{1}{8}$

  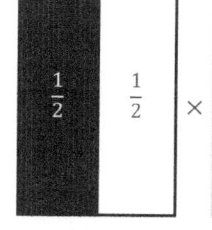 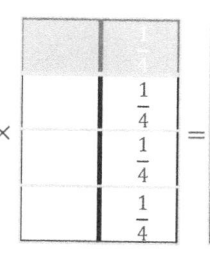 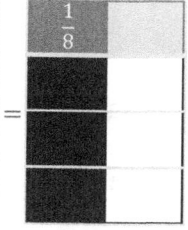

  $$\frac{1}{2} \times \frac{1}{4} = \frac{1}{8}$$

  - Simplify if necessary.

Example:

Use the model to find the product. $\frac{3}{4} \times \frac{1}{3} = ?$

Solution: The model has 4 columns and has 3 rows. So, 3 out of 4 columns are shaded, which represents the factor $\frac{3}{4}$. And 1 out of 3 rows are shaded, which represents the factor $\frac{1}{3}$. The part where the shaded columns and rows overlap represents the product: $\frac{3}{4} \times \frac{1}{3} = ?$

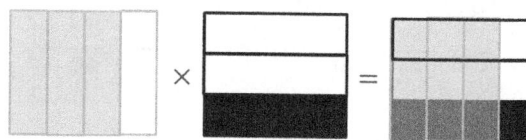

So, you can see there are 3 sections with overlap. And for the denominator, the whole model has 4 columns and 3 rows. So, there are 4 × 3 = 12 sections in total. Thus, you have 3 sections with an overlap out of 12 sections in total, $\frac{3}{12}$. Then, simplify the product. Therefore, $\frac{3}{4} \times \frac{1}{3} = \frac{3}{12} = \frac{1}{4}$

Multiplying and Dividing Fractions

- **Multiplying fractions:** multiply the top numbers and multiply the bottom numbers. Simplify if necessary. $\frac{a}{b} \times \frac{c}{d} = \frac{a \times c}{b \times d}$

- **Dividing fractions:** Keep, Change, Flip

- Keep the first fraction, change the division sign to multiplication, and flip the numerator and denominator of the second fraction. Then, solve!

$$\frac{a}{b} \div \frac{c}{d} = \frac{a}{b} \times \frac{d}{c} = \frac{a \times d}{b \times c}$$

Examples:

Example 1. Multiply. $\frac{2}{3} \times \frac{3}{5} =$

Solution: Multiply the top numbers and multiply the bottom numbers.
$\frac{2}{3} \times \frac{3}{5} = \frac{2 \times 3}{3 \times 5} = \frac{6}{15}$, now, simplify: $\frac{6}{15} = \frac{6 \div 3}{15 \div 3} = \frac{2}{5}$

Example 2. Solve. $\frac{3}{4} \div \frac{2}{5} =$

Solution: Keep the first fraction, change the division sign to multiplication, and flip the numerator and denominator of the second fraction.
Then: $\frac{3}{4} \div \frac{2}{5} = \frac{3}{4} \times \frac{5}{2} = \frac{3 \times 5}{4 \times 2} = \frac{15}{8}$

Example 3. Calculate. $\frac{4}{5} \times \frac{3}{4} =$

Solution: Multiply the top numbers and multiply the bottom numbers.
$\frac{4}{5} \times \frac{3}{4} = \frac{4 \times 3}{5 \times 4} = \frac{12}{20}$, simplify: $\frac{12}{20} = \frac{12 \div 4}{20 \div 4} = \frac{3}{5}$

Example 4. Solve. $\frac{5}{6} \div \frac{3}{7} =$

Solution: Keep the first fraction, change the division sign to multiplication, and flip the numerator and denominator of the second fraction.
Then: $\frac{5}{6} \div \frac{3}{7} = \frac{5}{6} \times \frac{7}{3} = \frac{5 \times 7}{6 \times 3} = \frac{35}{18}$

Word Problem for Explaining Fractions as Division

- Here, you learn the simplest method of dividing fractions. You must follow 3 easy steps:
- Reverse the divisor into a reciprocal.
- Then the division sign has to be changed to a multiplication sign.
- Then multiply.

Examples:

Example 1. Carmen sells pieces of cakes at the confectionery market. To make the pieces, she cuts a big 3 −pound block of cake into 19 pieces. How much does each piece of cake weigh? Write your answer as a proper fraction or mixed number.

Solution: Start by listing the information:

The block of cake weighs 3 pounds.

Carmen cuts the block of cake into 19 equal pieces.

There are 3 pounds of a cake divided into 19 pieces $3 \div 19 = \frac{3}{19}$. So, each piece of cake weighs $\frac{3}{19}$ pounds.

Example 2. Zack is making soup for his whole family. He wants to make 20 bowls using 8 carrots. How many carrots will be in each bowl? Write as a proper fraction or mixed number.

Solution: The given information says, used 8 carrots for 20 bowls of soup. Then, $8 \div 20 = \frac{8}{20} = \frac{2}{5}$. So, there will be $\frac{2}{5}$ carrots in each bowl.

Word Problem of Dividing Fractions

- Step 1: Use keywords and phrases to identify the problem. In division, we look for phrases like "go into" or "get out of" that ask how much or how many of something can fit into something else.

- Step 2: When dividing fractions, the quickest and easiest way to solve is to invert the second fraction and multiply instead of dividing.

- Step 3: Just multiply the numerators across and multiply the denominators across. If your problem involves mixed numbers, you will want to convert them to improper fractions first.

- Step 4: Simplify (reduce) the fraction if possible.

Examples:

Example 1. Jussie uses $\frac{3}{4}$ of a roll of wrapping paper to warp three equal-sized presents. What fraction of the roll wrapping paper does each present use?

Solution: Divide the total amount of used wrapping paper rolls by the number of presents, $\frac{3}{4} \div 3$. And write 3 as an improper fraction, $\frac{3}{4} \div \frac{3}{1}$. Then, turn this from a division problem into a multiplication problem by multiplying by the reciprocal. And simplify product:

$$\frac{3}{4} \times \frac{1}{3} = \frac{3 \times 1}{4 \times 3} = \frac{3}{12} = \frac{1}{4}$$

Example 2. Karolina uses $\frac{4}{5}$ of a jar of peach jam to make six muffins. What fraction of the jar of peach jam does each muffin contain?

Solution: Divide the total amount of a used peach jam by the number of muffins, $\frac{4}{5} \div 6$. And write 6 as an improper fraction, $\frac{4}{5} \div \frac{6}{1}$. Then, turn this from a division problem into a multiplication problem by multiplying by the reciprocal. And simplify product:

$$\frac{4}{5} \times \frac{1}{6} = \frac{4 \times 1}{5 \times 6} = \frac{4}{30} = \frac{2}{15}$$

Multiplication and Division of Decimals by Powers of Ten

- In order to multiply using the power of 10, merely move the decimal toward the right of the identical number of spaces as the exponent or as the number of zeros.

- Determining ten times as many are identical to multiplying by 10 (if you are using positive numbers); in order to multiply any whole number via 10, put a zero after the final digit in this number.

- In order to divide any multiple of 10 by 10, take out the last zero digit (in the ones place) from the number.

- Example: In order to divide via the power of 10, merely move its decimal over to the left-hand side with the identical number of spaces as the exponent or as the number of zeros.

Examples:

Example 1. Divide: $8.8 \div 10 = ?$

Solution: First, count the zeros in 10. And there is 1 zero in 10. Then, move the decimal point 1 place to the left in 8.8. So, $8.8 \rightarrow 0.88$

$$8.8 \div 10 = 0.88$$

Example 2. Multiply: $100 \times 0.853 = ?$

Solution: First, count the zeros in 100. And there are 2 zeros in 100. Then, move the decimal point 2 places to the right in 0.853. So, $0.853 \rightarrow 85.3$.

$$100 \times 0.853 = 85.3$$

Estimate Products of Mixed Numbers

- Mixed numbers are whole numbers, along with a proper fraction represented together. It usually signifies a number in between any 2 whole numbers.

- To approximate the product, you must round a mixed number to the closest whole number, after that you multiply. The resulting product is an estimate.

Examples:

Example 1. Estimate the result by rounding each number to the nearest whole number. $12\frac{3}{5} \times 19\frac{3}{4} = ?$

Solution: $12\frac{3}{5}$ rounded to the nearest whole number is 13. $19\frac{3}{4}$ rounded to the nearest whole number is 20.

Then: $13 \times 20 = 260$

Example 2. Estimate the multiplication by rounding the first factor to the nearest whole number and the second factor to the nearest hundred. $9 \times 211\frac{1}{7} = ?$

Solution: 9 rounded to the nearest ten is 10. $211\frac{1}{7}$ rounded to the nearest one is 200.

Then: $10 \times 200 = 2{,}000$

Scaling by Fractions and Mixed Numbers

- Rules for scaling:

    • Whenever a fraction gets multiplied by a number SMALLER THAN ONE WHOLE, its size gets scaled down.

    • Whenever a fraction is multiplied via a number LARGER THAN ONE WHOLE, its size gets scaled up.

- When you know this concept, you can find out if your answer is reasonable.

Examples:

Example 1. Which expression is greater or least? $3 \times 4\frac{2}{5}$ ☐ 12

Solution: First, calculate: $3 \times 4\frac{2}{5} = 3 \times \frac{22}{5} = \frac{66}{5} = 13\frac{1}{5}$. According to, 13 is greater than 12. Then, $3 \times 4\frac{2}{5}$ is greater than 12.

Example 2. Which expression is greater or least? $2 \times 5\frac{1}{8}$ ☐ 5

Solution: First, calculate: $2 \times 5\frac{1}{8} = 2 \times \frac{41}{8} = \frac{82}{8} = 10\frac{2}{8}$. According to, 10 is greater than 5. Then, $2 \times 5\frac{1}{8}$ is greater than 5.

Example 3. Which expression is greater or least? $7 \times 3\frac{3}{2}$ ☐ 10

Solution: First, calculate: $7 \times 3\frac{3}{2} = 7 \times \frac{9}{2} = \frac{63}{2} = 31\frac{1}{2}$. According to, 31 is greater than 10. Then, $7 \times 3\frac{3}{2}$ is greater than 10.

Multiplying Mixed Numbers

- Use the following steps for multiplying mixed numbers:
- Convert the mixed numbers into fractions. $a\frac{c}{b} = a + \frac{c}{b} = \frac{ab+c}{b}$
- Multiply fractions. $\frac{a}{b} \times \frac{c}{d} = \frac{a \times c}{b \times d}$
- Write your answer in lowest terms.
- If the answer is an improper fraction (numerator is bigger than denominator), convert it into a mixed number.

Examples:

Example 1. Multiply. $4\frac{1}{2} \times 2\frac{2}{5} =$

Solution: Convert mixed numbers into fractions, $4\frac{1}{2} = \frac{4 \times 2 + 1}{2} = \frac{9}{2}$ and $2\frac{2}{5} = \frac{2 \times 5 + 2}{5} = \frac{12}{5}$. Apply the fractions rule for multiplication: $\frac{9}{2} \times \frac{12}{5} = \frac{9 \times 12}{2 \times 5} = \frac{108}{10} = \frac{54}{5}$

The answer is an improper fraction. Convert it into a mixed number. $\frac{54}{5} = 10\frac{4}{5}$

Example 2. Multiply. $3\frac{2}{3} \times 2\frac{5}{6} =$

Solution: Converting mixed numbers into fractions, $3\frac{2}{3} \times 2\frac{5}{6} = \frac{11}{3} \times \frac{17}{6}$

Apply the fractions rule for multiplication: $\frac{11}{3} \times \frac{17}{6} = \frac{11 \times 17}{3 \times 6} = \frac{187}{18} = 10\frac{7}{18}$

Example 3. Find the product. $5\frac{1}{4} \times 3\frac{3}{8} =$

Solution: Convert mixed numbers to fractions: $5\frac{1}{4} = \frac{21}{4}$ and $3\frac{3}{8} = \frac{27}{8}$. Multiply two fractions:

$\frac{21}{4} \times \frac{27}{8} = \frac{21 \times 27}{4 \times 8} = \frac{567}{32} = 17\frac{23}{32}$

Dividing Mixed Numbers

- Use the following steps for dividing mixed numbers:
- Convert the mixed numbers into fractions. $a\frac{c}{b} = a + \frac{c}{b} = \frac{ab+c}{b}$
- Divide fractions: Keep, Change, Flip: Keep the first fraction, change the division sign to multiplication, and flip the numerator and denominator of the second fraction. Then, solve! $\frac{a}{b} \div \frac{c}{d} = \frac{a}{b} \times \frac{d}{c} = \frac{a \times d}{b \times c}$
- Write your answer in lowest terms.
- If the answer is an improper fraction (numerator is bigger than denominator), convert it into a mixed number.

Examples:

Example 1. Solve. $2\frac{1}{3} \div 1\frac{1}{2}$

Solution: Convert mixed numbers into fractions: $2\frac{1}{3} = \frac{2 \times 3 + 1}{3} = \frac{7}{3}$ and $1\frac{1}{2} = \frac{1 \times 2 + 1}{2} = \frac{3}{2}$
Keep, Change, Flip: $\frac{7}{3} \div \frac{3}{2} = \frac{7}{3} \times \frac{2}{3} = \frac{7 \times 2}{3 \times 3} = \frac{14}{9}$. The answer is an improper fraction. Convert it into a mixed number: $\frac{14}{9} = 1\frac{5}{9}$

Example 2. Solve. $3\frac{3}{4} \div 2\frac{2}{5}$

Solution: Convert mixed numbers to fractions, then solve:
$3\frac{3}{4} \div 2\frac{2}{5} = \frac{15}{4} \div \frac{12}{5} = \frac{15}{4} \times \frac{5}{12} = \frac{75}{48} = 1\frac{9}{16}$

Example 3. Solve. $2\frac{4}{5} \div 1\frac{2}{3}$

Solution: Converting mixed numbers to fractions: $2\frac{4}{5} \div 1\frac{2}{3} = \frac{14}{5} \div \frac{5}{3}$
Keep, Change, Flip: $\frac{14}{5} \div \frac{5}{3} = \frac{14}{5} \times \frac{3}{5} = \frac{14 \times 3}{5 \times 5} = \frac{42}{25} = 1\frac{17}{25}$

Word Problem of Multiplying Mixed Numbers

- Mixed numbers have a whole number as well as a fraction.
- For multiplying mixed numbers:
  - Write down the number as an improper fraction.
  - Write mixed numbers as an improper fraction.
- Multiply the numerators, then multiply the denominators.
- Simplify the product.

Examples:

Example 1. Jessi collected $\frac{1}{4}$ of a bin of glass bottles to recycle. Luci collected $5\frac{1}{2}$ times as many bins as Jessi. How many bins of bottles did Luci collect? Simplify your answer and write it as a fraction or as a whole or mixed number.

Solution: Since Luci collected $5\frac{1}{2}$ times $\frac{1}{4}$ of a bin of bottles, multiply $5\frac{1}{2}$ in $\frac{1}{4}$: $5\frac{1}{2} \times \frac{1}{4} =?$ And write $5\frac{1}{2}$ as an improper fraction, $5\frac{1}{2} = \frac{(5\times 2)+1}{2} = \frac{11}{2}$. Then, multiply the numerators and the denominators, $\frac{11}{2} \times \frac{1}{4} = \frac{11}{8}$. Now, simplify and write as a mixed number: $\frac{11}{8} = 1\frac{3}{8}$

Luci collected $1\frac{3}{8}$ bins of buttles.

Example 2. Sara planted an apple tree and an orange tree. The apple tree is 6 feet tall. The orange tree is $4\frac{3}{4}$ times as tall as the apple tree. How tall is Sara's orange tree?

Solution: Since the apple tree is $4\frac{3}{4}$ times 6 feet tall. Multiply $4\frac{3}{4}$ in 6: $4\frac{3}{4} \times 6 =$?, $4\frac{3}{4} = \frac{(4\times 4)+3}{4} = \frac{19}{4}$. And write 6 as an improper fraction too. Then, multiply the numerators and the denominators, $\frac{19}{4} \times \frac{6}{1} = \frac{114}{4}$. Now, simplify and write as a mixed number: $\frac{57}{2} = 28\frac{1}{2}$

The apple tree is $28\frac{1}{2}$ feet tall.

Multiplying and Dividing Decimals

For multiplying decimals:

- Ignore the decimal point and set up and multiply the numbers as you do with whole numbers.
- Count the total number of decimal places in both of the factors.
- Place the decimal point in the product.

For dividing decimals:

- If the divisor is not a whole number, move the decimal point to the right to make it a whole number. Do the same for the dividend.
- Divide similar to whole numbers.

Examples:

Example 1. Find the product. $0.65 \times 0.24 =$

Solution: Set up and multiply the numbers as you do with whole numbers. Line up the numbers: $\begin{array}{r} 65 \\ \times 24 \end{array}$ → Start with the ones place then continue with other digits → $\dfrac{\begin{array}{r} 65 \\ \times 24 \end{array}}{1,560}$. Count the total number of decimal places in both of the factors. There are four decimal's digits. (two for each factor 0.65 and 0.24) Then: $0.65 \times 0.24 = 0.1560 = 0.156$

Example 2. Find the quotient. $1.20 \div 0.4 =$

Solution: The divisor is not a whole number. Multiply it by 10 to get 4: → $0.4 \times 10 = 4$

Do the same for the dividend to get 12. → $1.20 \times 10 = 12$

Now, divide $12 \div 4 = 3$. The answer is 3.

Multiplying Three Rational Numbers, and Whole Numbers

- Write down the mixed numbers as well as the whole numbers in the form of improper fractions.
- Afterwards; multiply the numerators as well as multiply the denominators.
- Simplify the product.

Examples:

Example 1. Multiply $2\frac{1}{4} \times 3\frac{1}{2} \times 4 = ?$

Solution: Converting mixed numbers to fractions, $2\frac{1}{4} = \frac{9}{4}$ and $3\frac{1}{2} = \frac{7}{2}$. And write 4 as an improper fraction, $\frac{4}{1}$. Then, apply the fractions formula for multiplication. First, multiply 1st factor by 2nd factor. After that multiply the new and 3rd factor: $\frac{9}{4} \times \frac{7}{2} \times \frac{4}{1} = \frac{63}{8} \times \frac{4}{1} = \frac{252}{8}$.

Simplify the product: $\frac{252}{8} = \frac{63}{2} = 31\frac{1}{2}$

Example 2. Multiply $5\frac{2}{3} \times 3 \times \frac{3}{4} = ?$

Solution: Converting mixed numbers to fractions, $5\frac{2}{3} = \frac{17}{3}$. And write 3 as an improper fraction, $\frac{3}{1}$. Then, apply the fractions formula for multiplication. First, multiply 1st factor by 2nd factor. After that multiply the new and 3rd factor: $\frac{17}{3} \times \frac{3}{1} \times \frac{3}{4} = \frac{51}{3} \times \frac{3}{4} = \frac{153}{12}$.

Simplify the product: $\frac{153}{12} = \frac{51}{4} = 12\frac{3}{4}$

Chapter 12: Practices

✎ **Which expression is greater or least?**

1) $4 \square 4 \times \frac{7}{4}$

2) $2 \square 2 \times \frac{1}{15}$

3) $8 \square 8 \times \frac{8}{3}$

4) $3 \square 3 \times \frac{3}{5}$

5) $2 \square 5 \times \frac{2}{3}$

6) $4 \square 2 \times \frac{7}{4}$

7) $6 \square 6 \times \frac{7}{2}$

8) $9 \square 5 \times \frac{10}{6}$

✎ **Divide. Use the models to help you.**

9) $2 \div \frac{1}{2}$

10) $1 \div \frac{2}{5}$

11) $4 \div \frac{2}{3}$

12) $1 \div \frac{1}{6}$

13) $2 \div \frac{3}{5}$

14) $1 \div \frac{4}{7}$

15) $3 \div \frac{1}{3}$

16) $1 \div \frac{1}{4}$

✎ **According to the recipes solve the word problems.**

17) What quantity of **popcorn** would you need to make a third of the original sweet and salty snack mix recipe?

18) What quantity of **pretzels** would you need to make a half sweet and salty snack mix recipe?

19) What quantity of **chocolate chips** would you need to make a fifth of the original sweet and salty snack mix recipe?

Sweet and salty snack mix
$\frac{1}{2}$ cup popcorn
$4\frac{3}{5}$ cups pretzels
$\frac{1}{3}$ cup peanuts
2 cups chocolate chips
$\frac{2}{5}$ cup gumdrops

20) What quantity of **gumdrops** would you need to make a quarter sweet and salty snack mix recipe?

21) What quantity of **cherries** would you need to make a third of the original very cherry pie recipe?

22) What quantity of **flour** would you need to make a half very cherry pie recipe?

23) What quantity of **pie crust** would you need to make a half very cherry pie recipe?

24) What quantity of **sugar** would you need to make a quarter very cherry pie recipe?

Very cherry pie
5 cups cherries
$\frac{2}{3}$ cup sugar
$\frac{1}{4}$ cup flour
$2\frac{1}{3}$ teaspoons vanilla
$\frac{3}{4}$ teaspoon cinnamon
2 pie crust

✎ Write the multiplication expression and solve.

25)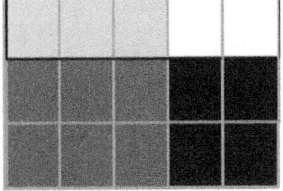

26)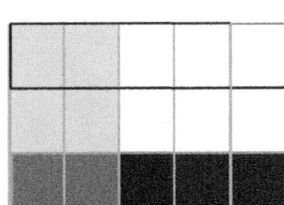

27)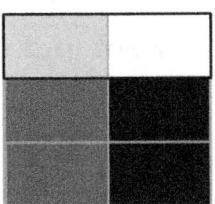

28)

✎ Multiply by model.

29) $\frac{5}{6} \times \frac{1}{3} = ?$

30) $\frac{1}{4} \times \frac{1}{2} = ?$

31) $\frac{1}{5} \times \frac{3}{4} = ?$

32) $\frac{1}{3} \times \frac{1}{3} = ?$

Chapter 12: Operations of Fraction, Decimal, and Mixed Numbers

✏ Find the products or quotients.

33) $\frac{2}{9} \div \frac{4}{3} =$

34) $\frac{14}{5} \div \frac{28}{35} =$

35) $\frac{9}{25} \times \frac{5}{27} =$

36) $\frac{65}{72} \times \frac{12}{15} =$

✏ Solve.

37) In a fish market, there are 9 gallons of water in the main tank. The water of this tank is shared between sixteen fish tanks. What fraction of a gallon of water is shared in each tank?

38) Adams shares his 15 − pack of football cards with his four friends. What fraction of the pack of football cards does each friend receive?

39) Luci uses 7 laboratory tubes to do 25 tests. What fraction of tests have been performed with each tube?

40) Sara planted 4 of a packet of orchid flower seeds in eighteen equal rows. What fraction of the packet of orchid flower seeds does each row contain?

✏ Solve the word problems. And simplify your answer and write it as a fraction or as a whole or mixed number.

41) Workmen used $\frac{3}{4}$ of the paving pallet to pave the inner path of the park. They used $\frac{1}{8}$ of a pallet for each step. How many steps did they build?

42) A factory uses $\frac{2}{5}$ of a barrel of oatmeal in each batch of biscuits. The factory used $\frac{1}{10}$ of a barrel of oatmeal yesterday. How many batches of biscuits did the factory make?

43) Martha bought some potatoes and $\frac{1}{2}$ of a gallon of oil to fry the potatoes. She used $\frac{1}{18}$ gallon of oil per kilogram of potatoes. In the end, all the purchased oil is used up. How many kilograms of potatoes did Martha buy?

44) A restaurant put a bottle of pepper sauce at each table. They divided $\frac{1}{4}$ of a kilogram of pepper sauce evenly to put $\frac{1}{28}$ of a kilogram in each dish. How many bottled peppers sauce did they fill?

✎ Multiply.

45) $0.98 \times 1000 =$

46) $0.5 \times 10 =$

47) $7.5 \times 100 =$

48) $100 \times 1.83 =$

✎ Divide.

49) $6.1 \div 10 =$

50) $75.5 \div 100 =$

51) $1.4 \div 100 =$

52) $35.2 \div 1000 =$

✎ Estimate the multiplication by rounding the first factor to the nearest whole number and the second factor to the nearest ten.

53) $3\frac{3}{5} \times 51\frac{1}{5} = ?$

54) $9\frac{5}{7} \times 19\frac{1}{8} = ?$

55) $2\frac{8}{10} \times 38\frac{1}{5} = ?$

56) $8\frac{1}{9} \times 43\frac{1}{2} = ?$

Estimate the multiplication by rounding each number to the nearest whole number.

57) $11\frac{1}{2} \times 45\frac{1}{4} = ?$

58) $1\frac{1}{5} \times 14\frac{7}{8} = ?$

59) $21\frac{1}{25} \times 4\frac{3}{4} = ?$

60) $\frac{5}{8} \times 2\frac{6}{10} = ?$

 Which expression is greater or least?

61) $4 \; \square \; 4 \times 3\frac{1}{2}$

62) $4 \; \square \; 2 \times 2\frac{1}{5}$

63) $9 \; \square \; 8 \times 1\frac{2}{4}$

64) $6 \; \square \; 3 \times 1\frac{3}{9}$

65) $9 \; \square \; 4 \times 1\frac{2}{3}$

66) $4 \; \square \; 3 \times 1\frac{1}{10}$

67) $6 \; \square \; 6 \times \frac{1}{2}$

68) $6 \; \square \; 5 \times 1\frac{1}{6}$

Find the products.

69) $1\frac{1}{2} \times 2\frac{3}{7} =$

70) $1\frac{3}{4} \times 1\frac{3}{5} =$

71) $4\frac{1}{2} \times 1\frac{5}{6} =$

72) $1\frac{2}{7} \times 3\frac{1}{5} =$

73) $2\frac{1}{5} \times 5\frac{1}{2} =$

74) $2\frac{1}{2} \times 4\frac{4}{5} =$

75) $3\frac{1}{5} \times 4\frac{1}{2} =$

76) $4\frac{9}{10} \times 4\frac{1}{2} =$

Solve.

77) $1\frac{1}{3} \div 1\frac{2}{3} =$

78) $2\frac{1}{4} \div 1\frac{1}{2} =$

79) $5\frac{1}{3} \div 3\frac{1}{2} =$

80) $3\frac{2}{7} \div 1\frac{1}{8} =$

81) $4\frac{1}{5} \div 2\frac{2}{3} =$

82) $1\frac{2}{3} \div 1\frac{3}{8} =$

83) $4\frac{1}{2} \div 2\frac{2}{3} =$

84) $1\frac{2}{11} \div 1\frac{1}{8} =$

✎ **Solve, simplify your answer and write it as a fraction or as a whole or mixed number.**

85) Kevin collected $2\frac{1}{3}$ pounds of his notebooks for the recycling drive. John collected $3\frac{1}{4}$ times as many notebooks as Kevin. How many pounds of notebooks did John collect?

86) A house is $14\frac{1}{2}$ yards wide. Its length is $3\frac{2}{3}$ times as long as it is wide. How long is the length house?

87) Last weekend, Ciara spent $2\frac{1}{5}$ hours watching movies. Bridgette watched movies for 2 times as many hours as Ciara did. How many hours did Bridgette spend watching movies?

88) Daniel owns $7\frac{3}{2}$ acres of farmland. He grows corn on $\frac{1}{5}$ of the land. On how many acres of land does Daniel grow corn?

✎ **Find the product or quotient.**

89) 3.3 × 0.2 =

90) 2.4 ÷ 0.3 =

91) 8.1 × 1.4 =

92) 4.8 ÷ 0.2 =

93) 4.1 × 0.3 =

94) 8.6 ÷ 0.2 =

95) 9.9 × 0.8 =

96) 1.84 ÷ 0.2 =

97) 2.1 × 8.4 =

98) 1.6 × 4.5 =

99) 9.2 × 3.1 =

100) 36.6 ÷ 1.6 =

101) 1.91 × 5.2 =

102) 3.65 × 1.4 =

103) 24.82 ÷ 0.4 =

104) 12.4 × 4.20 =

Multiply, simplify your answer and write it as a fraction or as a whole or mixed number.

105) $1\frac{1}{2} \times 2 \times \frac{1}{4} =$

106) $4 \times \frac{2}{5} \times 2\frac{1}{2} =$

107) $\frac{3}{5} \times 1\frac{5}{7} \times 0 =$

108) $7 \times 3\frac{2}{7} \times 2\frac{1}{5} =$

109) $4\frac{2}{3} \times \frac{1}{7} \times \frac{4}{5} =$

110) $19\frac{1}{5} \times 4\frac{3}{8} \times \frac{3}{4} =$

111) $3\frac{5}{8} \times 2\frac{5}{9} \times 8 =$

112) $5\frac{1}{5} \times 3\frac{3}{4} \times 2\frac{1}{3} =$

Chapter 12: Answers

1) $4 < 4 \times \frac{7}{4}$
2) $2 > 2 \times \frac{1}{15}$
3) $8 < 8 \times \frac{8}{3}$
4) $3 > 3 \times \frac{3}{5}$
5) $2 < 5 \times \frac{2}{3}$
6) $4 > 2 \times \frac{7}{4}$
7) $6 < 6 \times \frac{7}{2}$
8) $9 > 5 \times \frac{10}{6}$

9) 4

13) $\frac{10}{3}$

10) $\frac{5}{2}$

14) $\frac{7}{4}$

11) 6

15) 9

12) 6

16) 4

17) $\frac{1}{6}$
18) $2\frac{3}{10}$
19) $\frac{2}{5}$
20) $\frac{1}{10}$

21) $1\frac{2}{3}$
22) $\frac{1}{8}$
23) 1
24) $\frac{1}{6}$

25) $\frac{3}{5} \times \frac{2}{3} = \frac{6}{15}$
26) $\frac{2}{5} \times \frac{1}{3} = \frac{2}{15}$
27) $\frac{1}{2} \times \frac{2}{3} = \frac{2}{6} = \frac{1}{3}$
28) $\frac{1}{2} \times \frac{2}{5} = \frac{2}{10} = \frac{1}{5}$

29) $\frac{5}{18}$ 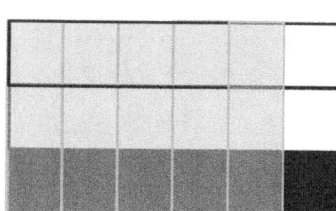 30) $\frac{1}{8}$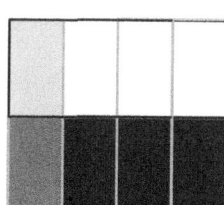

31) $\frac{3}{20}$  32) $\frac{1}{9}$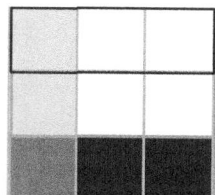

33) $\frac{1}{6}$

34) $\frac{7}{2} = 3\frac{1}{2}$

35) $\frac{1}{15}$

36) $\frac{13}{18}$

37) $\frac{9}{16}$

38) $3\frac{3}{4}$

39) $3\frac{4}{7}$

40) $\frac{2}{9}$

41) 6

42) 4

43) 9

44) 7

45) 980

46) 5

47) 750

48) 183

49) 0.61

50) 0.755

51) 0.014

52) 0.0352

53) $4 \times 50 = 200$

54) $10 \times 20 = 200$

55) $3 \times 40 = 120$

56) $8 \times 40 = 160$

57) $12 \times 45 = 540$

58) $1 \times 15 = 15$

59) $21 \times 5 = 105$

60) $1 \times 3 = 3$

61) $4 < 4 \times 3\frac{1}{2}$

62) $4 < 2 \times 2\frac{1}{5}$

63) $9 < 8 \times 1\frac{2}{4}$

64) $6 > 3 \times 1\frac{3}{9}$

65) $9 > 4 \times 1\frac{2}{3}$

66) $4 > 3 \times 1\frac{1}{10}$

67) $6 > 6 \times \frac{1}{2}$

68) $6 > 5 \times 1\frac{1}{6}$

69) $3\frac{9}{14}$

70) $2\frac{4}{5}$

71) $8\frac{1}{4}$

72) $4\frac{4}{35}$

73) $12\frac{1}{10}$

74) 12

75) $14\frac{2}{5}$

76) $22\frac{1}{20}$

77) $\frac{4}{5}$

78) $1\frac{1}{2}$

79) $1\frac{11}{21}$

80) $2\frac{58}{63}$

81) $1\frac{23}{40}$

82) $1\frac{7}{33}$

83) $1\frac{11}{16}$

84) $1\frac{5}{99}$

85) $7\frac{7}{12}$

86) $53\frac{1}{6}$

87) $4\frac{2}{5}$

88) $1\frac{7}{10}$

89) 0.66

90) 8

91) 11.34

92) 24

93) 1.23

94) 43

95) 7.92

96) 9.2

97) 17.64

98) 7.2

99) 28.52

100) 22.875

101) 9.932

102) 5.11

103) 62.05

104) 52.08

105) $\frac{3}{4}$

106) 4

107) 0

108) $50\frac{3}{5}$

109) $\frac{8}{15}$

110) 63

111) $74\frac{1}{9}$

112) $45\frac{1}{2}$

Chapter 13 Fraction, Decimals and Mixed Numbers

Math topics that you'll learn in this chapter:

- ☑ Using Number Lines to Represent Fractions
- ☑ Using Strip Diagrams to Represent Fractions
- ☑ Fractions Word Problems
- ☑ Word Problems Involving Fractions of a Group
- ☑ Simplifying Fractions
- ☑ Using Number Lines to Present Decimal
- ☑ Repeating Decimals
- ☑ Convert Between Fractions and Decimals
- ☑ Unit Prices with Decimals and Fractions
- ☑ Convert Between Decimals and Mixed Numbers
- ☑ Convert Between Improper Fractions and Mixed Numbers
- ☑ Order of Decimals, Mixed Numbers and Fractions

Using Number Lines to Represent Fractions

- Fractions are part of the whole. They have two parts: a numerator and a denominator.

  • A numerator is the number that is on top.

  • A denominator is a number that is on the bottom.

- For instance, with $\frac{1}{3}$, 1 is a numerator, and 3 is a denominator. So, its denominator is 3 which means the unit length in between 2 numbers get divided into three identical parts. $\frac{1}{3}$ signifies one part out of three. Therefore, it's marked on a number line at $\frac{1}{3}$ and this number sits between 0 and 1.

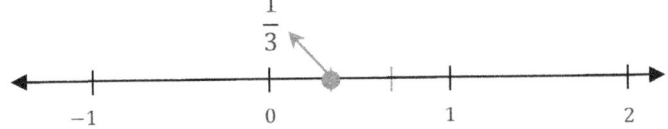

Its denominator is 3 which means the unit length in between 2 numbers get divided into three identical parts.

Examples:

Example 1. Graph $\frac{3}{4}$ on the number line.

Solution: Divide the distance between 0 and 1 by 4 (the denominator). Then jump to the third part (the numerator).

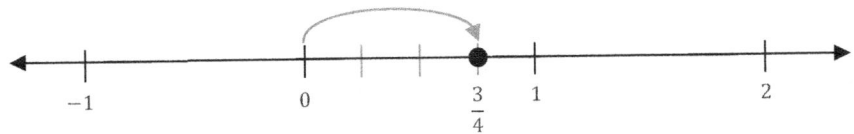

Example 2. Graph $\frac{6}{2}$ on the number line.

Solution: Divide the distance between positive numbers by 2 (the denominator). Then jump to the sixth part (the numerator).

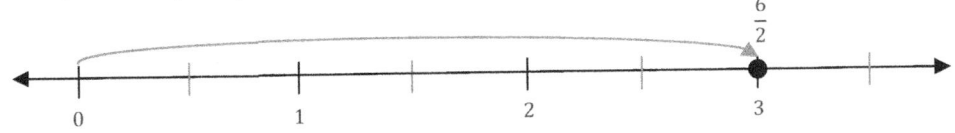

Using Strip Diagrams to Represent Fractions

- It's a rectangular model utilized to represent numerical relationships. It can be utilized to show fractions or solve problems that involve operations. Additional names for it consist of bar model, length model, or fraction strip.

- They're intended to be utilized as a method of representing relationships so one has a simpler time in deciding what operation(s) to utilize.

One whole	1
One half	$\frac{1}{2}$
One third	$\frac{1}{3}$
One quarter	$\frac{1}{4}$
One fifth	$\frac{1}{5}$

Examples:

Example 1. Shade 1 part of the fraction bar and write what fraction it represents.

Solution: First, count parts of the strip model, it is 4. And each part is $\frac{1}{4}$ of the whole. So, 1 part of the fraction is $\frac{1}{4}$. And draw that.

Example 2. Shade 4 part of the fraction bar and write what fraction it represents.

Solution: First, count parts of the strip model, it is 5. And each part is $\frac{1}{5}$ of the whole. So, 4 parts of the fraction are $\frac{4}{5}$. And draw that.

Fractions Word Problems

- The fraction problem-solving consist of a few sentences describing a real-life scenario where a mathematical calculation of fraction formulas is used to solve a problem.
- Some of the word problems on fractions that uses fraction formula are listed below:
- Word problems on simplification of fractions.
- Word problems on addition and subtraction of fractions.
- Word problems on multiplication of fractions.
- Word problems on dividing fractions.
- Word problems on fractions, percentages, and decimals.
- Word problems on simplification of fractions.

Examples:

Example 1. Alice's sushi recipe calls for $\frac{2}{5}$ of a cup of rice. How much rice would Alice use to make 5 batches of sushi? Write your answer as a fraction or as a whole or mixed number.

Solution: Multiply 5 batches in $\frac{2}{5}$ cups of rice: $5 \times \frac{2}{5} = \frac{5}{1} \times \frac{2}{5} = \frac{5 \times 2}{1 \times 5} = \frac{10}{5}$

Then, simplify the product: $\frac{10}{5} = 2$. Alice would use 2 cups of rice.

Example 2. Kelly has 7 candy bars. She wants to share them with 3 brothers. How much will each get?

Solution: Divide 7 candy bars by $3 + her = 4$:

$$7 \div 4 = \frac{7}{1} \div \frac{4}{1} = \frac{7}{1} \times \frac{1}{4} = \frac{7 \times 1}{1 \times 4} = \frac{7}{4}$$

Then, simplify the product: $\frac{7}{4} = 1\frac{3}{4}$. They get $1\frac{3}{4}$ candy bars each.

Word Problems Involving Fractions of a Group

- The number on top (numerator) results from the number of items desired. The number on the bottom (denominator) results from the total amount of items in a group.

Examples:

Example 1. There were 15 butterflies in the garden. 10 flew away. What fraction of the butterflies flew away? Write the fraction in the lowest terms.

Solution: Since 10 out of 15 flew away. Then, $\frac{10}{15}$ flew away. To write the fraction in the lowest terms, divide both the numerator and denominator by 5.

$$\frac{10 \div 5}{15 \div 5} = \frac{2}{3}$$

Example 2. Eli and her sister went for a walk. They saw 12 ducks along the way. 3 of the ducks they saw were white. What fraction of the ducks were white? Write the fraction in the lowest terms.

Solution: Since 3 out of 12 ducks were white. Then, $\frac{3}{12}$ of the ducks were white. To write the fraction in the lowest terms, divide both the numerator and denominator by 3.

$$\frac{3 \div 3}{12 \div 3} = \frac{1}{4}$$

Example 3. There are 16 books in Sarah's library. 8 of the books are historical. What fraction of books are historical? Write the fraction in the lowest terms.

Solution: Since 8 out of 16 books are historical book. Then, $\frac{8}{16}$ of the books are historical. To write the fraction in the lowest terms, divide both the numerator and denominator by 8

$$\frac{8 \div 8}{16 \div 8} = \frac{1}{2}$$

Simplifying Fractions

- A fraction contains two numbers separated by a bar between them. The bottom number, called the denominator, is the total number of equally divided portions in one whole. The top number, called the numerator, is how many portions you have. And the bar represents the operation of division.

- Simplifying a fraction means reducing it to the lowest terms. To simplify a fraction, evenly divide both the top and bottom of the fraction by $2, 3, 5, 7$, etc.

- Continue until you can't go any further.

Examples:

Example 1. Simplify $\frac{18}{30}$

Solution: To simplify $\frac{18}{30}$, find a number that both 18 and 30 are divisible by. Both are divisible by 6. Then: $\frac{18}{30} = \frac{18 \div 6}{30 \div 6} = \frac{3}{5}$

Example 2. Simplify $\frac{32}{80}$

Solution: To simplify $\frac{32}{80}$, find a number that both 32 and 80 are divisible by. Both are divisible by 8 and 16. Then: $\frac{32}{80} = \frac{32 \div 8}{80 \div 8} = \frac{4}{10}$, 4 and 10 are divisible by 2, then: $\frac{4}{10} = \frac{2}{5}$ or $\frac{32}{80} = \frac{32 \div 16}{80 \div 16} = \frac{2}{5}$

Example 3. Simplify $\frac{40}{120}$

Solution: To simplify $\frac{40}{120}$, find a number that both 40 and 120 are divisible by. Both are divisible by 40, then: $\frac{40}{120} = \frac{40 \div 40}{120 \div 40} = \frac{1}{3}$

Using Number Lines to Present Decimal

- Decimal numbers have a whole number and a fractional part which is separated by the decimal point.

- To indicate decimal numbers on the number line, you must divide the unit length between 0 and 1 into 10 identical parts. In between any 2 integers, for instance, 1 and 2 you get 1.1, 1.2, 1.3, 1.4, 1.5, 1.6, 1.7, 1.8 and 1.9.

Examples:

Example 1. Find number 1.7 on the number line.

Solution: First, with the number line, you must jump one number, after that you must divide the unit length between 1 and 2 into 10 identical parts. Then you must jump to the *7th* part.

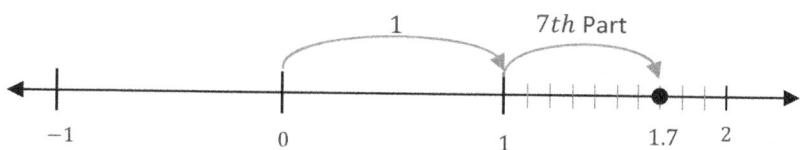

Example 2. Find the value of a. Write your answer as a decimal number.

Solution: The number line is divided into 10 equal parts between 2 and 3, then each interval represents 0.1. Count the intervals from 2 to a. There are 2 intervals. So, $a = 2.2$.

Repeating Decimals

- The description for a decimal that repeats is a fractional number where one or more of the numbers after a decimal point keeps repeating forever.

- A fractional depiction of $\frac{1}{6}$ is shown as 0.1666666 (the number 6 repeats forever) is an illustration of a decimal that repeats.

- It shows one must put down each of the fractions via utilizing a decimal. Divide its numerator by its denominator to get the fraction. Thus, $1 \div 6 = 0.1666666$

Examples:

Example 1. How do you write $\frac{1}{3}$ as a decimal?

Solution: First, divide the numerator by the denominator.

$1 \div 3 = 0.333 \ldots$

$\frac{1}{3}$ is about equal to 0.333 ….

$$\begin{array}{r} 0.3333 \\ 3 \overline{)1.0000} \\ -9 \\ \hline 10 \\ -9 \\ \hline 10 \\ -9 \\ \hline 10 \\ -9 \\ \hline 1 \end{array}$$

Example 2. How do you write $\frac{1}{6}$ as a decimal?

Solution: First, divide the numerator by the denominator.

$1 \div 6 = 0.1666 \ldots$

$\frac{1}{6}$ is about equal to 0.1666 ….

$$\begin{array}{r} 0.1666 \\ 6 \overline{)1.0000} \\ -6 \\ \hline 40 \\ -36 \\ \hline 40 \\ -36 \\ \hline 40 \\ -36 \\ \hline 4 \end{array}$$

Convert Between Fractions and Decimals

The simplest method of converting fractions to decimals is via dividing their numerator by its denominator via a calculator. The subsequent answer is the fraction's value written as a decimal number.

- How do you convert decimals to fractions?

    - Firstly, write down the particular decimal as a ratio ($\frac{p}{q}$), in which its denominator equals 1.

    - Then you must multiply its denominator and the numerator via multiples of 10 for each decimal point, so the decimal for the numerator ends up a whole number.

$$0.2 = \frac{0.2}{1} = \frac{0.2 \times 100}{1 \times 100} = \frac{20 \div 20}{100 \div 20} = \frac{1}{5}$$

Examples:

Example 1. Write 0.5 as a fraction.

Solution: First, add 1 to the denominator of the decimal number. Then you must multiply its denominator and the numerator by multiples of 10, for each decimal point. Then simplify: $0.5 = \frac{0.5}{1} = \frac{0.5 \times 10}{1 \times 10} = \frac{5}{10} = \frac{1}{2}$

Example 2. Write $\frac{1}{4}$ as a decimal number.

Solution: Divide the numerator by the denominator:

$1 \div 4 = 0.25$

$$\begin{array}{r} 0.25 \\ 4 \overline{\smash{)}1.00} \\ -8 \\ \hline 20 \\ -20 \\ \hline 00 \end{array}$$

Unit Prices with Decimals and Fractions

- Utilize multiplication for discovering the total price utilizing unit prices and amounts in fractions and decimals.

- You must divide the cost of a certain amount of units of an item by the number of units to discover the item's unit price.

- Unit rates are rates with a 1 in their denominator.

- If there is a rate, like something's cost per some amount of items, and the denominator's quantity isn't 1, then determine the unit rate or price per unit via a division operation: numerator divided via the denominator.

Examples:

Example 1. According to the given table:

Sophia went to the store and bought $5\frac{1}{2}$ kilograms of the banana. How much did she spend?

fruits	Per kilogram
Blueberries	$1
Raspberries	$1
Blackberries	$5
Banana	$2
Mango	$3

Solution: Find the cost of the banana. Multiply the price per kilogram by the number of kilograms.

$\$2 \times 5\frac{1}{2} = \$2 \times 5.5 = \$11$, So, she spends $11.

Example 2. According to the given table in the previous example, Sophia went to the store and bought 0.75 kilograms of blackberries. How much did she spend?

Solution: Find the cost of the blackberries. Multiply the price per kilogram by the number of kilograms.

$\$5 \times 0.75 = \$3.75$. So, she spends $3.75.

Convert Between Decimals and Mixed Numbers

- If the decimal has a number on the left-hand side of the decimal point it signifies, there's a whole part as well as several pieces of a whole.

- With decimals, the numbers on the left-hand side of a decimal point stand for the whole part and any numbers on the right-hand side of a decimal point stand for the decimal or the fraction part.

- If you wish to convert any decimal into a mixed number, you have to keep the whole number the same and then convert its decimal portion.

Examples:

Example 1. Write 2.9 as a mixed fraction.

Solution: Add 1 to the denominator of the decimal number. Then you must multiply its denominator and the numerator by multiples of 10. $2.9 = \frac{2.9}{1} = \frac{2.9 \times 10}{1 \times 10} = \frac{29}{10}$.

Now write the improper fraction as a mixed fraction: $\frac{29}{10} = 2\frac{9}{10}$

Example 2. Write $3\frac{1}{4}$ as a decimal number.

Solution: Multiply the denominator and numerator until the denominator becomes a power of 10. Therefore, the integers in the mixed fractions are the numbers to the left of the decimal point, and the fractional numbers are the decimal numbers to the right of the decimal:

$3\frac{1}{4} = 3\frac{1 \times 25}{4 \times 25} = 3\frac{25}{100} \rightarrow 3\frac{1}{4} = 3.25$

Convert Between Improper Fractions and Mixed Numbers

- Improper fractions are fractions where the numerator equals or is higher than the denominator. Mixed numbers are made up of a fraction and a whole number.

$$\frac{5}{2} = 2\frac{1}{2}$$

- An improper fraction can additionally be shown via a mixed number.

- In order to translate an improper fraction to a mixed number:

  • You divide its numerator by its denominator. The result is the whole number, plus the rest is now the new fraction's numerator.

  • The new fraction's denominator is the same number as the original denominator.

  • If no remainder is present, there's not a fraction and a resulting number is merely a whole number.

Examples:

Example 1. Write $5\frac{3}{5}$ as an improper fraction.

Solution: First, multiply the whole number in the denominator, then add with the numerator and write in the numerator. In this way, an improper fraction is obtained from a mixed fraction: $5\frac{3}{5} = \frac{(5\times5)+3}{5} = \frac{28}{5}$

Example 2. Write $\frac{48}{7}$ as a mixed fraction.

Solution: First, divide the numerator by denominator $48 \div 7$. The result is the whole number 6, plus the rest is now the new fraction's numerator 6: $\frac{48}{7} = \frac{(6\times7)+6}{7} = 6\frac{6}{7}$

$$\begin{array}{r} 0.1666 \\ 7\overline{)48} \\ -42 \\ \hline 6 \end{array}$$

Order of Decimals, Mixed Numbers and Fractions

- For a comparison of mixed numbers and decimals, you must change all these numbers into a decimal format.

- The lowest number must be placed first on the list, as well as the highest number must be the last one. The rest of the numbers must be put in between in rising order.

- For instance, numbers that go from lowest to highest will be $2\frac{1}{2} = 2.5, 3.5, 5.85$ and 7.5.

- They can also be written via the utilize of the less than symbol as $2.5 < 3.5 < 5.85$ and < 7.5.

Examples:

Example 1. Order this set of numbers from least to greatest. $4\frac{7}{9}, 1.5, \frac{5}{2}, 2.1$

Solution: The smallest number is 1.5 and the largest number is $4\frac{7}{9}$.

Now compare the integers and order them from least to greatest:

$$1.5 < 2.1 < \frac{5}{2} < 4\frac{7}{9}$$

Example 2. Order each set of integers from greatest to least. $1.3, \frac{11}{3}, 6\frac{7}{9}, 9.8$

Solution: The largest number is 9.8 and the smallest number is 1.3.

Now compare the integers and order them from greatest to least:

$$9.8 > 6\frac{7}{9} > \frac{11}{3} > 1.3$$

Chapter 13: Practices

✎ Find fractions on the number line.

3)

✎ Which models show fractions? Attention one of the models is redundant.

1) $\frac{3}{4}$
2) $\frac{3}{20}$
3) $\frac{9}{20}$
4) $\frac{7}{8}$
5) $\frac{2}{10}$
6) $\frac{1}{2}$
7) $\frac{1}{5}$
8) $\frac{1}{4}$

Chapter 13: Fraction, Decimals and Mixed Numbers

✏ **Solve.**

9) Mary needs to order fried chicken for 18 students. Each student should get $\frac{1}{3}$ of a fried chicken. How many fried chickens should Mary order?

10) Three friends want to share 5 bananas so that they each get the same amount. How much would each friend get?

11) Two children are sharing $\frac{1}{2}$ of a bottle of milk. How much will each child get?

12) Samuel operates an orange juice stand. On Sunday he used 3 bags of oranges. On Friday he used $\frac{5}{7}$ as many oranges as on Sunday. How many bags of oranges did Samuel use on Friday? Write your answer as a fraction or as a whole or mixed number.

✏ **Solve and write the fraction in the lowest terms.**

21) Jules baked 21 cookies. He placed some sprinkles on 7 cookies. What fraction of these cookies are covered in sprinkles?

22) Neil painted his room walls. He segmented walls into 8 parts. And painted purple 2 parts of them. What fraction of the walls are purple?

23) The fruit baskets contained 30 apples on the table. 6 of them were eaten by children in the afternoon. What fraction of the apples are eaten? Write the fraction in the lowest terms.

24) 24 students went on a trip to New York City. 14 of them went to Broadway. What fraction of the students went to Broadway?

25) There are 7 bottles on a shelf. 3 of bottles are empty. What fraction of the bottles are empty?

26) A refrigerator has 5 sections for organizing. 2 sections of them are for vegetables. What fraction of sections are for vegetables?

27) Karolina makes a necklace with 26 black and white beads. If she creates that with 8 black beads. What fraction of necklace is black beads?

28) Liam has $48. He bought 5 books and paid $18. What fraction of the dollars is paid to buy books?

✍ Simplify each fraction.

29) $\frac{2}{8} =$

30) $\frac{5}{15} =$

31) $\frac{10}{90} =$

32) $\frac{12}{16} =$

33) $\frac{25}{45} =$

34) $\frac{42}{54} =$

35) $\frac{48}{60} =$

36) $\frac{52}{169} =$

✍ Find the decimal number on the number line.

37) 1.8

38) −1.7

39) −2.1

40) 0.6

41) −3.8

42) 5.1

43) −4.4

44) −0.9

Chapter 13: Fraction, Decimals and Mixed Numbers

✏ **Write fractions as a decimal.**

45) $\frac{1}{15}$

46) $\frac{4}{6}$

47) $\frac{2}{6}$

48) $\frac{2}{3}$

49) $\frac{4}{9}$

50) $\frac{2}{15}$

51) $\frac{1}{9}$

52) $\frac{4}{15}$

✏ **Write decimal as a fraction.**

113) 0.85

114) 0.33

115) 0.95

116) 0.68

✏ **Write fraction as a decimal.**

117) $\frac{7}{100}$

118) $\frac{3}{5}$

119) $\frac{26}{50}$

120) $\frac{3}{8}$

✏ **According to the list, solve the word problems.**

List of the price of each book	
Art/architecture	$4
Cookbook	$2
Dictionary	$13
History	$6
Encyclopedia	$25

121) If the history book has a discount of 0.15, how much money discount for 1 book?

122) If the dictionary book has a discount of 0.25, how much money is in the total discount for 3 books?

123) If you pay $\frac{5}{8}$ of the total amount of the cookbook, what is its new cost?

124) If you pay $\frac{3}{4}$ of the total amount for the encyclopedia book, what is its new cost for 5 volumes?

125) Emma buys 3.5 pounds of vegetable oil, what is the total cost?

126) Sara buys $1\frac{3}{8}$ pounds of canola oil, what is the total cost?

List of the price of oil per pound	
peanut oil	$4
vegetable oil	$5
olive oil	$4
canola oil	$10
soybean oil	$3
sunflower seed oil	$6

127) Eve buys $3\frac{4}{2}$ pounds of sunflower seed oil, what is the total cost?

128) Williams buys 1.25 pounds of peanut oil, what is the total cost?

✍ Write decimal as a mixed fraction.

69) 2.85

70) 5.44

71) 1.65

72) 3.15

✍ Write a mixed fraction as a decimal

73) $8\frac{3}{100}$

74) $2\frac{2}{5}$

75) $4\frac{26}{50}$

76) $5\frac{3}{4}$

✍ Write improper fraction as a mixed fraction.

77) $\frac{47}{9}$

78) $\frac{12}{5}$

79) $\frac{32}{7}$

80) $\frac{8}{3}$

Write fractions as an improper fraction.

81) $5\frac{7}{9}$

82) $3\frac{1}{5}$

83) $4\frac{2}{7}$

84) $1\frac{3}{8}$

Order each set of rational numbers from least to greatest.

85) $6\frac{3}{5}, 6.3, 6\frac{1}{8}, 5.8 \rightarrow$ ___, ___, ___, ___

86) $4\frac{3}{4}, 2.5, 4\frac{1}{2}, 3.8 \rightarrow$ ___, ___, ___, ___

87) $9\frac{6}{9}, 9.6, 8\frac{1}{2}, 1.1 \rightarrow$ ___, ___, ___, ___

88) $6.5, 6\frac{9}{10}, 4.3, 4\frac{1}{2} \rightarrow$ ___, ___, ___, ___

Order each set of rational numbers from greatest to least.

89) $3.3, 3\frac{2}{9}, 3.5, 3\frac{3}{5} \rightarrow$ ___, ___, ___, ___

90) $1.9, 1\frac{8}{9}, 1\frac{1}{2}, 2.2 \rightarrow$ ___, ___, ___, ___

91) $0.4, \frac{8}{9}, 0.3, 0.8 \rightarrow$ ___, ___, ___, ___

92) $\frac{7}{10}, \frac{3}{6}, \frac{2}{7}, \frac{4}{5} \rightarrow$ ___, ___, ___, ___

Chapter 13: Answers

1) $\frac{14}{10}$
2) $\frac{11}{4}$
3) $\frac{2}{5}$
4) $\frac{3}{2}$
5) $\frac{8}{3}$
6) $\frac{15}{20}$
7) $\frac{13}{21}$
8) $\frac{5}{7}$
9) e
10) i
11) d
12) f
13) c
14) h
15) b
16) g
17) 6
18) $1\frac{2}{3}$
19) $\frac{1}{4}$
20) $2\frac{1}{7}$
21) $\frac{1}{3}$
22) $\frac{1}{4}$
23) $\frac{1}{5}$
24) $\frac{7}{12}$
25) $\frac{3}{7}$
26) $\frac{2}{5}$
27) $\frac{4}{13}$
28) $\frac{3}{8}$
29) $\frac{1}{4}$
30) $\frac{1}{3}$
31) $\frac{1}{9}$
32) $\frac{3}{4}$
33) $\frac{5}{9}$
34) $\frac{7}{9}$
35) $\frac{4}{5}$
36) $\frac{4}{13}$

37) [number line with point at 1.8]

38) [number line with point at −1.7]

39) [number line with point at −2.1]

40) [number line with point at 0.6]

41) [number line with point at −3.8]

42) [number line with point at 5.1]

43)

44)

45) 0.0666 ...
46) 0.666 ...
47) 0.333 ...
48) 0.666 ...
49) 0.444 ...
50) 0.1333 ...
51) 0.111 ...
52) 0.2666 ...
53) $\frac{17}{20}$
54) $\frac{33}{100}$
55) $\frac{19}{20}$
56) $\frac{17}{25}$
57) 0.07
58) 0.6
59) 0.52
60) 0.375
61) $0.9
62) $9.75
63) $1.25

64) $18.75
65) $17.5
66) $13.75
67) $30
68) $5
69) $2\frac{17}{20}$
70) $5\frac{11}{25}$
71) $1\frac{13}{20}$
72) $3\frac{3}{20}$
73) 8.03
74) 2.4
75) 4.52
76) 5.75
77) $5\frac{2}{9}$
78) $2\frac{2}{5}$
79) $4\frac{4}{7}$
80) $2\frac{2}{3}$

81) $\frac{52}{9}$
82) $\frac{16}{5}$
83) $\frac{30}{7}$
84) $\frac{11}{8}$
85) $5.8 < 6\frac{1}{8} < 6.3 < 6\frac{3}{5}$
86) $2.5 < 3.8 < 4\frac{1}{2} < 4\frac{3}{4}$
87) $1.1 < 8\frac{1}{2} < 9.6 < 9\frac{6}{9}$
88) $4.3 < 4\frac{1}{2} < 6.5 < 6\frac{9}{10}$
89) $3\frac{3}{5} > 3.5 > 3\frac{2}{9} > 3.3$
90) $2.2 > 1.9 > 1\frac{8}{9} > 1\frac{1}{2}$
91) $\frac{8}{9} > 0.8 > 0.4 > 0.3$
92) $\frac{4}{5} > \frac{7}{10} > \frac{3}{6} > \frac{2}{7}$

CHAPTER

14 Rational Numbers and Integers

Math topics that you'll learn in this chapter:

- ☑ Using a Diagram to Classify Rational Numbers
- ☑ Opposite Integers
- ☑ Using Number Lines to Present Integers
- ☑ Using Vertical and Horizontal Number Lines to Represent Integers

Using a Diagram to Classify Rational Numbers

- Whole numbers: a series of natural numbers are whole numbers, which includes zero. In other words, begin at zero, then go up. W is the symbol used to represent whole numbers.
- Integers: Integers are comprised of negative natural numbers (for instance, -3), positive natural numbers (for instance, 3), and zero.
- Rational numbers: these kinds of numbers are seen as one fraction of a pair of integers.

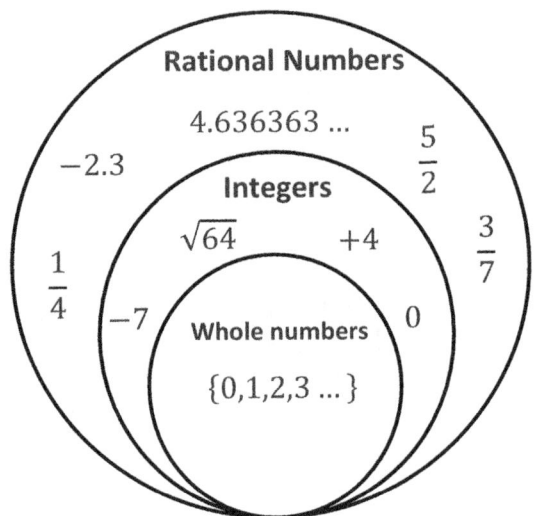

Examples:
Use the following diagram to find the answers:

Example 1. Which of the following numbers is a rational number but not an integer?

Solution: All integers are rational numbers, but all rational numbers aren't integers. $\frac{3}{2}$ in the picture is outside the range of integers and is only in the range of rational numbers. So, $\frac{3}{2}$ is only a rational number but not an integer.

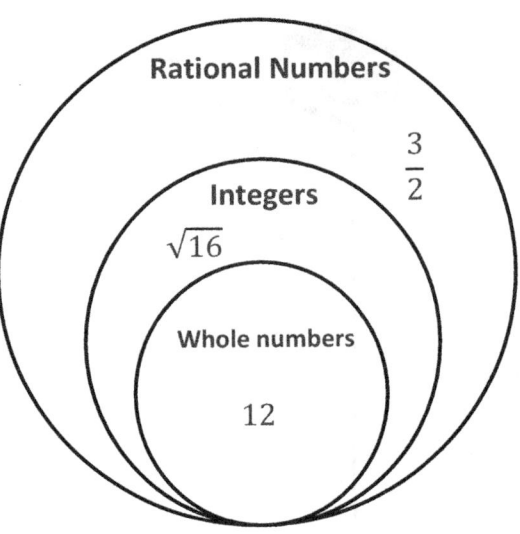

Example 2. Which of the following numbers is both an integer and a whole number?

Solution: All whole numbers are integers, but all integers aren't whole numbers. In the picture, 12 is both in the range of integers and whole numbers. So, 12 is both an integer and a whole number.

Opposite integers

- Opposite numbers are the same distance from zero, except it is from the opposite direction on a number line.

- An integer is a number that doesn't have fractional or decimal parts. The number may be negative, positive, or 0. Opposite integers are positive or negative forms of numbers.

- For instance, 8 and −8 are opposite integers. They're labeled as opposites since they're on opposite sides of a number line. Thus, 8 is on the right-hand side of 0. And −8 is on the left-hand side of 0.

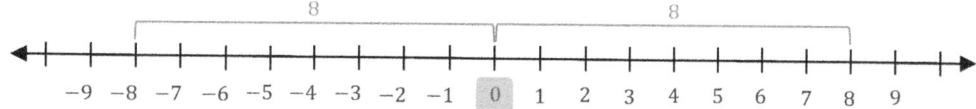

Examples:

Example 1. Example 1. What is the opposite of −6? Graph it on the number line.

Solution: Since the 6 is negative, the opposite of −6 will be the right-hand side of 0. Thus, the opposite of −6 is 6.

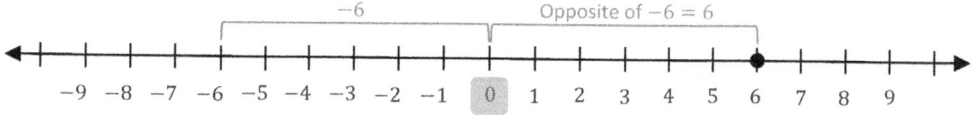

Example 2. What is the opposite of 0? And graph on the number line.

Solution: Zero is the only integer that is its opposite. The opposite of 0 is 0.

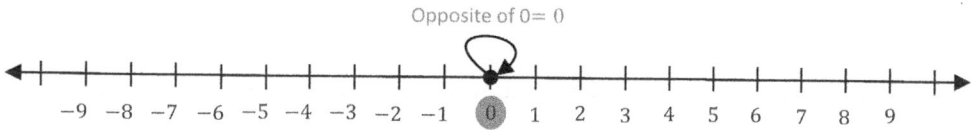

Using Number Lines to Present Integers

- In what way are integers shown on the number line? Integers are whole numbers (not fractional numbers) and these may be shown as negative, positive, or as zero. For example, numbers $-4, 1, 4, 9, 87$ and $5,705$ are all integers.

- To find integers on a number line: The 0 integer is placed in the middle of a number line.

- All of the positive integers on the number line are placed on the right-hand side of 0 and all negative integers get placed on the left-hand side of 0.

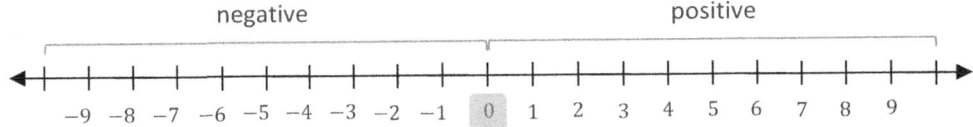

Examples:

Example 1. What number does the g point on the graph show?

Solution: The g is larger than 0 (positive number), and each interval represents 1. Count the interval from 0. Since $0 + 5 = 5$, then $g = 5$.

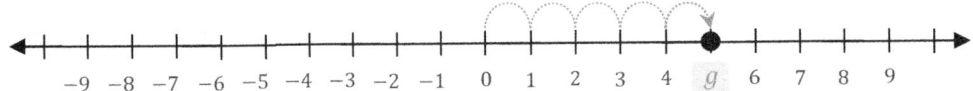

Example 2. What number does the x point on the graph show?

Solution: The x is smaller than 0 (negative number), and each interval represents 1. Count the interval from 0. Since $0 - 7 = -7$, then $g = -7$.

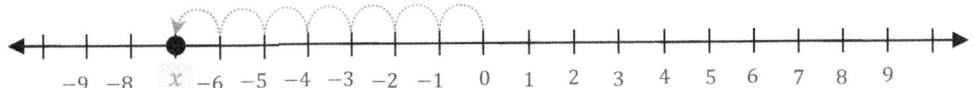

Integers and Vertical and Horizontal Number Lines

- Many times, the words vertical and horizontal denote directions: vertical lines go up and down, while horizontal lines go across.

- Horizontal number lines: Draw a horizontal line, then put a few points at identical distances on the line. Make one of the points 0. All the points on the right-hand side will be positive integers, while all of them on the left-hand side will be negative integers.

- Vertical number lines: Draw a vertical line, then place on it a few points at identical distances. Make one of these points zero. The points to the upward side of 0 will be positive integers, while the ones to the downward side of 0 will be negative integers.

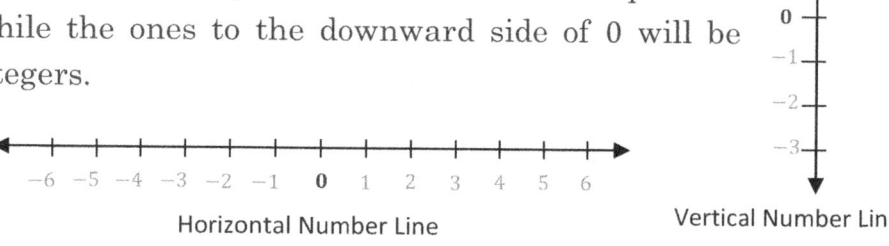

Horizontal Number Line   Vertical Number Line

Examples:

Example 1. Graph 0 on the horizontal number line.

Solution: Find 0 on the number line, then graph it with a point.

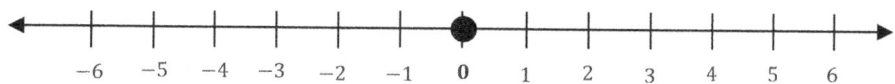

Example 2. Graph -2 on the vertical number line.

Solution: Find 0 on the number line, then scroll down on the number line. Count 2 numbers of the distance and draw it with a dot.

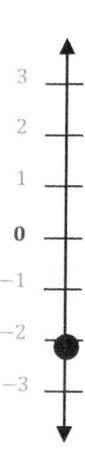

Chapter 14: Practices

✎ Use the following diagram to find the answers.

1) Which of the following numbers is a rational number but not an integer?
2) Which of the following numbers is both an integer and a rational number but isn't a whole number?
3) Which of the following numbers is an integer, whole number, and a rational number?
4) Which of the following numbers is an integer, but not a whole number?

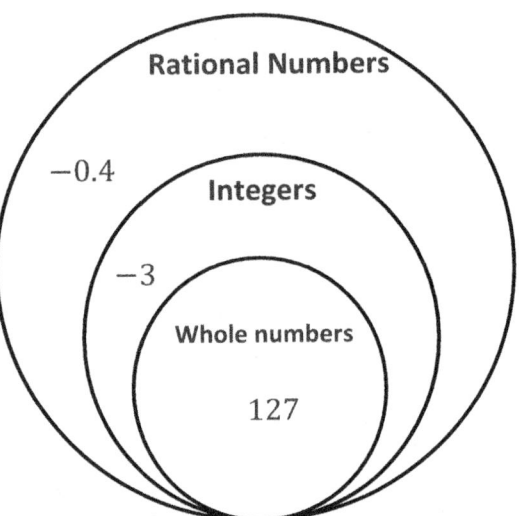

✎ Write the opposite of each integer.

5) −8 = ___

6) +33 = ___

7) −12 = ___

8) +101 = ___

9) −77 = ___

10) +1 = ___

11) +8 = ___

12) −3 = ___

✎ Graph integers on the number line.

13) 2

14) −4

15) −12

16) 3

Chapter 14: Rational Numbers and Integers

✏️ **What number does the x point on the graph show?**

17)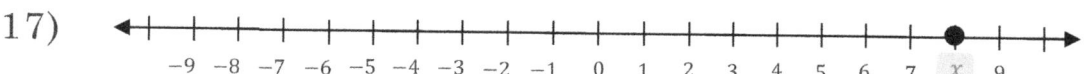

18)

19)

20)

✏️ **Graph integers on the horizontal number line.**

21) −5

22) 1

23) −10

24) −8

25) 6

26) 19

✏️ **Graph integers on the vertical number line.**

27) −2

28) 6

Chapter 14: Answers

13) −0.4
14) −3
15) 127
16) −3
17) +8
18) −33
19) +12
20) −101
21) +77
22) −1
23) −8
24) +3

13)
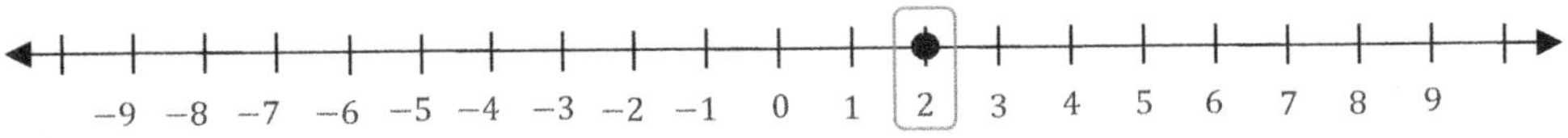

14)
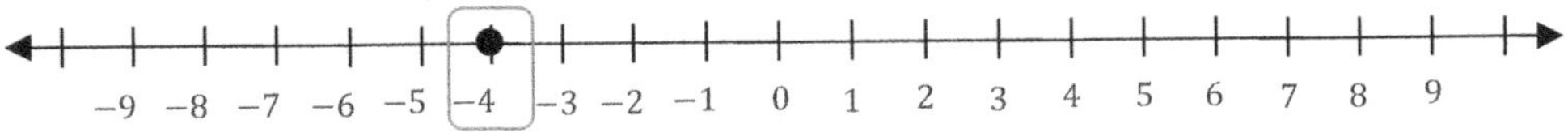

15)
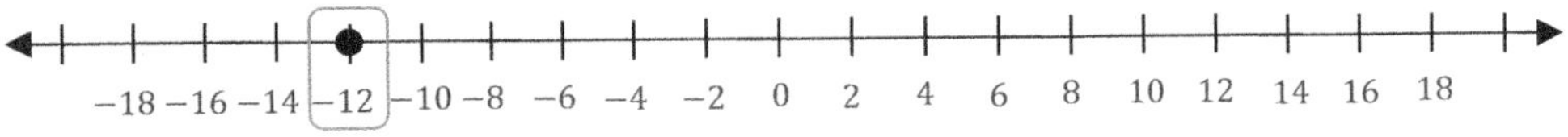

16)
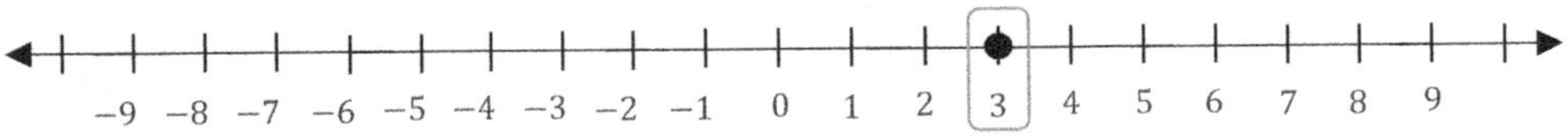

17) 8
18) −1
19) −5
20) −24

21)
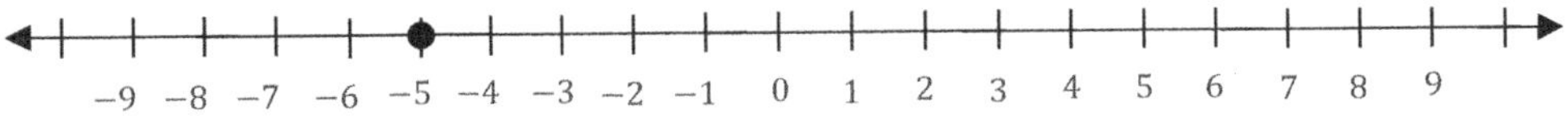

22)
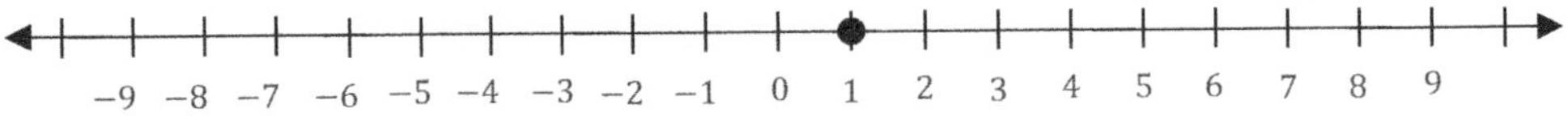

23)
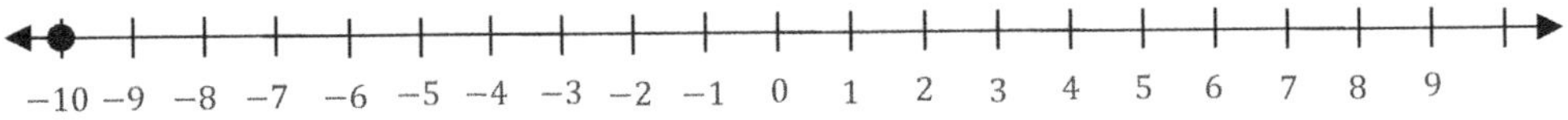

24)
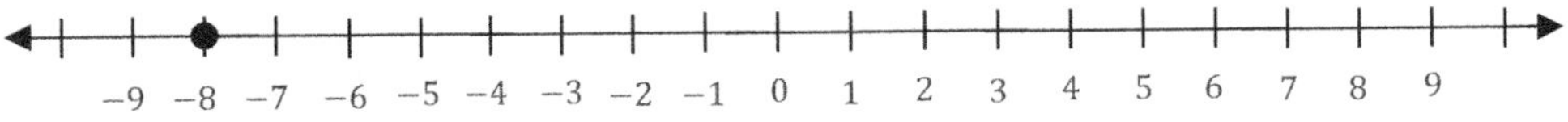

25)
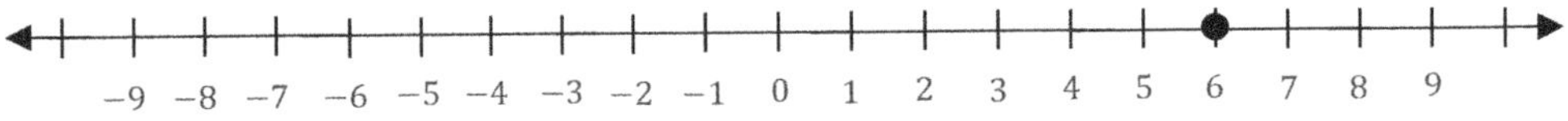

26)
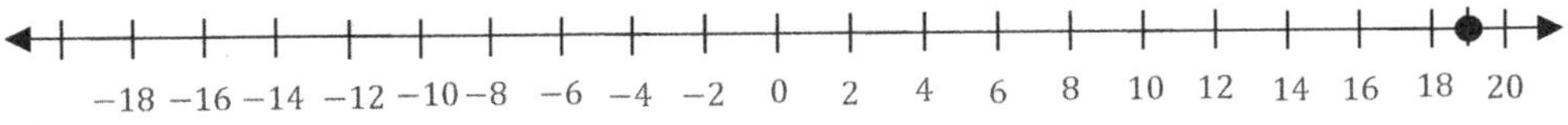

27)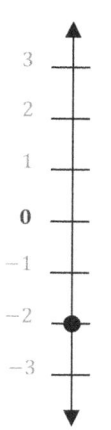

28)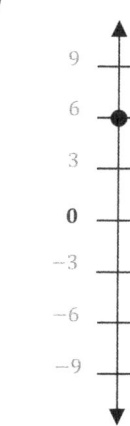

CHAPTER
15 Coordinate Plane

Math topics that you'll learn in this chapter:

- ☑ Objects on a Coordinate Plane
- ☑ Understanding Quadrants
- ☑ Coordinate Planes as Maps

Objects on a Coordinate Plane

- Coordinate planes are created via a horizontal number line known as an x–axis along with a vertical number line known as a y–axis.

- Each of the axis lines crosses the other one at zero. The point at which these axis lines converge is known as its origin.

- An ordered pair (x, y) illustrates the location of a point on a coordinate plane. The 1st number is known as an x–coordinate and the 2nd number is known as a y–coordinate.

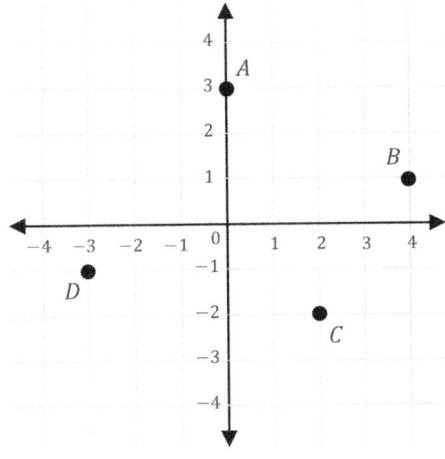

$A = (0,3), B = (4,1)$
$C = (2,-2), D = (-3,-1)$

- The points get identified through a capital letter or via their x and y values as ordered pairs.

Examples:

Example 1. What is the y–coordinate of point B?

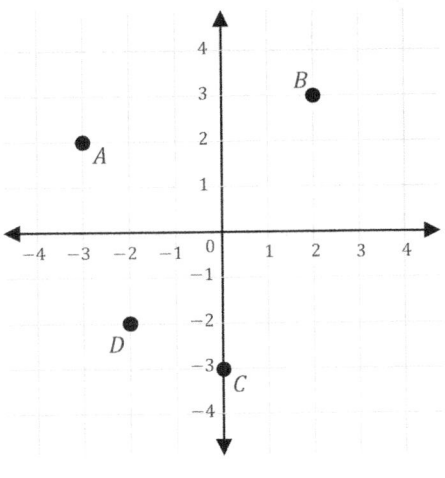

Solution: Draw a line perpendicular to the y–coordinate from point B. This position on the y-axis is 3 units above the origin. All y–coordinate above the origin are positive.

So, the y–coordinate of point B is 3.

Example 2. Based on the previous example, what is the x–coordinate of point C?

Solution: Draw a line perpendicular to the x–coordinate from point C. This position on the x-axis is on the origin.

So, the x–coordinate of point C is 0.

Understanding Quadrants

- Quadrants are the area enclosed by the x and y axes; therefore, a graph has 4 quadrants.

- To describe, the 2−dimensional Cartesian plane gets divided by the x and y axes into 4 quadrants. Beginning at the top right-hand corner is *Quadrant I* and then moving counterclockwise you find *Quadrants II* through *IV*.

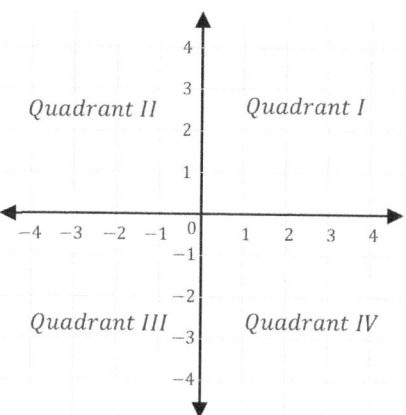

Examples:

Example 1. Which shape is in *Quadrant III*?

Solution: Quadrant III is the bottom left quadrant. So, ♡ is in *Quadrant III*.

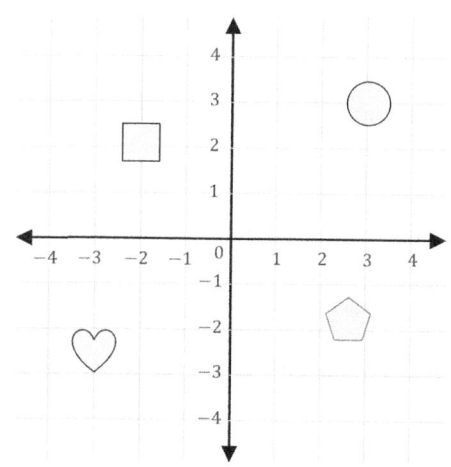

Example 2. According to the coordinate plane, in which quadrant is the ◯ located?

Solution: the shape is the top right quadrant, which is *Quadrant I*.

Coordinate Planes as Maps

- Coordinate planes are 2−dimensional planes created via the intersection of a vertical line known as a y−axis along with a horizontal line known as an x−axis. This lesson will teach you more about coordinate planes as maps.

- They are perpendicular lines that overlap one another at 0, and that point is known as its origin.

- It's utilized to indicate the location of various places on the earth's surface.

Examples:

Example 1. Where is the fire station?

Solution: Find the point of the fire station on the map. Determine, the x and y−coordinates of the fire station point.

x−coordinates of F: 1

y−coordinates of F: −1

Then, write the answer as an ordered pair.

So, the fire station is at $(1, -1)$.

Example 2. Where is the Bank?

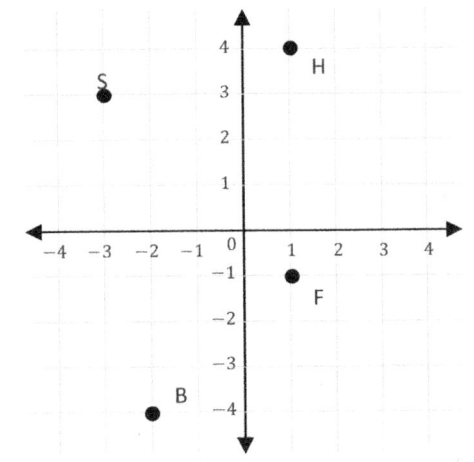

S: School
F: Fire Station
B: Bank
H: Home

Solution: Find the point of the bank on the map. Determine, the x and y−coordinates of the bank point.

x−coordinates of B: −2

y−coordinates of B: −4

Then, write the answer as an ordered pair.

So, the bank is at $(-2, -4)$.

Chapter 15: Practices

✏ **According to the coordinate plane, determine the requested coordinates.**

1) y –coordinate of point A

2) y – coordinate of point F

3) x –coordinate of point E

4) y –coordinate of point C

5) y – coordinate of point D

6) x –coordinate of point A

7) x –coordinate of point G

8) y – coordinate of point E

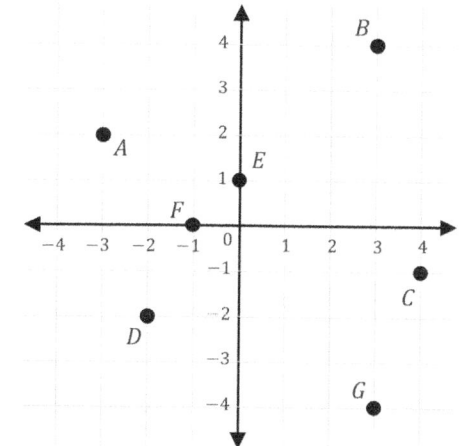

✏ **Determine.**

9) Which shape is in *Quadrant III*?

10) Which shape is in *Quadrant I*?

11) Which shape is in *Quadrant IV*?

12) Which shape is in *Quadrant II*?

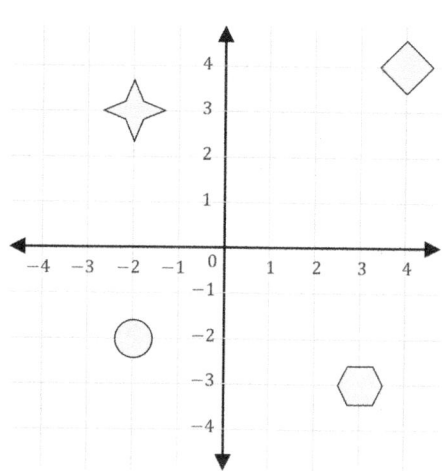

✎ **Write the coordinates of the specified points.**

13) Where is the pet store?

14) Where is the hospital?

15) Where is the theater?

16) Where is the science lab?

17) Where is the locksmith?

18) Where is the game store?

19) Where is the restaurant?

20) Where is the fire station?

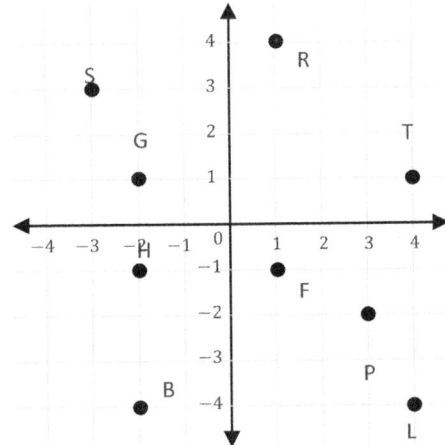

G: Game store

F: Fire Station

B: Bank

H: Hospital

T: Theater

R: Restaurant

L: Locksmith

S: Science lab

P: Pet store

Chapter 15: Answers

1) +2
2) 0
3) 0
4) −1
5) −2
6) −3
7) +3
8) +1

9) ○
10) ◇
11) ⬡
12) ✦

13) (3, −2)
14) (−2, −1)
15) (4, 1)
16) (−3, 3)
17) (4, −4)
18) (−2, 1)
19) (1, 4)
20) (1, −1)

CHAPTER
16 Rational Numbers

Math topics that you'll learn in this chapter:

☑ Using Number Lines to Represent Rational Numbers
☑ Using Number Lines to Order Rational Numbers
☑ Word Problems of Ordering Rational Numbers
☑ Convert Rational Numbers to a Fraction

Using Number Lines to Represent Rational Numbers

- There are both negative and positive rational numbers. All of the numbers higher than 0 are considered positive, while all of them lower than 0 will be negative.

- A rational number is one you can write as a fraction of 2 integers. For instance, to signify $\frac{3}{4}$ on the number line; firstly, divide the line between 0 to 1 into four parts. Since $\frac{3}{4}$ is positive you place this number on the right-hand side of 0.

- The rational number $\frac{3}{4}$ is placed at the 3rd point from zero.

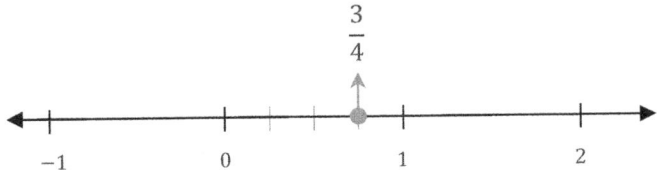

Divide the line between 0 to 1 into four parts.

Examples:

Example 1. Graph $\frac{7}{10}$ on the number line.

Solution: Divide the distance between 0 and 1 by 10 (the denominator). Then jump to the seventh part (the numerator).

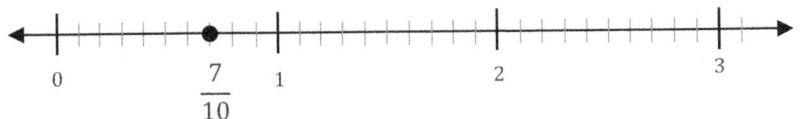

Example 2. Graph -1.75 on the number line.

Solution: First, you must jump one number to the left, after that the length between -1 and -2 is divided into 4 parts. So, the length of each part is $\frac{1}{4}$ or 0.25. Now find -0.75. Count 3 tick marks to the left of -1.

Using Number Lines to Order Rational Numbers

- Number lines make it possible for comparing and ordering of negative rational numbers.

- The number line gets divided into gaps which signify the relationship between these numbers. For instance, −1.5 and 0.4 can be graphed by utilizing a number line.

- −1.5 appears on the left-hand side of 0.4, therefore, −1.5 < 0.4.

- Whenever one goes to the right-hand side of 0, all the numbers will be higher.

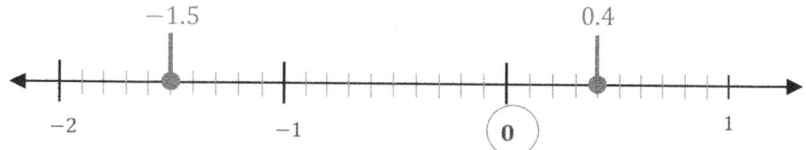

The right-hand side of 0, all the numbers will be higher, then −1.5 < 0.4.

Examples:

Example 1. Order this set of rational numbers from least to greatest. And utilize number lines. $-0.5, -\frac{3}{4}, 1.25, \frac{1}{2}$

Solution: Find the numbers on the line. The largest number is on the right side and the smallest number is left side. Then, compare the rational numbers and order them from least to greatest: $-\frac{3}{4} > -0.5 > \frac{1}{2} > 1.25$

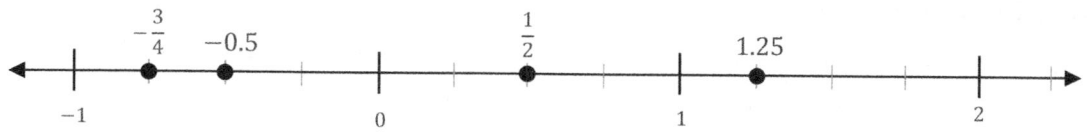

Example 2. Compare the numbers $-\frac{3}{5}, 0.2$.

Solution: Find the numbers on the line. $-\frac{3}{5}$ is left of 0.2 on the number line. Then $-\frac{3}{5}$ is smaller than 0.2: $-\frac{3}{5} < 0.2$

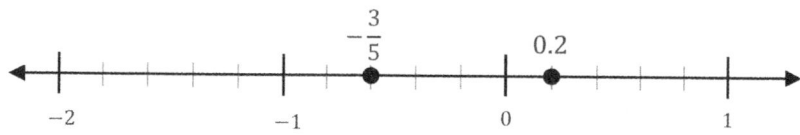

Word Problems of Ordering Rational Numbers

- You utilize word problems in order to learn a lesson better.

- For a word problem solution:

    - 1st step: review the problem, then determine what is being asked of you.

    - 2nd step: highlight the details of the problem.

    - 3rd step: Specify the numbers that should be written in order.

    - 4th step: Compare which of the numbers is bigger and which is smaller. Sort the numbers accordingly.

Examples:

Example 1. Bettie and Matt discovered they both have the same breed of cat, a Scottish Fold. Bettie said she gives her Scottish Fold, Bubba, 2.5 cups of cat food each day. Matt gives his Scottish Fold, Copper, $1\frac{2}{3}$ cups of cat food each day. Which Scottish Fold gets more cat food?

Solution: First, write 2.5 as a mixed number: $2.5 \rightarrow 2\frac{1}{2}$

And $2\frac{1}{2}$ or 2.5, is greater than $1\frac{2}{3}$. So, Bubba gets more cat food.

Example 2. Tessa and her brother Timothy decided to bake cookies. Timothy makes his cookies utilizing a 1.75 −ounce scoop, while his sister makes hers utilizing a $1\frac{1}{4}$ scoop size. Which of the cookies is larger?

Solution: In order to figure out which cookie is larger, calculate which of the numbers is bigger.

Put down $1\frac{1}{4}$ as a decimal: $1\frac{1}{4} \rightarrow 1.25$

1.25, or $1\frac{1}{4}$ is smaller than 1.75. Hence, Timothy's cookies are larger.

Chapter 16: Rational Numbers

Convert Rational Numbers to a Fraction

- Numbers written in the format of $\frac{a}{b}$, or any number that can be written as the format $\frac{a}{b}$, in which '**a**' and '**b**' are integers plus **b ≠ 0**, are known as rational numbers.

- So, rational numbers are any number in which it's possible to express it as the quotient of 2 integers with the situation being that its divisor isn't 0.

- For instance, each one of these numbers $\frac{4}{5}$, $-\frac{7}{13}$, $\frac{-9}{-7}$, and $\frac{-9}{-20}$ is considered to be a rational number.

Examples:

Example 1. Write 0.4 in the form $\frac{a}{b}$, where a and b are integers.

Solution: 0.4 is 4 tenths. So, write 4 in the numerator and 10 in the denominator: $0.4 = \frac{4}{10}$
Then, simplify that: $\frac{4}{10} = \frac{2}{5}$

Example 2. Write -9 in the form $\frac{a}{b}$, where a and b are integers.

Solution: -9 is an integer. So, you can write -9 in the numerator and 1 in the denominator: $-9 = -\frac{9}{1}$

Example 3. Write 1.1 in the form $\frac{a}{b}$, where a and b are integers.

Solution: 0.7 is 7 tenths. So, write 7 in the numerator and 10 in the denominator: $0.7 = \frac{7}{10}$

Chapter 16: Practices

✎ **Graph rational numbers on the number line.**

1) -0.5

2) 1.3

3) $-\frac{1}{5}$

4) $\frac{3}{7}$

5) 0.7

6) -2.25

7) $\frac{9}{15}$

8) $-\frac{5}{2}$

✎ **Order each set of rational numbers from least to greatest.**

9) $-\frac{1}{8}, -\frac{3}{4}, -0.25 \to$ ___, ___, ___

10) $0.125, \frac{9}{4}, -1.25 \to$ ___, ___, ___

11) $\frac{1}{3}, 0.5, -\frac{1}{2} \to$ ___, ___, ___

12) $2.2, -0.3, 0.7 \to$ ___, ___, ___

✎ **Compare rational numbers utilizing number lines.**

13) $1.25, \frac{3}{4}, -1.25$

14) $-\frac{3}{10}, 0, -0.8$

15) $-\frac{5}{3}, -\frac{4}{9}, \frac{1}{3}$

16) $-0.4, 0.1, -0.8$

✎ **Solve.**

17) There was a blizzard yesterday. Paul heard that it snowed 11.3 inches, and Janet heard that it snowed $11\frac{3}{5}$ inches. Who heard that it snowed less?

18) Three gamers completed a game that included discovering material, building, and buying. To compare their activity times,

Chapter 16: Rational Numbers

they created a table that shows the difference between each person's time and the total time. Who finished the game faster?

	Discovering Material (h)	Building (h)	Buying (h)	Total Activity (h)
Gamer −1	1.8	0.8	2.5	5.1
Gamer −2	$1\frac{1}{5}$	0.5	$2\frac{8}{10}$	$4\frac{5}{10}$
Gamer −3	2.1	$\frac{7}{10}$	1.3	4.1

19) Estelle and her mother are debating how many creams to add to their strawberry-nut bread. Estelle wants to add $\frac{2}{5}$ of a cup, and her mother wants to add 0.75 cups. Who wants to add more cream to the bread?

20) Mason and Liam just hiked towards each other in a 2-mile walk. Mason hikes the 1.5 hours, and Liam hikes it in $1\frac{5}{6}$ hours. Who has been on the road the most?

✏️ **Write the rational number in the form $\frac{a}{b}$.**

21) 0.35

22) 85

23) 1.58

24) −0.12

25) −3

26) 0.95

27) −4.44

28) −0.5

Chapter 16: Answers

1) 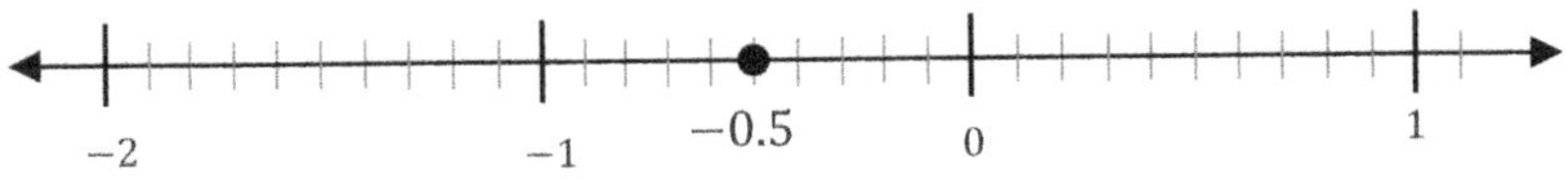

2) 

3) 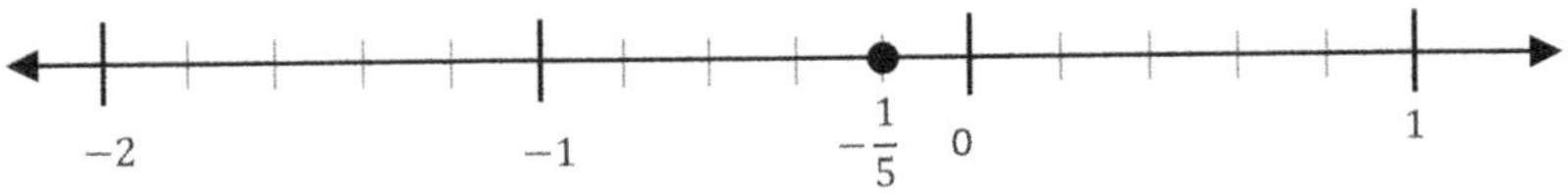

4) 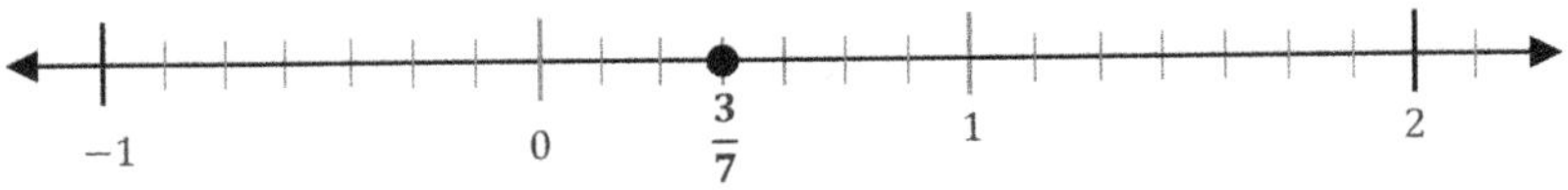

5) 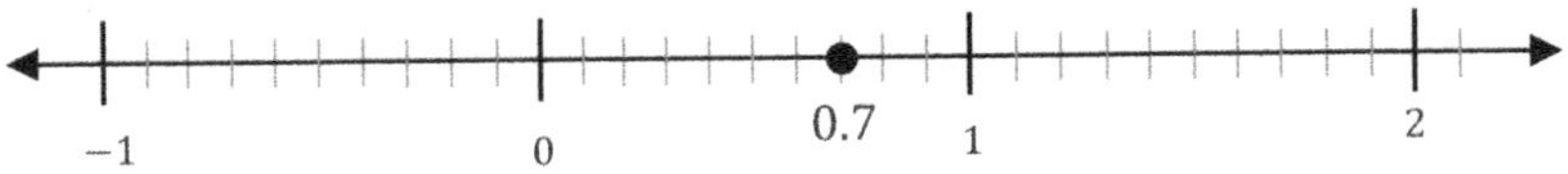

6) 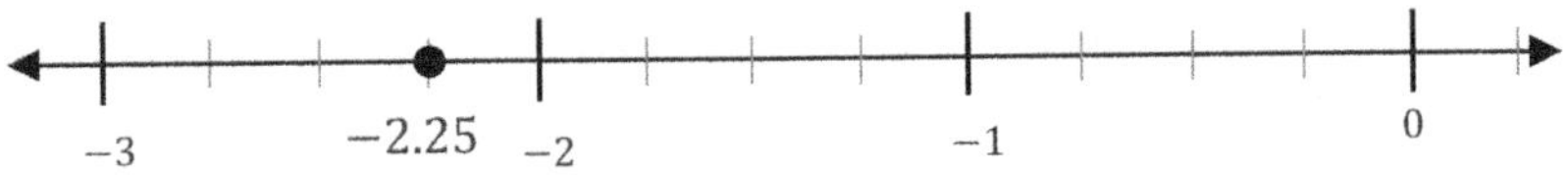

7) 

8) 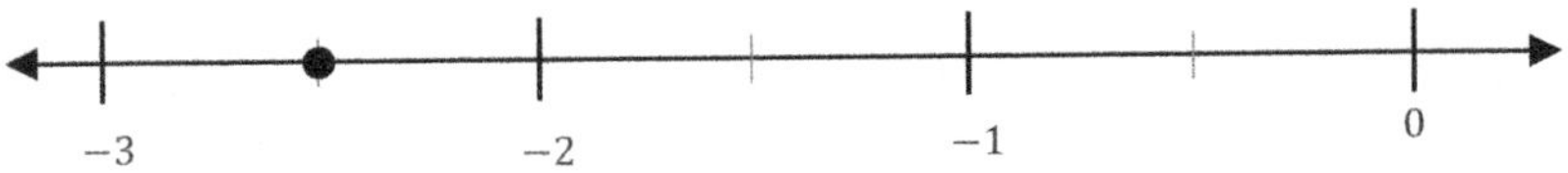

9) $-\frac{3}{4} < -0.25 < -\frac{1}{8}$

10) $-1.25 < 0.125 < \frac{9}{4}$

11) $-\frac{1}{2} < \frac{1}{3} < 0.5$

12) $-0.3 < 0.7 < 2.2$

Chapter 16: Rational Numbers

13)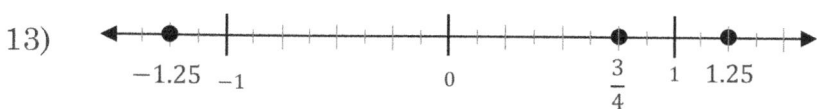

14)

15)

16)

17) Paul

18) Gamer −1

19) Her mother

20) Liam

21) $\dfrac{7}{20}$

22) $\dfrac{85}{1}$

23) $\dfrac{79}{50}$

24) $-\dfrac{3}{25}$

25) $-\dfrac{3}{1}$

26) $\dfrac{19}{20}$

27) $-\dfrac{111}{25}$

28) $-\dfrac{1}{2}$

Chapter 17 Absolute Value

Math topics that you'll learn in this chapter:

- ☑ Absolute Value Definition
- ☑ Integers and Absolute Value
- ☑ Using Number Lines to Present Absolute Value
- ☑ Integer Inequalities Involving Absolute Values
- ☑ Word Problems of Absolute Value and Integers
- ☑ Absolute Value of Rational Numbers
- ☑ Absolute Values and Opposites of Rational Numbers

Absolute Value Definition

- The absolute value of a number is its distance from 0 on a number line.

- Absolute value of a number is the non-negative value of the number, no matter its sign. As a result, the absolute value of any real number is positive.

- For instance, the number 9 has an absolute value of 9 since it's placed nine units away from zero.

- Plus, the absolute value of -9 is additionally 9 since it's nine units from zero. Thus, $|-9| = 9$

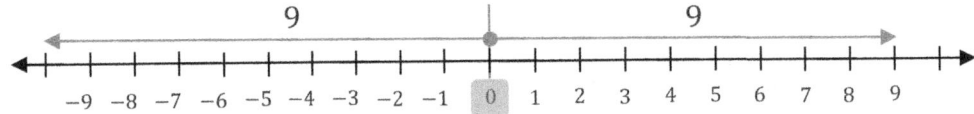

Absolute value of $9 = 9$

Absolute value of $-9 =$

Examples:

Example 1. Find the absolute value of $|-11|$.

Solution: According to $11 \geq 0$, the absolute value of -11 is eleven units away from 0. Thus, $|-11| = 11$.

Example 2. Find the absolute value of $|-2|$.

Solution: According to $2 \geq 0$, the absolute value of -2 is placed two units away from 0. Thus, $|-2| = 2$.

Integers and Absolute Value

- The absolute value of a number is its distance from zero, in either direction, on the number line. For example, the distance of 9 and -9 from zero on number line is 9.
- The absolute value of an integer is the numerical value without its sign. (Negative or positive)
- The vertical bar is used for absolute value as in $|x|$.
- The absolute value of a number is never negative; because it only shows, "how far the number is from zero".

Examples:

Example 1. Calculate. $|14 - 2| \times 5 =$

Solution: First, solve $|14 - 2|$, $\rightarrow |14 - 2| = |12|$, the absolute value of 12 is 12, $|12| = 12$, Then: $12 \times 5 = 60$

Example 2. Solve. $\frac{|-24|}{4} \times |5 - 7| =$

Solution: First, find $|-24| \rightarrow$ the absolute value of -24 is 24. Then: $|-24| = 24$, $\frac{24}{4} \times |5 - 7| =$

Now, calculate $|5 - 7|$, $\rightarrow |5 - 7| = |-2|$, the absolute value of -2 is 2. $|-2| = 2$ Then: $\frac{24}{4} \times 2 = 6 \times 2 = 12$

Example 3. Solve. $|8 - 2| \times \frac{|-4 \times 7|}{2} =$

Solution: First, calculate $|8 - 2|$, $\rightarrow |8 - 2| = |6|$, the absolute value of 6 is 6, $|6| = 6$. Then: $6 \times \frac{|-4 \times 7|}{2}$

Now calculate $|-4 \times 7|$, $\rightarrow |-4 \times 7| = |-28|$, the absolute value of -28 is 28, $|-28| = 28$, Then: $6 \times \frac{28}{2} = 6 \times 14 = 84$

Using Number Lines to Present Absolute Value

- Absolute value is the gap between zero and a number.

- To find absolute value of 6 and −6, firstly, a number line is drawn. Then:

    • Write down the numbers going from 0 to 6 on the right-hand side of 0.

    • Write down the numbers from 0 to −6 on the left-hand side of 0.

- After that, start with zero and count the number of jumps from 0 it is.

- Therefore, the amount of number is its absolute value, and this is always going to be positive.

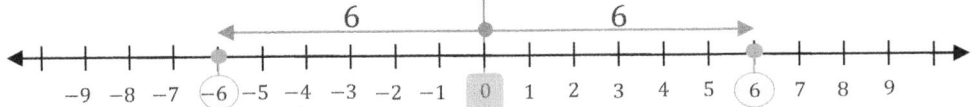

Absolute value of $6 = +6$

Absolute value of $-6 = +6$

Examples:

Example 1. Find the absolute value of $|7|$, and graph on the number line.

Solution: According to $7 \geq 0$, the absolute value of a positive number is the distance to the right side from 0. Thus, $|7| = 7$.

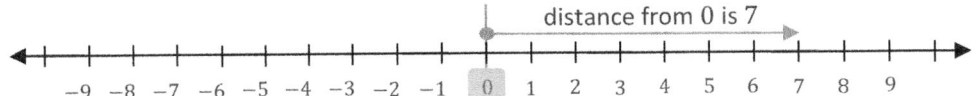

Example 2. Find the absolute value of $|-4|$, and graph it on the number line.

Solution: According to $-4 \leq 0$, the absolute value of a negative number is the distance to the left side from 0. Thus, $|-4| = 4$.

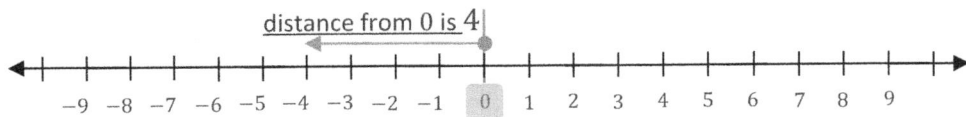

Integer Inequalities Involving Absolute Values

- An absolute value of any number is the distance it is from 0 on the number line.

- An easy absolute value example would be |10|. This signifies it's ten spaces from 0. Therefore, the absolute value of it is also 10.

- An absolute value is either zero or positive.

- For instance, |−8| and |3|. First, simplify its absolute value. Then the resulting numbers would be 8 and 3. Thus, $8 > 3$.

Examples:

Example 1. Compare the absolute value of the numbers: |−3|, |1|

Solution: Simplify the absolute value, then decide which number is greatest, least or they are equal.

|−3| = 3 and |1| = 1. So, $3 > 1$

Example 2. Compare the absolute value with the integer: |−5|, 7

Solution: Simplify the absolute value, then decide which number is greatest, least or they are equal.

|−5| = 5. So, $5 < 7$.

Example 3. Compare the absolute value of the numbers: |−1|, 4

Solution: Simplify the absolute value, then decide which number is greatest, least or they are equal.

|−1| = 1. So, $1 < 4$.

Word Problems of Absolute Value and Integers

- In mathematics, word problems can be described as exercises where background details are presented by way of text, as opposed to a mathematical notation.

- For a word problem solution:

  • **Review:** Review the problem, then determine what is being asked of you.

  • **Coordinate:** After determining what you are being asked, isolate the information you provided. Now determine what you don't know.

  • **Deduce:** What strategy should be used to get any information that is missing? Will it require division, multiplication, subtraction, or addition?

Example:

A scientist uses a tracking device to study animal behavior. The table shows the elevations of a hawk and a sea dolphin at $12:00\ A.M.$

Animal	Elevation ($ft.$)
Hawk	40
Dolphin	−28

Which animal is farthest from the sea level?

Solution: The hawk's elevation is positive, so it is above sea level. The dolphin's elevation is negative, so it is below sea level. And to find which animal is farther from sea level, use absolute value.

Hawk: $|40| = 40$

Dolphin: $|-28| = 28$

Then, $40 > 28$. Thus, the hawk is 40 feet above sea level, but the dolphin is 28 feet below sea level. The hawk is farthest from sea level.

Absolute Value of Rational Numbers

- Absolute value of rational numbers means the distance of rational numbers from zero. Absolute values are always positive (distance cannot be negative!).

- A rational number is a number that you can write as a fraction of 2 integers. An integer can be either negative or positive. For example, $\frac{2}{3}$ or $-\frac{3}{4}$ are both rational numbers. Therefore:

  - Absolute value of $\frac{2}{3}$ equals $\left|\frac{2}{3}\right| = \frac{2}{3}$.
  - Absolute value of $-\frac{3}{4}$ is $\left|-\frac{3}{4}\right| = \frac{3}{4}$.

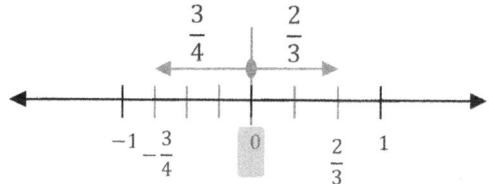

Absolute value of $\frac{2}{3} = \frac{2}{3}$

Absolute value of $-\frac{3}{4} =$

Examples:

Example 1. Find the absolute value of $-\frac{7}{5}$.

Solution: The absolute value of rational numbers is the distance from zero and distance cannot be negative; thus, $\left|-\frac{7}{5}\right| = \frac{7}{5} = 1\frac{2}{5}$

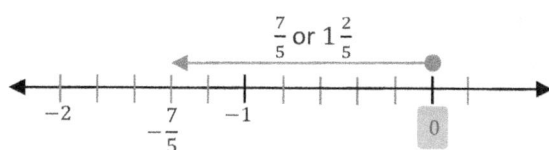

Example 2. What is |2.6|?

Solution: The absolute value of rational numbers is the distance from zero and distance cannot be negative; thus, $|2.6| = 2.6$

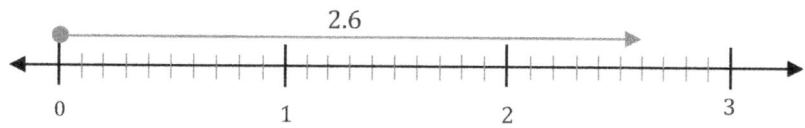

Absolute Values and Opposites of Rational Numbers

- A positive number's opposite will be negative and a negative number's opposite is always positive.

- Absolute value is the number of spaces it is from 0.

- A rational number is written as a fraction of 2 integers.

- A rational number's opposite is either positive or negative. For instance, the opposite of $-\frac{2}{3}$ is $\frac{2}{3}$.

Examples:

Example 1. What is the opposite of $-\frac{3}{5}$?

Solution: $-\frac{3}{5}$ is $\frac{3}{5}$ units to the left of 0. So, $\frac{3}{5}$ is the opposite of $-\frac{3}{5}$.

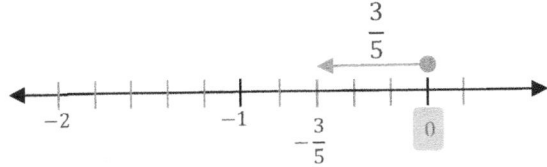

Example 2. What is the absolute value of 0.25?

Solution: 0.25 is 0.25 units to the right of 0. So, 0.25 is the absolute value of 0.25.

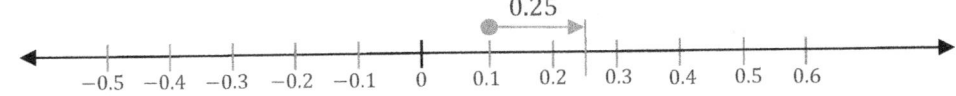

Chapter 17: Practices

✎ **Find the absolute value.**

1) $|+63| = $ ___

2) $|-13| = $ ___

3) $|0| = $ ___

4) $|-5| = $ ___

5) $|+37| = $ ___

6) $|-123| = $ ___

7) $|-25| = $ ___

8) $|+50| = $ ___

✎ **Find the answers.**

9) $|-5| + |7 - 10| = $

10) $|-4 + 6| + |-2| = $

11) $|-9| + |1 - 9| = $

12) $|-7| - |8 - 12| = $

13) $|9 - 11| + |8 - 15| = $

14) $|-7 + 10| - |-8 + 3| = $

15) $|-12 + 6| - |3 - 9| = $

16) $5 + |2 - 6| + |3 - 4| = $

17) $-4 + |2 - 6| + |1 - 9| = $

18) $\frac{|-42|}{7} \times \frac{|-64|}{8} = $

19) $\frac{|-100|}{10} \times \frac{|-36|}{6} = $

20) $|4 \times (-2)| \times \frac{|-27|}{3} = $

21) $|-3 \times 2| \times \frac{|-40|}{8} = $

22) $\frac{|-54|}{6} - |-3 \times 7| = $

23) $\frac{|-72|}{8} + |-7 \times 5| = $

24) $\frac{|-121|}{11} + |-6 \times 4| = $

25) $\frac{|(-6) \times (-3)|}{9} \times \frac{|2 \times (-20)|}{5} = $

26) $\frac{|(-3) \times (-8)|}{6} \times \frac{|9 \times (-4)|}{12} = $

✎ **Find the absolute value on the number line.**

27) $|-6| = $ ___

28) $|+19| = $ ___

29) $|-17| = $ ___

30) $|-14| = $ ___

31) $|+2| = $ ___

32) $|-3| = $ ___

33) $|+10| = $ ___

34) $|-44| = $ ___

✎ Compare.

35) $|5|, |-2|$

36) $|-10|, |-7|$

37) $-6, |-8|$

38) $11, |-11|$

39) $|4|, -4$

40) $|-9|, |5|$

41) $0, |-2|$

42) $|1|, |-1|$

✎ Solve.

43) A hiker starts hiking at the beginning of a trail that is 150 feet below sea level. She hikes to a location on the trail that is 490 feet above sea level and stops for some rest. How far did she hike?

44) In the lab, Mike is measuring the temperature of different chemical liquids. The temperature of liquid -1 is -4 and liquid -2 is 8. Which liquid's temperature is closest to zero?

45) Becky has two cats, Jake and Rob. He is worried because Jake keeps eating Rob's food. She asks their vet how much each cat's weight has changed since their last visit. Weight change for Jake is $5\ oz$ and for Rob is $-3\ oz$. Which cat has changed the most?

46) Bob's cottage is close to two cities. A path passes through a lake at the bottom of a small mountain. The other trail passes at a mountain peak. The elevation of the lake destination is $-240\ ft$ and the mountain peak destination is $380\ ft$ that is shown on the map. Which trail's destination is farther from sea level?

Chapter 17: Absolute Value

✎ **Find the absolute value.**

47) $|-4.83| = $ ___

48) $|60| = $ ___

49) $\left|-4\frac{2}{7}\right| = $ ___

50) $\left|8\frac{1}{2}\right| = $ ___

51) $\left|\frac{-1}{5}\right| = $ ___

52) $|9.963| = $ ___

53) $\left|-\frac{7}{3}\right| = $ ___

54) $\left|\frac{5}{9}\right| = $ ___

✎ **Find the absolute value of the following rational numbers.**

55) $\left|\frac{2}{7}\right| = $ ___

56) $|-0.8| = $ ___

57) $\left|-1\frac{3}{20}\right| = $ ___

58) $|-92| = $ ___

59) $\left|\frac{-5}{7}\right| = $ ___

60) $|3.31| = $ ___

61) $\left|-\frac{9}{12}\right| = $ ___

62) $|19| = $ ___

✎ **What is the opposite of the following rational numbers?**

63) $-53 = $ ___

64) $-9\frac{2}{3} = $ ___

65) $1.333\ldots = $ ___

66) $3\frac{3}{5} = $ ___

67) $0.44 = $ ___

68) $-\frac{7}{6} = $ ___

69) $\frac{1}{21} = $ ___

70) $-48.7 = $ ___

Chapter 17: Answers

1) 63
2) 13
3) 0
4) 5
5) 37
6) 123
7) 25
8) 50
9) 8
10) 4
11) 17
12) 3
13) 9
14) −2
15) 0
16) 10
17) 8
18) 48
19) 60
20) 72
21) 30
22) −12
23) 44
24) 35
25) 16
26) 12

27)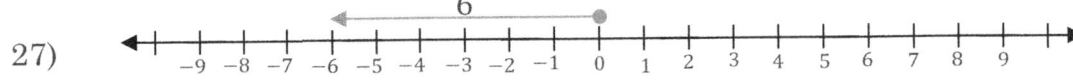

28)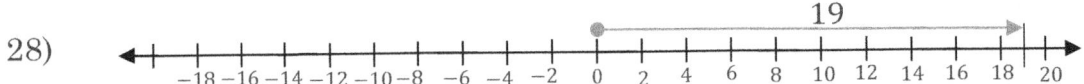

29)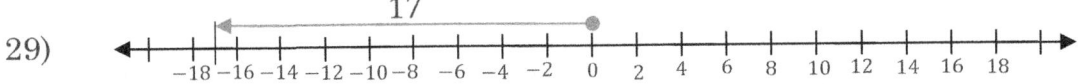

30)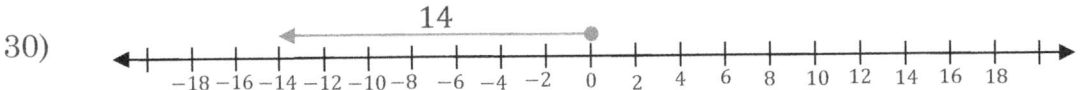

31)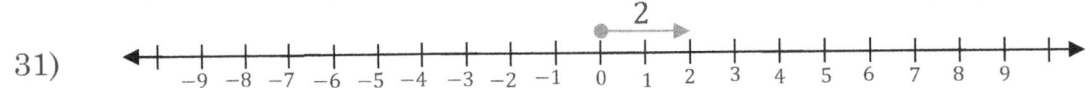

32)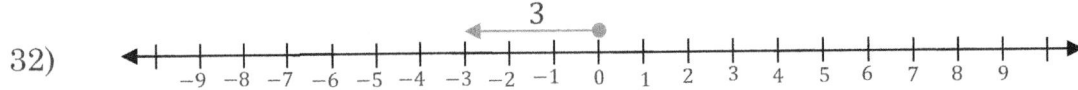

33)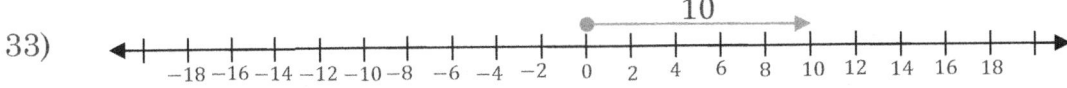

34)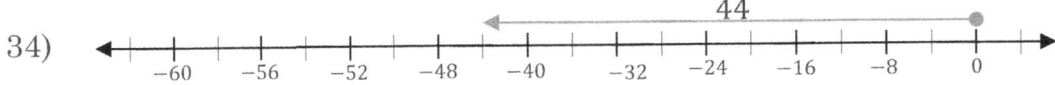

Chapter 17: Absolute Value

35) $5 > 2$

36) $10 > 7$

37) $-6 < 8$

38) $11 = 11$

39) $4 > -4$

40) $9 > 5$

41) $0 < 2$

42) $1 = 1$

43) 640

44) 1

45) 5

46) 380

47) 4.83

48) 60

49) $4\frac{2}{7}$

50) $8\frac{1}{2}$

51) $\frac{1}{5}$

52) 9.963

53) $\frac{7}{3}$

54) $\frac{5}{9}$

55) $\frac{2}{7}$

56) 0.8

57) $1\frac{3}{20}$

58) 92

59) $\frac{5}{7}$

60) 3.31

61) $\frac{9}{12}$

62) 19

63) 53

64) $9\frac{2}{3}$

65) $-1.333\ldots$

66) $-3\frac{3}{5}$

67) $-0.44 =$

68) $\frac{7}{6}$

69) $-\frac{1}{21}$

70) 48.7

Time to Test

Time to refine your skill with a practice examination.

Take a practice North Carolina EOG Math Test to simulate the test day experience. After you've finished, score your test using the answer key.

Before You Start

- You'll need a pencil and scratch papers to take the test.
- There are two types of questions:

  Multiple choice questions: for each of these questions, there are four or more possible answers. Choose which one is best.

  Grid-ins questions: for these questions, write your answer in the box provided.
- It's okay to guess. You won't lose any points if you're wrong.
- The North Carolina EOG Mathematics test contains a formula sheet, which displays formulas relating to geometric measurement and certain algebra concepts. Formulas are provided to test-takers so that they may focus on application, rather than the memorization, of formulas.
- After you've finished the test, review the answer key to see where you went wrong and what areas you need to improve.

North Carolina EOG Grade 6 Math Practice Test 1

2022 – 2023

Two Parts

Total number of questions: 40

Part 1 (No Calculator): 20 questions

Part 2 (Calculator): 20 questions

Total time for two parts: 120 Minutes

North Carolina EOG Grade 6 Mathematics Reference Materials

AREA

Triangle $\qquad A = \dfrac{1}{2}bh$

Rectangle Parallelogram $\qquad A = bh$

Trapezoid $\qquad A = \dfrac{1}{2}h(b_1 + b_2)$

VOLUME

Rectangle Prism $\qquad V = Bh$

LENGTH

Customary
- 1 mile = 1,760 yards (yd)
- 1 yard = 3 feet (ft)
- 1 foot (ft) = 12 inches (in.)

Metric
- 1 kilometer (km) = 1,000 meter (m)
- 1 meter (m) = 100 centimeters (cm)
- 1 centimeter (cm) = 10 millimeters (mm)

VOLUME AND CAPACI

Customary
- 1 gallon (gal) = 4 quarts (qt)
- 1 quart (qt) = 2 pints (pt)
- 1 pint (pt) = 2 cups (c)
- 1 cup (c) = 8 fluid ounces (fl oz)

Metric
- 1 liter (L) = 1,000 millimeters (mL)

WEIGHT AND MASS

Customary
- 1 ton (T) = 2,000 Pounds (lb)
- 1 pound (lb) = 16 ounces (oz)

Metric
- 1 kilogram (kg) = 1,000 grams (g)
- 1 gram (g) = 1,000 milligrams (mg)

North Carolina EOG Mathematics Practice Test 1

Part 1

(No Calculator)

Total number of questions: 20

Total time for Part 1 (No Calculator): 60 Minutes

You may not use a calculator on this part.

1) $4(1.052) - 3.126 = \cdots$?

A. 0.926

B. 1.082

C. 1.122

D. 1.134

2) Which list shows the integer numbers listed in order from least to greatest?

A. $-12, -4, -1, -2, 1, 3, 7$

B. $-12, -1, -2, -4, 1, 3, 7$

C. $-12, -4, -2, -1, 1, 3, 7$

D. $-1, -2, -4, -12, 1, 3, 7$

3) There are 55 blue marbles and 143 red marbles. We want to place these marbles in some boxes so that there is the same number of red marbles in each box and the same number of blue marbles in each of the box. How many boxes do we need?

A. 8

B. 9

C. 10

D. 11

4) What is the value of the following expression?

$$2{,}205 \div 315$$

A. 5

B. 6

C. 7

D. 8

5) Solve the following equation. $112 = 22 + x$

A. $x = -90$

B. $x = 90$

C. $x = -134$

D. $x = 134$

6) Car A travels $221.5\ km$ at a given time, while car B travels 1.2 times the distance car A travels at the same time. What is the distance car B travels during that time?

A. $222.7\ km$

B. $233.5\ km$

C. $241.5\ km$

D. $265.8\ km$

7) The perimeter of the trapezoid below (not drawn to scale) is $38\ cm$. What is its area?

A. $576\ cm^2$

B. $78\ cm^2$

C. $40\ cm^2$

D. $24 cm^2$

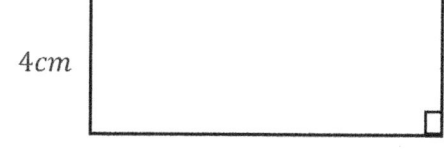

8) Which of the following expressions has the greatest value?

A. $3^1 + 12$

B. $3^3 - 3^2$

C. $3^4 - 60$

D. $3^5 - 218$

9) Which value is equivalent to the expression 5^4?

A. 9
B. 20
C. 625
D. 1024

10) Alfred has x apples. Alvin has 40 apples, which is 15 apples less than number of apples Alfred own. If Baron has $\frac{1}{5}$ times as many apples as Alfred has, how many apples does Baron have?

A. 5

B. 11

C. 55

D. 275

11) In the following triangle find α. (Figure not drawn to scale)

A. 100°

B. 90°

C. 60°

D. 30°

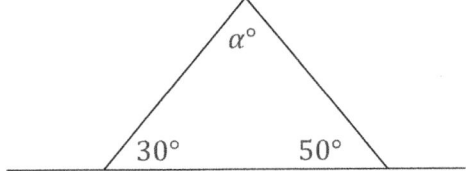

12) The price of a laptop is decreased by 15% to $425. What is its original price?

A. $283

B. $430

C. $500

D. $550

13) Find the perimeter of shape in the following figure? (All angles are right angles)

A. 21

B. 22

C. 24

D. 20

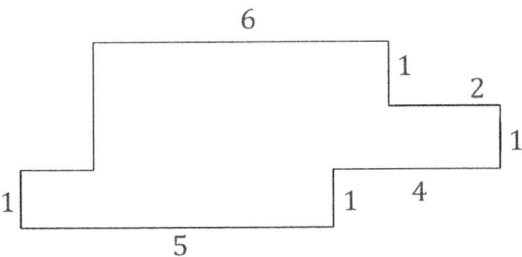

14) What is the probability of choosing a month starts with A in a year?

A. 1

B. $\frac{2}{3}$

C. $\frac{1}{2}$

D. $\frac{1}{6}$

15) What are the values of mode and median in the following set of numbers?

$$1, 3, 3, 6, 6, 5, 4, 3, 1, 1, 2$$

A. Mode: 1, 2, Median: 2

B. Mode: 1, 3, Median: 3

C. Mode: 2, 3, Median: 2

D. Mode: 1, 3, Median: 2.5

16) Which expression equivalent to $x \times 92$?

A. $(x \times 90) + 2$

B. $x \times 9 \times 2$

C. $(x \times 90) + (x \times 2)$

D. $(2 \times 90) + x$

17) The ratio of pens to pencils in a box is 3 to 5. If there are 96 pens and pencils in the box altogether, how many more pens should be put in the box to make the ratio of pens to pencils 1: 1?

A. 22

B. 23

C. 24

D. 25

18) If point A placed at $-\frac{24}{3}$ on a number line, which of the following points has a distance equal to 5 from point A?

A. −13

B. −3

C. −2

D. A and B

19) Which of the following shows the numbers in increasing order?

A. $\frac{3}{13}, \frac{4}{11}, \frac{5}{14}, \frac{2}{5}$

B. $\frac{3}{13}, \frac{5}{14}, \frac{4}{11}, \frac{2}{5}$

C. $\frac{3}{13}, \frac{5}{14}, \frac{2}{5}, \frac{4}{11}$

D. $\frac{5}{14}, \frac{3}{13}, \frac{2}{5}, \frac{4}{11}$

20) If $x = -4$, which of the following equations is true?

A. $x(3x - 1) = 50$

B. $5(11 - x^2) = -25$

C. $3(-2x + 5) = 49$

D. $x(-5x - 19) = -3$

STOP

This is the End of this Section. You may check your work on this section if you still have time.

North Carolina EOG Mathematics Practice Test 1

Part 2

(Calculator)

Total number of questions: 20

Total time for Part 2 (Calculator): 60 Minutes

You may use a calculator on this part.

1) What is the missing prime factor of number 450?

$$450 = 2^1 \times 3^2 \times \ldots$$

Write your answer in the box below?

2) Which situation is best represented by the inequality $\frac{x}{2} \leq 4$?

A. Sarah gave x pieces of candy to 2 kids, and each kid received fewer than 4 pieces of candy.

B. Sarah put x books on 4 shelves, and there were no more than 4 books on each shelf.

C. Sarah divided x pencils into 4 stacks, and each stack had at least 4 pencils.

D. Sarah shared 4 stickers with x friends, and each friend received fewer than 4 stickers.

3) 65 is what percent of 50?

A. 50%

B. 77%

C. 130%

D. 140%

4) Which of the following expressions has a value of -23?

A. $-10 + (-8) + \frac{-5}{2} \times 2$

B. $5 \times 3 + (-2) \times 18$

C. $-10 + 6 \times 8 \div (-4)$

D. $(-3) \times (-7) + 2$

5) 300 inches equal to ...?

A. 3600 ft

B. 900 ft

C. 100 ft

D. 25 ft

6) Which of the following equations is true?

A. $0.09 = \frac{9}{10}$

B. $\frac{20}{100} = 0.02$

C. $2.4 = \frac{24}{10}$

D. $\frac{35}{7} = 0.5$

7) What is the greatest common factor of 36 and 54?

A. 20

B. 19

C. 18

D. 17

8) Based on the table below, which of the following expressions represents any value of f in term of its corresponding value of x?

A. $f = x + 1\frac{7}{8}$

B. $f = x - 1\frac{7}{8}$

C. $f = 2x + 1\frac{7}{8}$

D. $f = 2x - 1\frac{7}{8}$

x	1.1	1.4	2.1
f	−0.775	−0.475	0.225

9) $10 \, mm = ...$?

A. $0.001 \, m$

B. $0.01 \, m$

C. $100 \, m$

D. $1000 \, m$

10) A football team won exactly 60% of the games it played during last session. Which of the following could be the total number of games the team played last season?

A. 63

B. 55

C. 48

D. 37

11) 8 less than twice a positive integer is 70. What is the integer?

A. 80

B. 78

C. 40

D. 39

Types of air pollutions in 10 cities of a country

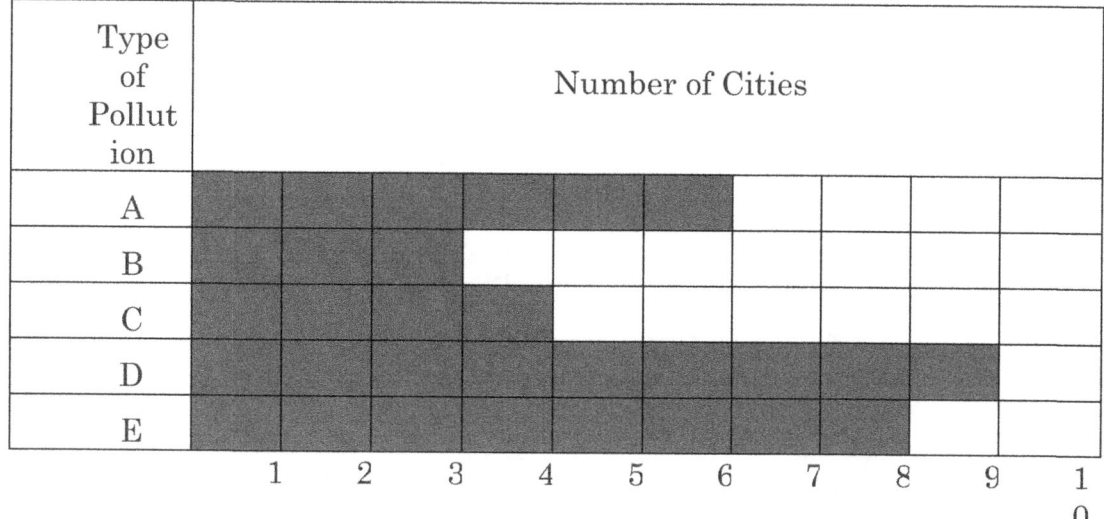

12) Based on the above data, what percent of cities are in the type of pollution A, C, and E respectively?

A. 60%, 40%, 90%

B. 30%, 40%, 90%

C. 30%, 40%, 60%

D. 40%, 60%, 90%

13) What is the missing term in the given sequence?

$$2, 7, 17, 37, 77, \_\_, 317$$

Write your answer in the box below.

14) If $4x - 1 = 9$, what is the value of $2x + 10$?

A. 30.5

B. 25

C. 20.5

D. 15

15) How many tiles of 9 cm^2 is needed to cover a floor of dimension 7 cm by 36 cm?

A. 26

B. 27

C. 28

D. 29

16) If there are 400 students at a school and nearly 37% of them prefer to learn Germany, approximately how many students want to learn Germany?

A. 400

B. 252

C. 148

D. 130

17) A shaft rotates 360 times in 12 seconds. How many times does it rotate in 18 seconds?

A. 540

B. 450

C. 360

D. 100

18) A card is drawn at random from a standard 52–card deck, what is the probability that the card is of the King? (There are 4 Kings in a standard 52 –card deck.)

A. $\frac{1}{3}$

B. $\frac{1}{13}$

C. $\frac{1}{6}$

D. $\frac{1}{52}$

19) Which of the following statement can describe the following inequality correctly?

$$\frac{x}{5} \geq 9$$

A. David put x books in 5 shelves, and each shelf had at least 9 books.

B. David placed 5 books in x shelves so that each shelf had less than 9 books.

C. David put 9 books in x shelves and each shelf had exactly 5 books.

D. David put x books in 5 shelves, and each shelf had more than 9 books.

20) Removing which of the following numbers will change the average of the numbers to 7.4?

$$1, 4, 5, 8, 11, 12$$

A. 4

B. 5

C. 8

D. 11

This is the end of Practice Test 1

North Carolina EOG Grade 6 Math Practice Test 2

2022 – 2023

Two Parts

Total number of questions: 40

Part 1 (No Calculator): 20 questions

Part 2 (Calculator): 20 questions

Total time for two parts: 120 Minutes

North Carolina EOG Grade 6 Mathematics Reference Materials

AREA

Triangle $\quad A = \dfrac{1}{2}bh$

Rectangle Parallelogram $\quad A = bh$

Trapezoid $\quad A = \dfrac{1}{2}h(b_1 + b_2)$

VOLUME

Rectangle Prism $\quad V = Bh$

LENGTH

Customary
- 1 mile = 1,760 yards (yd)
- 1 yard = 3 feet (ft)
- 1 foot (ft) = 12 inches (in.)

Metric
- 1 kilometer (km) = 1,000 meter (m)
- 1 meter (m) = 100 centimeters (cm)
- 1 centimeter (cm) = 10 millimeters (mm)

VOLUME AND CAPACITY

Customary
- 1 gallon (gal) = 4 quarts (qt)
- 1 quart (qt) = 2 pints (pt)
- 1 pint (pt) = 2 cups (c)
- 1 cup (c) = 8 fluid ounces (fl oz)

Metric
- 1 liter (L) = 1,000 millimeters (mL)

WEIGHT AND MASS

Customary
- 1 ton (T) = 2,000 Pounds (lb)
- 1 pound (lb) = 16 ounces (oz)

Metric
- 1 kilogram (kg) = 1,000 grams (g)
- 1 gram (g) = 1,000 milligrams (mg)

North Carolina EOG Mathematics Practice Test 2

Part 1

(No Calculator)

Total number of questions: 20

Total time for Part 1 (No Calculator): 60 Minutes

You may not use a calculator on this part.

1) In the following figure, the shaded squares are what fractional part of the whole set of squares?

A. $\frac{1}{2}$

B. $\frac{5}{8}$

C. $\frac{2}{3}$

D. $\frac{3}{5}$

2) In a party, 14 soft drinks are required for every 16 guests. If there are 160 guests, how many soft drinks are required?

A. 18

B. 104

C. 140

D. 1,440

3) Which of the following statement is False?

A. $2 \times 2 = 4$

B. $(4 + 1) \times 5 = 25$

C. $6 \div (3 - 1) = 1$

D. $6 \times (4 - 2) = 12$

4) What is the value of 3^4 ?

Write your answer in the box below.

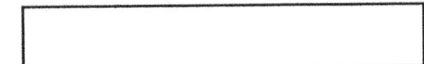

5) What is the volume of the following rectangle prism?

A. $19 \ m^3$

B. $40 \ m^3$

C. $50 \ m^3$

D. $200 \ m^3$

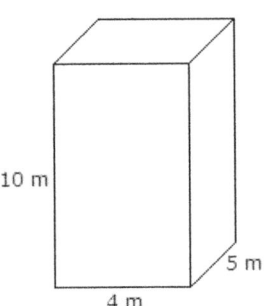

6) Which number line represents the solution to $4x - 1 < 11$?

A.

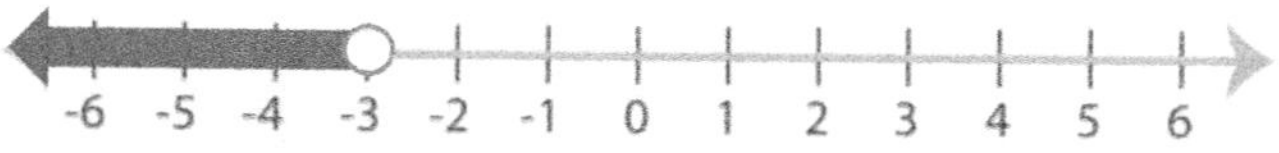

B.

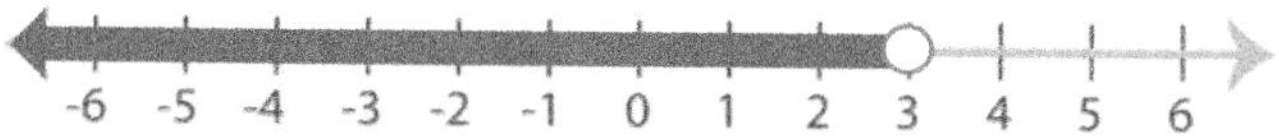

C.

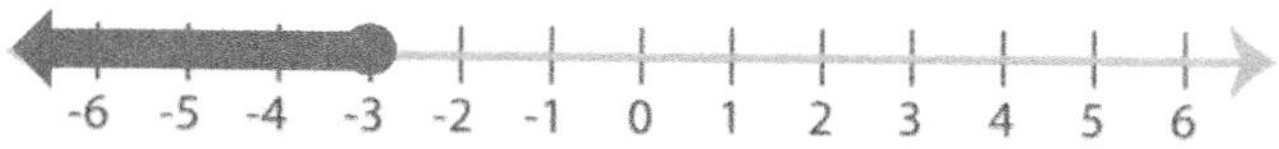

D.

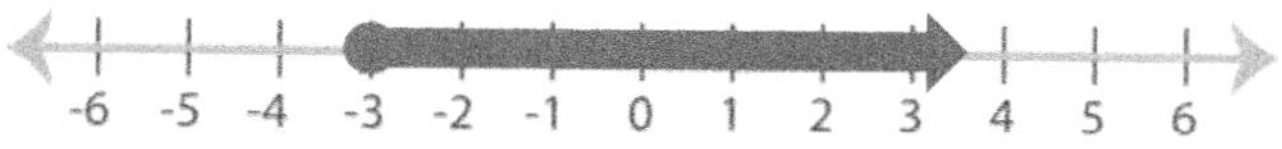

7) The area of a rectangle is x square feet and its length is 9 feet. Which equation represents y, the width of the rectangle in feet?

A. $y = \frac{x}{9}$

B. $y = \frac{9}{x}$

C. $y = 9x$

D. $y = 9 + x$

8) $(11 + 7) \div (3^3 \div 3) =$ __

A. 18

B. $\frac{5}{7}$

C. 2

D. 6

9) The area of the square shown is $144\ cm^2$. What is x?

A. $12\ cm$

B. $10\ cm$

C. $8\ cm$

D. $6\ cm$

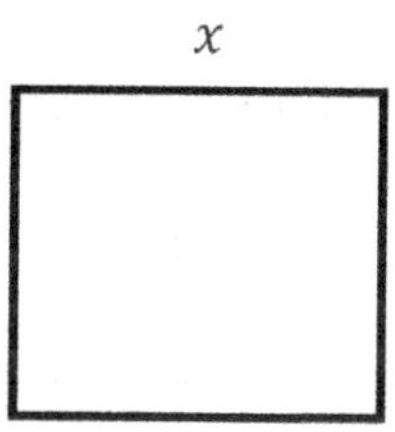

10) Which of the following shows the numbers from least to greatest?

$\frac{11}{15}, 75\%, 0.74, \frac{19}{25}$

A. $75\%, 0.74, \frac{11}{15}, \frac{19}{25}$

B. $75\%, 0.74, \frac{19}{25}, \frac{11}{15}$

C. $0.74, 75\%, \frac{11}{15}, \frac{19}{25}$

D. $\frac{11}{15}, 0.74, 75\%, \frac{19}{25}$

11) When 3 is added to four times a number M, the result is 24. Which of the following equations represents this statement?

A. $4 + 3M = 24$

B. $24M + 4 = 3$

C. $4M + 3 = 24$

D. $4M + 24 = 3$

12) The average of $13, 15, 20$ and x is 25. What is the value of x?

Write your answer in the box below.

13) What is the Area of the square shown in the following square?

A. 2

B. 4

C. 6

D. 8

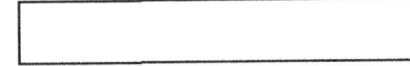

14) What is the value of this expression? $[3 \times (-14) - 48] - (-14) + [3 \times 8] \div 2$

Write your answer in the box below.

15) The price of a car was $28,000 in 2012. In 2013, the price of that car was $18,200. What was the rate of depreciation of the price of car per year?

A. 20%

B. 30%

C. 35%

D. 40%

16) How many possible outfit combinations come from five shirts, seven slacks, and five ties?

Write your answer in the box below.

$$\boxed{}$$

17) A construction worker needs 58.5 cubic yard of concrete to lay the foundation for a house. Each truck can hold 4.5 cubic yards of concrete. How many trucks will the worker need to transport the concrete?

A. 13

B. 15

C. 18

D. 28

18) John traveled 150 km in 6 hours and Alice traveled 180 km in 4 hours. What is the ratio of the average speed of John to average speed of Alice?

A. 3 : 2

B. 2 : 3

C. 5 : 9

D. 5 : 6

19) In five successive hours, a car travels 40 km, 45 km, 50 km, 35 km and 55 km. In the next five hours, it travels with an average speed of 50 km per hour. Find the total distance the car traveled in 10 hours.

   A. 425 km

   B. 450 km

   C. 475 km

   D. 500 km

20) How long does a 280-miles trip take moving at 50 miles per hour (mph)?

   A. 5 hours

   B. 5 hours and 24 minutes

   C. 5 hours and 36 minutes

   D. 5 hours and 48 minutes

STOP

This is the End of this Section. You may check your work on this section if you still have time.

North Carolina EOG Mathematics Practice Test 2

Part 2

(Calculator)

Total number of questions: 20

Total time for Part 2 (Calculator): 60 Minutes

You may use a calculator on this part.

1) Which set of angle measures can be the angle measures of triangle?

   A. 35, 45, 90

   B. 65, 70, 80

   C. 100, 35, 40

   D. 40, 50, 90

2) Which list shows the numbers in order from greatest value to least value?

   A. $\frac{3}{4}, \frac{2}{3}, \frac{4}{7}, \frac{1}{2}, \frac{2}{5}$

   B. $\frac{3}{4}, \frac{2}{3}, \frac{4}{7}, \frac{1}{2}, \frac{2}{5}$

   C. $\frac{3}{4}, \frac{2}{3}, \frac{4}{7}, \frac{1}{2}, \frac{2}{5}$

   D. $\frac{3}{4}, \frac{2}{3}, \frac{4}{7}, \frac{1}{2}, \frac{2}{5}$

3) The A store offered a 15% discount off the regular price of a desk. The amount of the discount is $6. What is the regular price of the desk?

   A. $35

   B. $40

   C. $45

   D. $50

4) What is the result of evaluating the expression $(-14) + 5(-4) + 4(5)$?

   A. -34

   B. -14

   C. 26

   D. 54

5) A $45 shirt now selling for $28 is discounted by about what percent?

   A. 20%

   B. 37.7%

   C. 40%

   D. 60%

6) In 1999, the average worker's income increased $3,000 per year starting from $24,000 annual salary. Which equation represents income greater than average?

(I = income, x = number of years after 1999)

A. $I > 3000x + 24000$

B. $I > -3000x + 24000$

C. $I < -3000x + 24000$

D. $I < 3000x - 24000$

7) From last year, the price of gasoline has increased from $1.40 per gallon to $1.75 per gallon. The new price is what percent of the original price?

A. 72%

B. 125%

C. 140%

D. 160%

8) Sophia purchased a sofa for $504. The sofa is regularly priced at $600. What was the percent discount Sophia received on the sofa?

A. 12%

B. 16%

C. 20%

D. 25%

9) A bag contains 20 balls: four green, five black, eight blue, a brown, a red and one white. If 19 balls are removed from the bag at random, what is the probability that a brown ball has been removed?

A. $\frac{1}{9}$

B. $\frac{1}{20}$

C. $\frac{4}{5}$

D. $\frac{19}{20}$

10) A rope weighs 600 grams per meter of length. What is the weight in kilograms of 15.2 meters of this rope? (1 $kilograms = 1,000\ grams$)

A. 0.0912

B. 0.912

C. 9.12

D. 91.20

11) If $x = -8$, which equation is true?

A. $x(2x - 4) = 120$

B. $8(4 - x) = 96$

C. $2(4x + 6) = 79$

D. $6x - 2 = -46$

12) The Which expression is equivalent to $-12 + (5 \times n)$?

A. $12n - 5$

B. $5n - 12$

C. $5n$

D. $n - 12$

13) What is the median of these numbers? $2, 27, 28, 19, 67, 44, 35$

A. 19

B. 28

C. 44

D. 35

14) In Los Angeles, California, 5 squirrels collected 100 acorns in one day. If they continued collecting acorns at the same rate, how many acorns would 30 squirrels collect in one day?

Write your answer in the box below.

15) A bank is offering 4.5% simple interest on a savings account. If you deposit $9,000, how much interest will you earn in five years?

A. $405

B. $720

C. $2,025

D. $3,600

16) A soccer field has a perimeter of 240 meters. What is the perimeter of the field in kilometers?

Write your answer in the box below.

17) Find the missing number in the sequence: 6, 9, 13, ..., 24

A. 15

B. 17

C. 18

D. 20

18) 55 students took an exam and 11 of them failed. What percent of the students passed the exam?

Write your answer in the box below.

19) What is the sum of $\frac{8}{12} + \frac{4}{3} + \frac{2}{6}$?

A. 2.1

B. 3

C. $2\frac{1}{3}$

D. 1

20) What is 8,923.2769 rounded to the nearest tenth?

A. 8923.3

B. 8923.277

C. 8923

D. 8923.27

This is the end of Practice Test 2

North Carolina EOG Grade 6 Math Practice Tests Answer Keys

Now, it's time to review your results to see where you went wrong and what areas you need to improve.

North Carolina EOG Math Practice Test 1 Answer Key			
Section 1		**Section 2**	
1	B	1	5
2	C	2	A
3	D	3	C
4	C	4	A
5	B	5	D
6	D	6	C
7	B	7	C
8	D	8	B
9	C	9	B
10	B	10	B
11	A	11	D
12	C	12	A
13	C	13	157
14	D	14	D
15	B	15	C
16	C	16	C
17	C	17	A
18	D	18	B
19	B	19	A
20	B	20	A

North Carolina EOG Math Practice Test 2 Answer Key

	Section 1		Section 2
1	D	1	D
2	C	2	A
3	C	3	B
4	81	4	B
5	D	5	B
6	B	6	A
7	A	7	B
8	C	8	B
9	A	9	D
10	D	10	C
11	C	11	B
12	52	12	B
13	B	13	B
14	−64	14	600
15	C	15	C
16	175	16	0.24
17	A	17	C
18	C	18	80
19	C	19	C
20	C	20	A

North Carolina EOG Grade 6 Math Practice Tests Answers and Explanations

North Carolina EOG Grade 6 Math Practice Test 1 Answers and Explanations

Section 1 – No Calculator

1) Choice B is correct

$4(1.052) - 3.126 = 4.208 - 3.126 = 1.082$

2) Choice C is correct

$-12 < -4 < -2 < -1 < 1 < 3 < 7$

Then choice C is correct

3) Choice D is correct

First, we need to find the GCF (Greatest Common Factor) of 143 and 55. $143 = 11 \times 13$

$55 = 5 \times 11 \rightarrow GFC = 11$. Therefore, we need 11 boxes.

4) Choice C is correct

$2,205 \div 315 = \dfrac{2,205}{315} = \dfrac{441}{63} = \dfrac{147}{21} = 7$

5) Choice B is correct

$112 = 22 + x$. Subtract 22 from both sides of the equation. Then: $x = 112 - 22 = 90$

6) Choice D is correct

Distance that car B travels = 1.2 × distance that car A travels

$= 1.2 \times 221.5 = 265.8 \, km$

7) Choice D is correct

The perimeter of the trapezoid is 38.

Therefore, the missing side (height) is $= 38 - 4 - 9 - 13 = 12$

Area of the trapezoid: $A = \frac{1}{2}h(b_1 + b_2) = \frac{1}{2}(12)(4+9) = 78$

8) Choice D is correct

A. $3^1 + 12 = 3 + 12 = 15$

B. $3^3 - 3^2 = 27 - 9 = 18$

C. $3^4 - 60 = 81 - 60 = 21$

D. $3^5 - 218 = 243 - 218 = 25$

9) Choice C is correct

The expression $5^4 = 5 \times 5 \times 5 \times 5 = 625$

10) Choice B is correct

Alfred has x apple which is 15 apples more than number of apples Alvin owns. Therefore:

$x - 15 = 40 \rightarrow x = 40 + 15 = 55$. Alfred has 55 apples. Let y be the number of apples that Baron has. Then: $y = \frac{1}{5} \times 55 = 11$

11) Choice A is correct

Complementary angles add up to 180 degrees. $\beta + 150° = 180° \rightarrow \beta = 180° - 150° = 30°$

The sum of all angles in a triangle is 180 degrees. Then: $\alpha + \beta + 50° = 180° \rightarrow$
$\alpha + 30° + 50° = 180° \rightarrow \alpha + 80° = 180° \rightarrow \alpha = 180° - 80° = 100°$

12) Choice C is correct

Let x be the original price. If the price of a laptop is decreased by 15% to $425, then: $85\% \ of \ x = 425 \Rightarrow 0.85x = 425 \Rightarrow x = 425 \div 0.85 = 500$

13) Choice C is correct

Let x and y be two sides of the shape. Then:

$x + 1 = 1 + 1 + 1 \rightarrow x = 2$

$y + 6 + 2 = 5 + 4 \rightarrow y + 8 = 9 \rightarrow y = 1$

Then, the perimeter is:

$1 + 5 + 1 + 4 + 1 + 2 + 1 + 6 + 2 + 1 = 24$

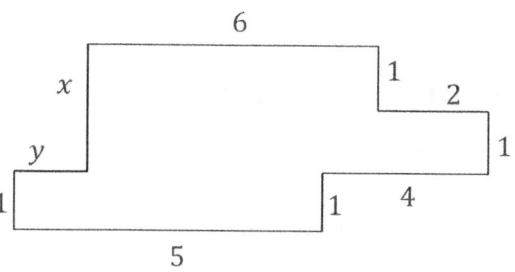

14) Choice D is correct

Two months, April and August, in 12 months start with A, then:

Probability $= \dfrac{number \ of \ desired \ outcomes}{number \ of \ total \ outcomes} = \dfrac{2}{12} = \dfrac{1}{6}$

15) Choice B is correct
First, put the numbers in order from least to greatest: 1, 1, 1, 2, 3, 3, 3, 4, 5, 6, 6

The Mode of the set of numbers is: 1 and 3 (the most frequent numbers)

Median is: 3 (the number in the middle)

16) Choice C is correct
$x \times 92 = x \times (90 + 2) = (x \times 90) + (x \times 2)$

17) Choice C is correct
The ratio of pens to pencils is $3:5$. Therefore there are 3 pens out of all 8 pens and pencils. To find the answer, first divide 96 by 8 then multiply the result by 3. $96 \div 8 = 12 \rightarrow 12 \times 3 = 36$

There are 36 pens and 60 pencils ($96 - 36$). Therefore, 24 more pens should be put in the box to make the ratio $1:1$

18) Choice D is correct
If the value of point A is greater than the value of point B, then the distance of two points on the number line is: value of A − value of B

A. $-\frac{24}{3} - (-13) = -8 + 13 = 5 = 5$

B. $-3 - \left(-\frac{24}{3}\right) = -3 + 8 = 5 = 5$

C. $-2 - \left(-\frac{24}{3}\right) = -2 + 8 = 6 \neq 5$

Both A and B are 5 points from $-\frac{24}{3}$. Choice D is correct.

19) Choice B is correct
$\frac{3}{13} \cong 0.23$ $\frac{5}{14} \cong 0.357$ $\frac{4}{11} \cong 0.36$ $\frac{2}{5} = 0.4$

Then: $\frac{3}{13} < \frac{5}{14} < \frac{4}{11} < \frac{2}{5}$

20) Choice B is correct
Plug in the value of x in the equations. $x = -4$, then:

A. $x(3x - 1) = 50 \rightarrow -4(3(-4) - 1) = -4(-12 - 1) = -4(-13) = 52 \neq 50$

B. $5(11 - x^2) = -25 \rightarrow 5(11 - (-4)^2) = 5(11 - 16) = 5(-5) = -25$

C. $3(-2x + 5) = 49 \rightarrow 3(-2(-4) + 5) = 3(8 + 5) = 39 \neq 49$

D. $x(-5x - 19) = -3 \rightarrow -4(-5(-4) - 19) = -4(20 - 19) = -4 \neq -3$

Section 2 – Calculator

1) **The answer is 5**

Let x be the missing prime factor of 450. $450 = 2 \times 3 \times 3 \times x \Rightarrow x = \frac{450}{18} \Rightarrow x = 25 = 5 \times 5$

$450 = 2^1 \times 3^2 \times 5^2$ The missing prime factor of 450 is 5.

2) **Choice A is correct**

Only choice A represent the inequality $\frac{x}{2} \leq 4$.

Sarah gave x pieces of candy to 2 kids, and each kid received fewer than 4 pieces of candy.

3) **Choice C is correct**

$\frac{65}{50} = 1.30 = 130\%$. The answer is 130%.

4) **Choice A is correct**

Let's check the options provided.

A. $-10 + (-8) + \frac{-5}{2} \times 2 \rightarrow -10 + (-8) + \frac{-5}{2} \times 2 = -10 + (-8) + (-5) = -10 - 13 = -23$

B. $5 \times 3 + (-2) \times 18 = 15 + (-38) = -21$

C. $-10 + 6 \times 8 \div (-4) = -10 + 48 \div (-4) = -10 - 12 = -22$

D. $(-3) \times (-7) + 2 = 21 + 2 = 23$

5) **Choice D is correct**

1 feet = 12 inches. Then: $300 \, in \times \frac{1 \, ft}{12 \, in} = \frac{300}{12} \, ft = 25 \, ft$

6) **Choice C is correct**

A. $0.09 = \frac{9}{100}$
B. $\frac{20}{100} = \frac{2}{10} = 0.2$
C. $2.4 = 2\frac{4}{10} = \frac{24}{10}$
D. $\frac{35}{7} = 5$

Only choice C is correct.

7) Choice C is correct

Prime factorizing of $36 = 2 \times 2 \times 3 \times 3$

Prime factorizing of $54 = 2 \times 3 \times 3 \times 3$

To find Greatest Common Factor, multiply the common factors of both numbers.

$GCF = 2 \times 3 \times 3 = 18$

8) Choice B is correct

Plug in the values of x in the equations provided.

A. $f = x + 1\frac{7}{8} = 1.1 + 1\frac{7}{8} = 1.1 + \frac{15}{8} = 2.975 \neq -0.775$

B. $f = x - 1\frac{7}{8} = 1.1 - 1\frac{7}{8} = -0.775$

C. $f = 2x + 1\frac{7}{8} = 2(1.1) + \frac{15}{8} = 4.075 \neq -0.775$

D. $f = 2x - 1\frac{7}{8} = 2(1.1) - \frac{15}{8} = 0.325 \neq -0.775$

9) Choice B is correct

$1\,m = 1000\,mm$ and $1\,mm = 0.001\,m$

Then, $10\,mm = 10 \times 0.001\,m = 0.01\,m$

10) Choice B is correct

Choices A, C and D are incorrect because 60% of each of the numbers is a non-whole number.

A. 63, 60% of $63 = 0.60 \times 63 = 37.8$

B. 55, 60% of $55 = 0.60 \times 55 = 33$

C. 48, 60% of $48 = 0.60 \times 48 = 28.8$

D. 37, 60% of $37 = 0.60 \times 37 = 22.2$

11) Choice D is correct

Let x be the integer. Then: $2x - 8 = 70$. Add 8 both sides: $2x = 78$. Divide both sides by 2: $x = 39$

12) Choice A is correct

Percent of cities in the type of pollution A: $\frac{6}{10} \times 100 = 60\%$

Percent of cities in the type of pollution C: $\frac{4}{10} \times 100 = 40\%$

Percent of cities in the type of pollution E: $\frac{9}{10} \times 100 = 90\%$

13) The answer is 157

Find the difference of each pairs of numbers: $2, 7, 17, 37, 77, \_\_, 317$

The difference of 2 and 7 is 5, 7 and 17 is 10, 17 and 37 is 20, 37 and 77 is 40, 77 and next number should be 80. The number is $77 + 80 = 157$

14) Choice D is correct

$4x - 1 = 9 \rightarrow 4x = 9 + 1 = 10 \rightarrow x = \frac{10}{4} = 2.5$

Then, $2x + 10 = 2(2.5) + 10 = 5 + 10 = 15$

15) Choice C is correct

The area of the floor is: $7\ cm \times 36\ cm = 252\ cm$

The number of tiles needed $= 252 \div 9 = 28$

16) Choice C is correct

Number of students prefer to learn Germany $= 37\%\ of\ 400 = \frac{37}{100} \times 400 = 148$

17) Choice A is correct

The shaft rotates 360 times in 12 seconds. Then, the number of rotates in 18 second equals to:

$$\frac{360 \times 18}{12} = 540$$

18) Choice B is correct

The probability of choosing a King is $\frac{4}{52} = \frac{1}{13}$

19) Choice A is correct
Let's write an inequality for each statement.

A. $\frac{x}{5} \geq 9$ (this is the same as the inequality provided)

B. $\frac{5}{x} < 9$

C. $\frac{9}{x} = 5$

D. $\frac{x}{5} > 9$

20) Choice A is correct
Check each choice provided:

A. 4 $\frac{1+5+8+11+12}{5} = \frac{37}{5} = 7.4$

B. 5 $\frac{1+4+8+11+12}{5} = \frac{36}{5} = 7.2$

C. 8 $\frac{1+4+5+11+12}{5} = \frac{36}{5} = 6.6$

D. 11 $\frac{1+4+5+8+12}{5} = \frac{30}{5} = 6$

North Carolina EOG Grade 6 Math Practice Test 2 Answers and Explanations

Section 1 – No Calculator

1) **Choice D is correct**

There are 10 squares and 6 of them are shaded. Therefore, 6 out of 10 or $\frac{6}{10} = \frac{3}{5}$ are shaded.

2) **Choice C is correct**

Let x be the number of soft drinks for 252 guests. It's needed to have a proportional ratio to find x. $\frac{14 \text{ soft drinks}}{16 \text{ guests}} = \frac{x}{160 \text{ guests}} \Rightarrow x = \frac{160 \times 14}{16} \Rightarrow x = 140$

3) **Choice C is correct**

Let's review the choices provided:

A. $2 \times 2 = 4$ This is true!

B. $(4 + 1) \times 5 = 25$ This is true!

C. $6 \div (3 - 1) = 1 \rightarrow 6 \div 2 = 3$ This is NOT true!

D. $6 \times (4 - 2) = 12 \rightarrow 6 \times 2 = 12$ This is true!

4) **The answer is 81**

$3^4 = 3 \times 3 \times 3 \times 3 = 81$

5) **Choice D is correct**

$V = lwh \rightarrow V = 4 \times 5 \times 10 = 200$

6) **Choice B is correct**

Add 1 to both sides of $4x - 1 < 11$: $4x - 1 + 1 < 11 + 1 \rightarrow 4x < 12$

Divide both sides of $4x < 12$ by 4: $x < 3$

7) **Choice A is correct**

Area $= L \times W \rightarrow x = 9 \times W \rightarrow W = y$

Then: $x = 9 \times W \rightarrow x = 9 \times y \rightarrow y = \frac{x}{9}$

8) Choice C is correct

$(11 + 7) \div (3^3 \div 3) = (18) \div (27 \div 3) = (18) \div (9) = 2$

9) Choice A is correct

Area of square equals $(one\ side)^2 \rightarrow x^2 = 144\ cm^2 \rightarrow x = 12\ cm$

10) Choice D is correct

Change the numbers to decimal and then compare. $\frac{11}{15} = 0.73\ldots, 0.74, 75\% = 0.75, \frac{19}{25} = 0.76$

Therefore: $\frac{11}{15} < 0.74 < 75\% < \frac{19}{25}$

11) Choice C is correct

$3 + (4 \times M) = 24 \rightarrow 4M + 3 = 24$

12) The answer is 52.

Average $= \frac{sum\ of\ terms}{number\ of\ terms} \Rightarrow 25 = \frac{13+15+20+x}{4} \Rightarrow 100 = 48 + x \Rightarrow x = 52$

13) Choice B is correct

$Area\ of\ a\ square = (one\ side) \times (one\ side) = 2 \times 2 = 4$

14) The answer is: -64

Use PEMDAS (order of operation): $[3 \times (-14) - 48] - 14 + [3 \times 8] \div 2 =$

$[-42 - 48] + 14 + 24 \div 2 = -90 + 14 + 12 = -64$

15) Choice C is correct

Use this formula: Percent of Change: $\frac{New\ Value - Old\ Value}{Old\ Value} \times 100\%$

$\frac{28,000 - 18,200}{28,000} \times 100\% = -35\%$. The negative sign means that the price decreased.

16) The answer is 175

To find the number of possible outfit combinations, multiply number of options for each factor: $5 \times 7 \times 5 = 175$

17) Choice A is correct

Divide the total amount of concrete needed by the capacity of each truck:

$$58.5 \div 4.5 = 13$$

18) Choice C is correct

The average speed of John is: $150 \div 6 = 25 \, km$

The average speed of Alice is: $180 \div 4 = 45 \, km$

Write the ratio and simplify: $25:45 \Rightarrow 5:9$

19) Choice C is correct

Add the first 5 numbers. $40 + 45 + 50 + 35 + 55 = 225$

To find the distance traveled in the next 5 hours, multiply the average by number of hours.

$Distance = Average \times Rate = 50 \times 5 = 250$

Add both numbers: $250 + 225 = 475$

20) Choice C is correct

Use distance formula: $Distance = Rate \times time \Rightarrow 280 = 50 \times T$, divide both sides by 50.

$\frac{280}{50} = T \Rightarrow T = 5.6$ hours. Change hours to minutes for the decimal part. 0.6 hours $= 0.6 \times 60 = 36$ minutes.

Section 2 – Calculator

1) Choice D is correct

The three angles in a triangle always add up to 180°. So, only choice D is correct.

$$40 + 50 + 90 = 180$$

2) Choice A is correct

First convert fractions to get decimals, then sort the decimals, greatest to lest:

$\frac{3}{4} = 0.75$, $\frac{2}{3} = 0.\bar{6}$, $\frac{4}{7} \approx 0.57$, $\frac{1}{2} = 0.5$, $\frac{2}{5} = 0.4 \rightarrow 0.75 > 0.\bar{6} > 0.57 > 0.5 > 0.4$

3) Choice B is correct

Let x be the regular price. $0.15x = 6 \rightarrow x = \frac{6}{0.15} = 40$

4) Choice B is correct

To solve this expression that involves addition and multiplication of numbers, we need to follow the "order of operations" rules. Let's break it down:

$(-14) + 5(-4) + 4(5)$. First, solve the multiplications: $5(-4) = 5 \times (-4) = -20$

$4(5) = 4 \times (5) = 20$. Then: $(-14) + 5(-4) + 4(5) = -14 - 20 + 20 = -14$

5) Choice B is correct

Use the formula for Percent of Change: $\frac{New\ Value - Old\ Value}{Old\ Value} \times 100\%$.

$\frac{28-45}{45} \times 100\% = -37.7\%$ (negative sign here means that the new price is less than old price).

6) Choice A is correct

Let x be the number of years. Therefore, $3,000 per year equals $3000x$.

starting from $24,000 annual salary means you should add that amount to $3000x$.

Income more than that is: $I > 3,000x + 24,000$

7) Choice B is correct

The question is this: 1.75 is what percent of 1.40?

$$\frac{1.75}{1.40} = 1.25 = 125\%$$

8) Choice B is correct

$\frac{504}{600} = 0.84 = 84\%$. 504 is 84% of 600. Therefore, the discount is: $100\% - 84\% = 16\%$

9) Choice D is correct

If 19 balls are removed from the bag at random, there will be one ball in the bag. The probability of choosing a brown ball is 1 out of 20. Therefore, the probability of not choosing a brown ball is 19 out of 20 and the probability of having not a brown ball after removing 19 balls is the same.

10) Choice C is correct

The weight of 15.2 meters of this rope is: $15.2 \times 600\ g = 9,120\ g$, $1\ kg = 1,000\ g$, therefore, $7,320\ g \div 1000 = 9.12\ kg$

11) Choice B is correct.

Only choice B is correct. Other choices don't work in the equation.
$8(4 - (-8)) = 96$

12) Choice B is correct

$-12 + (5 \times n) = 5n - 12$

13) Choice B is correct

Write the numbers in order: $2, 19, 27, 28, 35, 44, 67$.

Median is the number in the middle. So, the median is 28.

14) The answer is 600

30 squirrels would collect 600 acorns in one day (5 squirrels collected 100 acorns in one day, so 1 squirrel collected 20 acorns in one day. Therefore, 30 squirrels would collect $30 \times 20 = 600$ acorns in one day).

15) Choice C is correct

Use simple interest formula: $I = prt, I = interest, p = principal, r = rate, t = time$)

$I = (9,000)(0.045)(5) = 2,025$

16) The answer is 0.24

The perimeter of the soccer field in kilometers is 0.24 kilometers (since 1 kilometer = 1000 meters, the perimeter in kilometers is 240 meters ÷ 1000).

17) Choice C is correct

$6 + 3 = 9$, $\quad 9 + 4 = 13$, $\quad 13 + 5 = 18$, $\quad 18 + 6 = 24$

18) The answer is 80

The failing rate is 11 out of $55 = \frac{11}{55}$

Change the fraction to percent: $\frac{11}{55} \times 100\% = 20\%$

20 percent of students failed. Therefore, 80 percent of students passed the exam.

19) Choice C is correct

$\frac{8}{12} + \frac{4}{3} + \frac{2}{6} = \frac{8+4(4)+2(2)}{12} = \frac{28}{12} = \frac{7}{3} = 2\frac{1}{3}$

20) Choice A is correct

The tenth value is 2.

8923.27 is closer to 8923.3 than 8923.2

Effortless Math's North Carolina EOG Grade 6 Online Center

... So Much More Online!

Effortless Math Online North Carolina EOG Grade 6 Math Center offers a complete study program, including the following:

- ✓ Step-by-step instructions on how to prepare for the North Carolina EOG Grade 6 Math test

- ✓ Numerous North Carolina EOG Grade 6 Math worksheets to help you measure your math skills

- ✓ Complete list of North Carolina EOG Grade 6 Math formulas

- ✓ Video lessons for North Carolina EOG Grade 6 Math topics

- ✓ Full-length North Carolina EOG Grade 6 Math practice tests

- ✓ And much more...

No Registration Required.

Visit **EffortlessMath.com/NorthCarolinaEOG6** to find your online North Carolina EOG Grade 6 Math resources.

Receive the PDF version of this book or get another FREE book!

Thank you for using our Book!

Do you LOVE this book?

Then, you can get the PDF version of this book or another book absolutely FREE!

Please email us at:

info@EffortlessMath.com

for details.

Author's Final Note

I hope your student enjoyed reading this book.

First of all, thank you for purchasing this study guide. I know you could have picked any number of books to help your student prepares for the North Carolina EOG Grade 6 Math test, but you picked this book and for that I am extremely grateful.

It took me years to write this study guide for the NC EOG Grade 6 Math because I wanted to prepare a comprehensive study guide to help students make the most effective use of their valuable time while preparing for the test.

After teaching and tutoring math courses for over a decade, I've gathered my personal notes and lessons to develop this study guide. It is my greatest hope that the lessons in this book could help your student prepares for the test successfully.

If you have any questions, please contact me at reza@effortlessmath.com and I will be glad to assist. Your feedback will help me to greatly improve the quality of my books in the future and make this book even better. Furthermore, I expect that I have made a few minor errors somewhere in this study guide. If you think this to be the case, please let me know so I can fix the issue as soon as possible.

If your student enjoyed this book and found some benefit in reading this, I'd like to hear from you and hope that you could take a quick minute to post a review on the book's Amazon page.

I personally go over every single review, to make sure my books really are reaching out and helping students and test takers. Please help me help students, by leaving a review!

I wish you all the best in your future success!

Reza Nazari

Math teacher and author

Made in the USA
Middletown, DE
23 May 2025

Encountering God Through Soaking

By
Aileen Foos

ENCOUNTERING GOD THROUGH SOAKING
BY AILEEN FOOS

Copyright © 2011 by Aileen Foos

All rights reserved.
This book or parts thereof may not be reproduced in any form, stored in a retrieval system, or transmitted in any form by any means – electronic, mechanical, photocopy, recording, or otherwise – without prior written permission of the publisher, except as provided by United States of America copyright law.

Unless otherwise identified, Scripture quotations are taken from the NEW AMERICAN STANDARD BIBLE ®, Copyright © 1960, 1962, 1963, 1968, 1971, 1972, 1973, 1975, 1977, 1995 by the Lockman Foundation. Used by permission. Scripture quotations marked ESV are taken from The Holy Bible, English Standard Version ® (ESV®), Copyright © 2001 by Crossway, a publishing ministry of Good News Publishers. Used by permission. All rights reserved. Scripture quotations marked NIV are taken from the Holy Bible, New International Version ®, Copyright © 1973, 1978, 1984, Biblica. Used by permission of Zandervan. All rights reserved.

Published by Aileen Foos, Reseda, CA
Printed in the United States of America

Cover by Chris Molitor – www.ChrisMolitorPhotography.com.

ISBN-13: 978-1466457447

ISBN-10: 1466457449

Table of Contents

INTRODUCTION ii
NOTES FOR THE GROUP LEADER v
- 1 - SOAKING IN THE HEAVENLY REALM 1
- 2 - ASK FOR WISDOM - SOAKING FOR STRATEGY 7
- 3 - REVELATION THROUGH SCRIPTURE 11
- 4 - SOAKING FOR REVELATION ON JUSTICE 15
- 5 - SOAKING TO RELEASE CREATIVE EXPRESSION 19
- 6 - SOAKING WITH PROPHETIC PURPOSE 21
- 7 - SOAKING TO SOMEONE ELSE'S ENCOUNTER 25
- 8 - SOAKING THROUGH PROPHETIC WORSHIP 27
- BONUS - SOAKING FOR PHYSICAL HEALING 29
CONTINUING THE JOURNEY 33
ABOUT THE AUTHOR 34

Introduction

Encountering God

This manual was written for those who want to ***encounter*** God, who want to ***know*** Him more. As you probably know, this happens best when we spend time with Him and set aside time to actually listen to what He is saying. The path towards experiencing God today is not very different than it was for those who lived in the time Jesus walked the earth with His disciples. The ones who knew Him the best were those who spent time with Him and devoted themselves to encountering Him by ***observing*** Him, ***listening*** to Him, and ***letting themselves be changed and shaped*** by Him. They wanted to ***know*** Him.

What is soaking?
Soaking is a term used to reference being at peace in the presence of God. As we rest in His presence, we soak in the nature of who God is and who He's created us to be. It's a position that we take, where we purposefully stay still and rest with the expressed reason of spending time with our Creator. We create a space for God to encounter us. As we wait upon the Lord, we begin to hear His voice and experience who He is **(Ps. 46:10)**.

What does it mean to know Him?
There have been many men and women— throughout the Bible and all of time— who have had a significant shift in their lives after an encounter with God. Abraham, Isaac, Jacob, Moses, David, and Mary are just a few. The list goes on and on. For this manual, we will focus on the story of Moses. Moses had a personal relationship with God that came from encountering Him. First, he encountered God in the burning bush **(Exod. 3:2)**. As a result of that encounter, Moses went back to Egypt and demanded that Pharaoh set the children of Israel free.

While in the desert, Moses asked God a question:

> ***Then Moses said, "I pray You, show me Your glory!" And He said, "I Myself will make all My goodness pass before you, and will proclaim the name of the LORD before you; and I will be gracious to whom I will be gracious, and will show compassion on whom I will show compassion."*** *Exod. 33:18–19*

Moses hungered for God to encounter Him. God was moved by that hunger and let Moses see part of who He was. An amazing thing about this passage is that it occurred before God's people had what we call the Bible, and before Jesus died on the cross.

Moses had such a powerful relationship with God that it shifted even His physical appearance. Exod. 34:29–35 describes Moses's skin as shining from being in the presence of God. It shone so much Moses had to put a veil over his face when he talked with the Israelites. Another place the depths of Moses's relationship with God was shown was when he was able to change God's mind.

> *The Lord said to Moses, "I have seen this people, and behold, they are an obstinate people. Now then let Me alone, that My anger may burn against them and that I may destroy them; and I will make of you a great nation." Then Moses entreated the Lord his God and said, "O Lord, why does Your anger burn against Your people whom You have brought out from the land of Egypt with great power and with a mighty hand? Why should the Egyptians speak, saying, 'With evil intent He brought them out to kill them in the mountains and to destroy them from the face of the earth'? Turn from Your burning anger and change Your mind about doing harm to Your people. Remember Abraham, Isaac, and Israel, Your servants to whom You swore by Yourself, and said to them, 'I will multiply your descendants, as the stars or the heavens, and all this land of which I have spoken I will give to your descendants and they shall inherit it forever.'" So the Lord changed His mind about the harm which He said He would do to His people.* Exod. 32:9–14

This passage speaks of deep relationship where, through intimacy, Gods heart was moved towards mercy. Moses is just one example of many people in the Bible who encountered God, and through that encounter, developed a depth of friendship that impacted the outcome of people groups or situations.

After Jesus died on the cross and rose again, we were given access to the Father through Jesus like never before. Mark 15:38 says the veil in the temple was torn, symbolizing the separation that we once had from the presence of God which is no longer there. Paul puts it this way,

> *'But to this day whenever Moses is read, a veil lies over their heart; but whenever a person turns to the Lord, the veil is taken away. Now the Lord is the Spirit, and where the Spirit of the Lord is, there is liberty. But we all, with unveiled face, beholding as in a mirror the glory of the Lord, are being transformed into the same image from glory to glory, just as from the Lord, the Spirit.'*
> *2 Cor. 3:15–18*

Now we have access to God the Father in a greater way because we don't have anything separating us. In 2 Cor. 3:7–13 it states:

> *'But if the ministry of death, in letters engraved on stones, came with glory, so that the sons of Israel could not look intently at the face of Moses because of the glory of his face, fading as it was, how will the ministry of the Spirit fail to be even more with glory? For if the ministry of condemnation has glory, much more does the ministry of righteousness abound in glory. For indeed what had glory, in this case has no glory because of the glory that surpasses it. For if that which fades away was with glory, much more that which is in glory. Therefore having such hope, we use great boldness in our speech, and are not like Moses, who used to put a veil over his face so that the sons of Israel would not look intently at the end of what was fading away.' 2 Cor. 3:7-13*

This passage is mind blowing. Paul talks about how the glory that Moses had doesn't compare to what we have access to now through Jesus. Under the covenant of grace, we get to tap into eternal Glory. We get to come into the presence of God and live out of a place of deep relationship with Him. We get to know God in a way that many in history didn't. The children of Israel had to go through rituals, and even then the priests were the ones who encountered the Ark of the Covenant. After Jesus, it all changed. He was the ultimate sacrifice; never again will there be such a separation from God and His creation.

Let's explore what it means to build a relationship with God through encountering His presence.

Notes for the Group Leader

General Tips for Leading Soaking Sessions:

- During introductions and teaching, allow people time to process what they are learning, ask questions, and discuss.

- When doing the exercises, it is incredibly helpful to have soft, uplifting, instrumental music playing in the background. For some of Aileen's favorite music choices, see her website: www.AileenFoos.com.

- The facilitator can read the questions out loud to the group, one by one. Allow about 5 minutes between each question, giving people enough time to soak in God's presence and write.

- Be sure to participate in the encounter yourself, so you can share with the group what God has shown you. This can help to encourage others. During the teaching parts, it can also be helpful for you to include testimonies of your own personal encounters with God.

- At the end of each session, allow everyone to share their encounters if they would like. This can help affirm that what they are seeing or experiencing is really from God.

- Be aware of how people are doing during the teaching and encounter. If there are people struggling, coaching one on one can help.

- If people say they are feeling things, instead of seeing them that's fine. Allow God to speak in a personal language that is comfortable to each of the students.

- Pray over people who are experiencing darkness or violent images.

- Also please have art supplies ready for session #5. Crayons and paper are fine.

- Have inner healing options you can recommend to those who are having a hard time connecting with God. If someone continually has a hard time connecting with God, there is probably an issue that God wants to heal.

Teaching Notes for Introducing to Your First "Soaking Session"

Example: Pick out a Bible story that means a lot to you. Choose one that demonstrates the impact of a strong relationship with God. For example, you can take the story about Moses and talk about how his encounters with God changed his life and the lives of others.

Original Design: God originally created us to encounter Him. Adam was created, not only in the image of God, but for relationship with Him. **(Gen. 1, 2)**

Intimacy With God In the Old Testament: The Old Testament is full of stories about God encountering His people. Because of a word God spoke to him, Abraham left everything he had known and went to a land God showed him **(Gen. 12:1)**. It's because of that intimacy– Abraham was called God's friend **(James 2:23)**– God didn't think it right to hide His plans to destroy Sodom and Gomorrah from him **(Gen. 18:17-18)** Another example is David who was a man after God's own heart **(1Sam. 13:14)**. His psalms express a full range of emotions experienced in encounters with God. His heart after God did so much to establish a culture of worship among God's people. There are so many others, like Daniel, Abraham, Job, Isaiah, and Joshua. They made themselves available for relationship with God.

Intimacy With God in the New Testament and Beyond: How much more intimacy is available now that Jesus has come and left us His Spirit? Jesus made the ultimate way to encounter and hear God's voice. We have much more access in hearing God's voice and encountering Him because we are covered in the blood of Jesus and filled with His Spirit.

> *Therefore, brethren, since we have confidence to enter the holy place by the blood of Jesus, by a new and living way which He inaugurated for us through the veil, that is, His flesh, and since we have a great priest over the house of God, let us draw near with a sincere heart in full assurance of faith... Heb. 10:19–22.*

When God looks at us, He sees His Son. What Father wouldn't want to talk with His sons or daughters?

> *For you have died and your life is hidden with Christ in God. Col. 3:3*

> *"For everyone who asks receives, and he who seeks finds, and to him who knocks it will be opened. Or what man is there among you who, when his son asks for a loaf, will give him a stone?" Matt. 7:8–9*

Jesus is the reason we can boldly approach the throne of grace.

> *For we do not have a high priest who cannot sympathize with our weaknesses, but One who has been tempted in all things as we are, yet without sin. Therefore let us draw near with confidence to the throne of grace, so that we may receive mercy and find grace to help in time of need. Heb. 4:15–16*

God wants us to know, through experience, who He is. We want to know God and we want to be known by God.

> *The man who thinks he knows something does not yet know as he ought to know. But the man who loves God is known by God. I Cor. 8:2 NIV*

There's only so much you can learn through reading about someone. You need to encounter them if you really want to know them. You can encounter God through His word, because He IS the Word. But the Word is also a person who became flesh. We are to encounter God not just as the written Word, but as a living, breathing, glorified being. When you experience someone face to face, you can learn so much more about them. You learn how they smell, how they smile, how they feel, what their voice sounds like. It's similar with God. When we know Him through encounter, we experience a Person, not a theology. **(Jer. 31:31–34, Heb. 8:7–13)**

God can speak through many different ways. He's so massive, not only in size, but in His character, and nature. He can use whatever He wants to use to communicate with His people.

We know that the character and the voice of God towards His people is love **(1 John 4:8, 16)**. God calls us sons and daughters, and because of Jesus we have access to the Father **(John 14:6, 2 Cor. 6:18)**. How would the voice of God sound towards the Son who gave up everything so that He could be reconciled with His creation? Would it sound judgmental, angry, mean? No, God is life and life abundantly **(John 10:10)**. More then we can hope, think or imagine! He looked at creation and said that it's good **(Gen. 1:31, Eph. 3:20)**. We, His creation in the core of who we are, are created from Glory. God, the Creator of Heaven and Earth, thinks about you all the time **(Gen. 1:27)**. His thoughts towards you are like the sands of the sea and are good thoughts **(Ps. 139:17–18, Jer. 29:11)**.

As we go into experiencing God, we must remember that by faith we grab hold of the reality that God's voice can drown out all other voices. What are the other voices we can hear? Our voice, which will only protect ourselves, sounds self serving. The enemy's voice is filled with lies, pain, judgment, condemnation, fear, and doubt **(John 10:10, 1 Peter 5:8)**.

God's voice sounds like peace, love, joy, hope, trust– even in correction it sounds– safe **(Galatians 5:22–23)**. The result of the voice of God in your life is life and life abundantly **(John 10:10)**. If the voice that you hear doesn't bring life, then it's fundamentally not the voice of God. The nature of God is love and life **(1 John 4:7-8)**. Most of the times we hear God's voice through the filters of our experience. We've been wounded and have had hard things happen to us throughout life and it creates these lenses that we look through when we encounter God and hear His voice. For the sake of these exercises we are going to, by faith grab hold of the fact the God is good, He's in a good mood, He's for us, and He is Love.

The way that we are going to encounter God is through our imagination. God created everything we need to hear His voice and have relationship with Him. He can use our imagination to speak pictures to us, which would take Him much longer, if He said it one word at a time. You've heard the saying, "A picture is worth a thousand words." Because God is so infinite, language is quite limiting. He can say many things if He uses pictures **(Eze. 8:9, Joel 2:28, Acts 2:17, Acts 10:9–18, Revelation)**.

Because the Holy Spirit dwells within us we have direct access into the heart of God **(1 Cor. 2:11)**. We also have the mind of Christ **(1 Cor. 2:16)** and as such we can ask God to show us through our mind what He thinks.

Before we start these exercises, close your eyes and put your hand on your head and pray. "Holy Spirit, thank you that I have the mind of Christ. Wash my mind in the Blood of the Lamb. Break away any paradigms or lies that would hinder me from hearing and seeing what the Father of heaven would have to say to me. Fill me with peace and wash away all anxiety, fear, and unbelief. I'm here to encounter you and love you. Amen."

- 1 -
Soaking in the Heavenly Realm

You keep him in perfect peace
*whose **mind** is stayed on you, because he trusts in you.*
– Isaiah 26:3 (ESV)
The word used for "mind" in this verse
can also be translated "imagination."[1]

Imagination is the greatest gift God has given us
and it ought to be devoted entirely to Him.
– Oswald Chambers, "My Utmost for His Highest"[2]

The imagination is a beautiful thing, a part of us that God created to be used for His glory. There is a difference, however, between us imagining something and God giving us pictures IN our imagination. We are looking for the latter. Just as we have to learn to discern the difference between our own thoughts and the words of the Spirit, so we need to grow in discernment with our imagination. As we proceed, take care not to try and *direct* what you imagine. Instead, be *open* to the Holy Spirit and allow Him the freedom to speak to you not just in words, but also in pictures. You will be asked to picture general settings or actions, which may seem contradictory, but allow the Holy Spirit to guide you even in imagining what is being suggested. Do not try and superimpose what you think the image should look like. Allow the Holy Spirit to lead the way and fill in all the details.

Do not get caught up and lost trying to figure out what is of God and what is of you. Before starting your time of soaking, ask Jesus to purify your imagination. Ask for the purifying of your mind and imagination by the blood of Jesus. Since we are new creations in Christ, we carry the mind of Christ **(1 Cor. 2:16, 2 Cor. 5:17)**. We can have faith that what God is speaking to us in our mind or imagination is what He wants to reveal to us.

Let's practice using your imagination! Quickly close your eyes and picture a tree. Can you see it? That's the place God is going to use to talk with us today.

Now let's try it with the Holy Spirit. I suggest you play soft instrumental worship throughout your encountering time. This will help to invite God's presence into the room, as well as help you to keep your mind focused on God.

---

[1] Blue Letter Bible. "Dictionary and Word Search for *yetser (Strong's 3336)*". Blue Letter Bible. 1996-2011. 6 May 2011.
< http:// www.blueletterbible.org/lang/lexicon/lexicon.cfm?strongs=H3336 >

[2] Chambers, Oswald. "My Utmost for His Highest: Selections for the Year". Dodd, Mead & Company. 1964. New York. (p. 42)

Again, you will be asked to picture settings or actions. When you are asked, allow the Holy Spirit to guide you and show you things you might not imagine by yourself (**Eph. 3:20**).

We will start with picturing a couple of different scenes. (Make sure your music is playing if you haven't started it already.)

1) Picture a Garden (Song 4:16). Visualize Jesus standing in a garden ready to show you around. Let Him take you on a journey and reveal to you mysteries there. Ask Him why He is showing you certain things and what their manifestations are in your life. The garden is your safe place with the Lord. Allow Him to walk you through it. This first exercise will help you practice seeing, so don't be afraid to go wherever He's leading you.

Record what you see and hear so you can go back to it later. You can always go back to that encounter and ask Jesus more about what you were seeing. Asking God questions is like pulling tissues out of a tissue box. There's always more. And the more you ask the more you get.

_____

_____

_____

_____

_____

_____

_____

_____

_____

_____

_____

_____

_____

_____

_____

_____

_____

2) Picture a Castle (John 14:2). Picture Jesus standing in front of a huge castle. He takes your hand and leads you in the front door. Ask Him to show you around. As He shows you different rooms or places, ask Him what they have inside of them and what the items in the rooms are for. Ask Him to show you the room He's made specifically for you. Take a look around the room, and ask what each of the items in the room mean. Once He's walked you around the room take time to write down what you saw. Continue to ask about each item in the room. Why are they there? What do they symbolize or mean? Be like a child who asks question after question. It's God's pleasure to show you His Kingdom **(Luke 12:32).**

_____

_____

_____

3) Go back to the room that Jesus showed you that was just for you. As you're looking at Jesus, ask Him to give you a present (Matt. 7:11). When He hands you the present, open it up. Ask Him why He gave this item to you and its purpose.

_____

_____

_____

_____

_____

_____

_____

_____

4) Next we are going to picture the throne room of God (Ps. 47:8). Picture yourself as a little kid crawling onto Father God's lap. Stand on His lap and look into His face. Look into His eyes. Explore that for a moment. Then ask the Father what His favorite thing about you is. When you hear what that is, ask Him why He likes that about you. Then ask Father God if He will show you a mystery about Himself that you don't know yet. After He tells you what the mystery is, ask Him to tell you a secret. As a friend of God, you have access to His secrets, and this secret is just between you and Him (John 15:15).

_____

_____

_____

_____

_____

_____

_____

- 2 -
Ask for Wisdom - Soaking for Strategy

*But if any of you lacks wisdom, let him ask of God,
who gives to all generously and without reproach, and it will be given to him.*
— James 1:5

God has all the strategy that you will ever need. He's the one who knows all and has every answer. In this lesson, we are going to soak for the strategy of heaven. Think of a problem in your current season that you need an answer for. Nothing is too difficult for God!

1) Picture yourself in a library full of books that holds the wisdom and revelation of the Kingdom of heaven (Isa. 11:2). In the library is a desk. On that desk is a piece of blank paper. Go over to the piece of paper and write your problem down. Jesus is with you. Ask Him what He thinks and what the strategy for the problem is. (Prov. 4:7, Prov. 25:2)

_____

_____

_____

_____

_____

_____

_____

_____

_____

_____

_____

_____

_____

_____

2) Ask Him if there's anything that you can do to partner with heaven in releasing this strategy for your problem. Ask Him how you can align your heart with His heart for this season in your life.

3) Ask Jesus for one thing you need to know about the current season or time you're in.

4) Ask Jesus what your role is in this season of your life. Some seasons of life are for learning the revelation of being a child or a warrior, being royalty or a lover. When we understand the season God has us in, we can better prepare ourselves to receive the fullness of what heaven has for us.

_____
_____
_____
_____
_____
_____
_____
_____
_____
_____
_____
_____
_____

- 3 -
Revelation Through Scripture

The Spirit of the LORD will rest on Him, The spirit of wisdom and understanding,
The spirit of counsel and strength, The spirit of knowledge and the fear of the Lord.
— Isaiah 11:2
All Scripture is inspired by God and profitable for teaching, for reproof, for correction, for training in righteousness; so that the man of God may be adequate, equipped for every good work.
— 2 Timothy 3:16, 17

We have access to the Spirit of wisdom and revelation through our connection with God. One way that God releases that revelation is through Scripture. The Word of God is like a multi-layered cake. You can have the top layer, which is good, but there are deeper layers that are just as good if not better. As we explore the Word of God, we need the Holy Spirit to breathe on it to give us life through it. When God gives us revelation through the Word, it puts a solid foundation under us. It gives us something to stand on when circumstances and things in the natural realm don't line up with what the Lord has told us.

1) Ask the Holy Spirit to bring a scripture to mind He wants to explore with you. Write out the scripture. Read it a couple of times. When you contemplate something over and over again, it's called meditation. We can meditate on the Word of God by repeating it over and over again in our minds (Josh. 1:8, Ps. 119:148). Write the scripture in the lines below.

_____
_____
_____
_____
_____
_____
_____
_____
_____
_____
_____
_____

_____
_____

2) Picture yourself on a path with a Bible in your hand turned to the verse that the Holy Spirit has shown you. Holy Spirit is beside you. Ask Him to show you what the verse means.

_____
_____
_____
_____
_____
_____
_____
_____
_____
_____
_____
_____

3) Ask Holy Spirit how this verse applies to the season you are in right now.

_____
_____
_____
_____
_____
_____
_____
_____

4) Ask Holy Spirit how it applies to the body of Christ in this season.

5) Ask Holy Spirit what this verse looks like in action.

- 4 -
Soaking for Revelation on Justice

*He executes justice for the orphan and the widow,
and shows His love for the alien by giving him food and clothing.*
— Deuteronomy 10:18

As we learned earlier, God loves giving us strategy for our lives. Now we are going to move into seeking God's strategy for even bigger things. We can partner with God's heart for the world. The way we first partner with God is to fall in love with Him. When we fall in love with Him, we begin to fall in love with what He loves. There are many social justice issues in the world, and we know heaven has answers for them all. We just have to tap into the infinite wisdom God has for these global issues. Every solution and strategy must flow from a place of intimacy with God. Jesus only did what He saw His Father doing, so we must practice seeing what our Father is doing. Then we can co-labor with heaven and see Jesus get His full reward.

1) Picture a globe. Jesus is standing next to you. Ask Him which country He wants you to focus on. Then ask Him what He wants you to see about that country. Ask Him a couple more questions. Write down what you see.

_____
_____
_____
_____
_____
_____
_____
_____
_____
_____
_____
_____
_____

2) Ask Jesus to tell you the redemptive nature of this nation. Ask what this nation was created to do from heaven's perspective.

3) Ask Jesus what problem He wants to focus on related to this country. Ask for His strategy for the problem. Ask for His perspective, how He sees the issue.

4) Ask Jesus for one thing you can do in this season to partner with His heart to release this strategy on earth for this nation. Ask for one practical you can do.

5) Ask Jesus how He wants you to partner with His heart through prayer for this nation in this season. (Remember we want to pray what God is praying, and He sees the original design for each nation. Call out the best in that nation).

- 5 -
Soaking to Release Creative Expression

In the beginning God created the heavens and the earth.
– Genesis 1:1

God is creative, and when we are in His presence creativity flows. Sometimes, a lie we believe about ourselves is we are not creative. But God, the Creator, created us to be creative. Before we start this exercise, I want you to pray and break off any lies or word curses that may have been spoken against your creativity, either by yourself or by other people.

We are not being creative to have a masterpiece; we are being creative to connect with God. As we move through this lesson, speak life over your creative self. Get ready by having canvas or paper, paints, brushes, water, colored pencils, crayons, markers, or whatever you will need to be creative. Be encouraged to try out your creativity with different mediums and sources. Be creative!

1) Picture in your mind a blank canvas. Now ask Holy Spirit to show you what color to use first and where should it go. After He shows you something, start creating. Once you've finished that, continue to ask Him, "What next?" When you are finished, write down what you saw. You can use the space on the previous page to sketch any notes you want to as well.

_____
_____
_____
_____
_____
_____
_____

2) When you are finished, ask Holy Spirit what it is you've created, if you don't already know. Then ask Him what it means.

_____
_____
_____

_____
_____
_____
_____
_____
_____
_____
_____

3) Ask Holy Spirit to anoint your painting or art piece to bring healing, deliverance, and freedom. Ask God what His nature is through this art piece. Write a description of this experience, as well as what God showed you about Himself.

_____
_____
_____
_____
_____
_____
_____
_____
_____
_____
_____
_____
_____
_____

- 6 -
Soaking with Prophetic Purpose

*Pursue love, yet desire earnestly spiritual gifts,
but especially that you may prophesy.*
– 1 Corinthians 14:1

In this lesson we are going to soak with prophetic purpose. Let the Lord bring someone to mind. Or if you're doing a class, pick someone or have an assigned person to make sure everyone gets prophesied over.

1) Picture the person you chose on a path walking with Jesus. As they are walking beside Jesus, ask Jesus to tell or show you one thing about them He loves so much.

_____
_____
_____
_____
_____
_____
_____
_____

2) Ask Jesus if there's one thing He wants this person to know. When He tells you something, ask why this is important for the person to know.

_____
_____
_____
_____
_____
_____

___

3) Ask Jesus what kind of season they are in. Then ask for one piece of strategy for them in this season.

___

4) Give that person the word. Write it down and send or give it to them. Let them confirm or deny whatever it is you saw. We are learning how to connect with God, so it's okay if you missed it. Ask God for His heart for them and pray a blessing over them for the season they are in and the one they are going into. Let God encounter you through His heart for other people! Write any remaining thoughts.

___

- 7 -
Soaking to Someone Else's Encounter

*Then Elisha prayed and said, "O Lord, I pray, open his eyes that he may see.
And the Lord opened the servant's eyes and he saw;
and behold, the mountain was full of horses and chariots of fire all around Elisha.
—2 Kings 6:17*

For this lesson you're going to need to find music or a CD that has someone else's encounter on it. For example, Bob Jones, Jill Austin, and Todd Bentley have some of their encounters set to music.[3] As you listen to their encounter, go with them to that place of their encounter. Someone else's encounter is a place where you can experience God as well. We are the body of Christ (Rom. 12:5). Our breakthrough is someone else's breakthrough, and visa versa. When they are talking, allow Holy Spirit to fill your imagination with the same images they are seeing. See the vision with them. Throughout the encounter, ask the Lord how this relates to your life.

1) Ask God what revelation He wants you to see or hear from this encounter.

_____
_____
_____
_____
_____
_____
_____
_____
_____
_____
_____
_____

2) Ask God if there is any strategy you can get from this encounter for your life. Let the Lord shift your mindset and bring breakthrough into your life through someone else's encounter.

---
[3] See my website: www.AileenFoos.com for more resources, links, and information.

- 8 -
Soaking Through Prophetic Worship

What is the outcome then? I will pray with the spirit and I will pray with the mind also;
I will sing with the spirit and I will sing with the mind also.
— 1 Corinthians 14:15

One of the most powerful ways God can use to shift and declare things over our lives is prophetic worship. As God has moved to re-awaken our love for hearing His voice and trusting His character, prophetic song has taken flight. There are many ministries that have amazing prophetic worship soaking CDs out there.[4] You can go exploring and find what you like to soak to.

When you find the CD that you're going to use. Get yourself comfortable and let the presence of God soak into every part of your being. Listen to the words of the singer and let the instruments and words penetrate every part of you. As if you're drinking from a river, let God speak to you through the words and sounds. Be aware of phrases or lines in the music that stick out to you or resonate with you.

1) Write down what you feel God is saying to you throughout the entire experience. Let the words He speaks penetrate into your heart and break down walls or barriers. When you experience His love, it changes you forever!

_____
_____
_____
_____
_____
_____
_____
_____
_____
_____
_____
_____

---

[4] Two suggestions of people who have wonderful soaking CD's are: Grace Williams and Kimberly and Alberto Rivera. See my website: www.AileenFoos.com for more suggestions.

- Bonus -
Soaking for Physical Healing

But He was pierced through for our transgressions, He was crushed for our iniquities;
The chastening for our well-being fell upon Him, And by His scourging we are healed.
— Isaiah 53:5

Jesus, our Lord and Savior, made a way for us to be set free from our physical afflictions. When Jesus died on the cross, He not only paid for us to have salvation, but for us to be physically healed as well. 1 Peter 2:24 puts it this way:

and He Himself bore our sins in His body on the cross,
so that we might die to sin and live to righteousness;
for by His wounds you were healed.

Notice the past tense "were healed." What could this mean? It means that Jesus paid the price before we were ever sick. There is complete freedom from sickness because the price for divine healing was already paid for, by the shedding of His blood. The object of this lesson isn't to convince you theologically that healing is for today. It is to give you one way to access healing for your body. There are many ways God releases healing to our bodies. Jesus healed different ways all the time. However, what He always did do was answer people's emotional need as well as their physical sickness. In Luke 17:19, Jesus told the leper who was healed, "your faith has made you well." That word "well," in Greek, means whole, healed, delivered, and saved.[5] Not only did the man receive healing, he received wholeness of body and spirit.

The miracle of the cross is that we get complete wholeness. Every part of us that has been affected by sin and the kingdom of darkness is eradicated by His marvelous light.

With all these exercises, there is an element of meditation. While many Christians run away from the word "meditation," it was actually something to be done as a daily practice amongst the Israelites. According to Josh. 1:8, they were instructed to meditate on the law day and night. David talked frequently about meditating on God: His ways, laws, and works (Ps. 27:4; 63:6; 77:6,12; 119:15,27,48,78,148; 143:5; 145:5). With this soaking manual, we are basically doing the same thing. We are setting our hearts on things above and interacting with God, not only to receive all He has for us, but also to build a relationship with the One for whom we were created.

As we start this healing lesson, remember that **your sickness has already been paid for.** Nothing is impossible for God. Not even death could hold Jesus in the grave. Let us access all God has for us and walk in the fullness of healing!

---

[5] Blue Letter Bible. "Dictionary and Word Search for *sōzō (Strong's 4982)*". Blue Letter Bible. 1996-2011. 10 May 2011.
< http://www.blueletterbible.org/lang/lexicon/lexicon.cfm?Strongs=G4982&t=NASB >

1) First picture the organ or body part that is being afflicted by pain, disease, or maybe missing and you need that body part created. Invite Holy Spirit to wash you with His presence. Now picture every cell of your body being washed in the blood of Jesus. Meditate on that for a while.

Now picture your cells receiving the Light of Jesus. Every cell of your being is being filled with His Light. Now focus back on that place of your body that needs healing and ask Jesus to show you what His blood paid for. When He shows you in your heart, begin to worship Him and thank Him for your healing. When you're finished, write down what He has shown you.

_____

_____

_____

_____

_____

_____

_____

_____

2) Now we are going to go back into picturing your body and where you have been afflicted. The picture in your mind could look like you would see in an x-ray with God highlighting what He wants to focus His healing on. Ask Jesus if there's any way you can partner with heaven to release His healing into your body. Ask if there is something standing in the way of you receiving your full healing. Sometimes we have believed a lie about our healing, and He wants to give us the truth. Sometimes God wants you to do an action in the physical realm that releases healing in the Spirit realm. For example, Jesus put mud on the blind man's eyes, which released the miracle. Co-laboring with heaven builds relationship between God and us. Write down what He has shown and told you.

_____

_____

_____

_____

_____

_____

3) Picture Jesus standing before you. Ask Him for a promise regarding your healing. It could be a scripture or it could be a direct promise from Him. Let the words He speaks to you penetrate your heart until you feel the promise go into the depths of your heart. Meditate on His words. If it's a scripture read it over and over until you feel your heart agreeing with His promise. Write down what you heard and saw.

_____

_____

_____

_____

_____

_____

_____

4) Now picture Father God on His throne. You are standing before Him. Because of the price Jesus paid, you can ask for justice for every moment, dollar, or life that was stolen by pain, sickness, or disease. Father God sees His son when He looks at you. Ask Father God for justice. Ask Him what that justice will look like in your life. It could look like you releasing healing on many people who have the same affliction you had. It could look like finances returned to you sevenfold.

Each promise will come in a seed form, and you get to stand on it, declaring that Jesus is enough and He deserves His full reward. Write down what you see. Remember you get the privilege of partnering with heaven in your life to see justice released. So go after it. Pray for lots of people who have the same affliction you suffered with until you see the promise released. God is faithful and He will never go back on His Word.

_____

_____

_____

_____

_____

_____

_____

_____

_____
_____
_____
_____
_____

All of these lessons have been to build relationship with Jesus, Father God, and Holy Spirit. As you write your own story with Him and create your own history, your encounters with God will grow. These lessons are just platforms to launch into a lifestyle of encounter. God loves to connect with His people, and His desire is beyond what we could imagine.

**We could discover Him everyday for eternity
and never begin to scratch the surface of how extravagant He is!**

Enjoy the process in discovering how incredible our God is!

Continuing the Journey

God is spirit, and those who worship Him must worship in spirit and truth."
–John 4:24

Being a people who experience God is what changes us. Being in His presence will always transform us. We cannot leave the presence of God without having a shift in our lives. God longs to encounter us more than we want to encounter Him. As we make room in our lives for encounter, we get to experience a true relationship with our Creator. He becomes everything we long for when He's not just an idea but a real being in our lives who we have a personal relationship with.

As you finish this series, remember **this is only the beginning of the journey.** We have access to the Father because of what Jesus did on the cross, and now we can boldly approach the throne! We can go everyday before our Father to talk with Him and ask Him all sorts of questions.

This is not just a theology we believe, but we can become people who literally carry the presence of God. We are temples the Holy Spirit dwells in, but we have to make room for Him and allow Him to dwell in us. If we don't take the time to worship and let Him encounter us, we will miss a great invitation for intimacy with the One we were created to have relationship with. **As you continue this journey with Jesus, let Him show you the mysteries you were created to be a part of!**

About the Author

Aileen Foos is a children's pastor in the Los Angeles area. She has worked with children for several years and traveled to many nations. Since she was a child, Aileen has had numerous meaningful encounters with God.

As she has ministered over the years, she noticed a hunger for practical tools that can help someone have a lifestyle of encountering God. People are hungry not only to experience God's presence, but also to have relationship with the One for whom they were created. Her heart is to bring the Bride of Christ into Her fullness through encounter and intimacy with God. She desires to see Jesus get His full reward and see the Kingdom of Heaven invade earth with radical love.

If you would like to invite her to speak or share at your event, browse her recommended resources related to encountering God, or find out about her other publications, please visit:

www.AileenFoos.com

Made in the USA
Coppell, TX
10 December 2020